Download Forms on Nolo.com

You can download the forms in this book at:

 www.nolo.com/back-of-book/GRN.html

We'll also post updates whenever there's an important change to the law affecting this book—as well as articles and other related materials.

More Resources from Nolo.com

Legal Forms, Books, & Software

Hundreds of do-it-yourself products—all written in plain English, approved, and updated by our in-house legal editors.

Legal Articles

Get informed with thousands of free articles on everyday legal topics. Our articles are accurate, up to date, and reader friendly.

Find a Lawyer

Want to talk to a lawyer? Use Nolo to find a lawyer who can help you with your case.

15th Edition

How to Get a Green Card

Ilona Bray, J.D.

FIFTEENTH EDITION	JULY 2022
Editor	ILONA BRAY
Cover Design	SUSAN PUTNEY
Book Design	SUSAN PUTNEY
Proofreading	JOCELYN TRUITT
Index	NOTA BENE INDEXING
Printing	SHERIDAN

ISSN: 2371-9885 (print)
ISSN: 2371-9915 (online)

ISBN: 978-1-4133-2957-5 (pbk)
ISBN: 978-1-4133-2958-2 (ebook)

This book covers only United States law, unless it specifically states otherwise.

Please note

Accurate, plain-English legal information can help you solve many of your own legal problems. But this text is not a substitute for personalized advice from a knowledgeable lawyer. If you want the help of a trained professional—and we'll always point out situations in which we think that's a good idea—consult an attorney licensed to practice in your state.

Acknowledgments

The original authors of this book were Loida Nicolas Lewis and Len Madlansacay. Nolo thanks them for their efforts in producing a work of such ambitious scope, and one that has endured for many years.

Of course, massive and constant changes in immigration laws and practices have necessitated many rewrites and revisions of the original book.

For this edition, we owe tremendous debts of thanks to a number of highly skilled attorneys who offered their expertise in various areas of immigration law. Most recently, these include Kyle A. Knapp, an Ohio-based immigration attorney, attorney Taylor Jameson, of Legal Services of Eastern Michigan, and Catherine Seitz, attorney and Legal Director of Immigration Institute of the Bay Area (IIBA).

About the Author

Ilona Bray came to the practice of immigration law through her long interest in international human rights issues. Before joining Nolo as legal editor in charge of immigration, she ran a solo law practice and held positions at nonprofit immigration agencies including the International Institute of the East Bay (Oakland) and the Northwest Immigrant Rights Project (Seattle). Ms. Bray was also an intern in the legal office at Amnesty International's International Secretariat in London. She received her Bachelor's degree in philosophy from Bryn Mawr College, and her law degree and a Master's degree in East Asian (Chinese) Studies from the University of Washington. Ms. Bray is a member of the American Immigration Lawyers Association (AILA). She has authored other books for Nolo, including *Fiancé & Marriage Visas: A Couple's Guide to U.S. Immigration* and *Becoming a U.S. Citizen: A Guide to the Law, Exam & Interview.*

Table of Contents

Your Immigration Companion 1

   A. Types of Green Cards We Cover 2

   B. How Much You Can Do Without a Lawyer 2

   C. Using This Book 3

1 America: A Nation of Immigrants 5

   A. America's Earliest Settlers 6

   B. Early Immigration Restrictions 7

   C. Today's Immigration Laws 8

   D. Looking Forward 10

2 All Ways to Get a Green Card 11

   A. Family-Based Relationships 12

   B. Employment-Based Relationships 13

   C. Special Immigrants 14

   D. Entrepreneur Immigrants 14

   E. Asylum and Refugee Status 15

   F. Diversity Visa Lottery 15

   G. Amnesties 15

   H. Private Bills 16

3 Short-Term Alternatives to a Green Card 17

   A. How Do Foreign Nationals Enter the United States? 18

   B. Types of Visas 18

   C. Tourists Who Can Visit Without a Visa 21

   D. The Importance of Staying Legal 23

   E. How to Extend a Visitor Visa 23

   F. Changing Your Reason for Staying 24

   G. What to Do If USCIS Denies Your Extension Application 24

   H. Tips on Filling Out Form I-539 25

4 Will Inadmissibility Bar You From Getting a Green Card? 27

    A. What Is Inadmissibility? 28

    B. The Possibility of Waiving Inadmissibility 28

    C. Most Troublesome Grounds of Inadmissibility 34

    D. Reversing an Inadmissibility Finding 39

5 How Long You'll Have to Wait 45

    A. Immediate Relatives of U.S. Citizens: No Waiting for Eligibility 47

    B. Relatives in Preference Categories: Longer Waits 47

    C. Dealing With the Wait 48

    D. Can You Predict How Long You'll Wait? 49

    E. Revocation of a Petition or Application 53

6 Fiancé(e) Visas 55

    A. Who Qualifies for a Fiancé Visa 56

    B. Quick View of the Fiancé Visa Application Process 57

    C. Detailed Instructions for the Fiancé Visa Application Process 58

    D. How to Bring Your Children on a Fiancé Visa 63

    E. Marriage and After 64

7 Green Cards Through Marriage 65

    A. Who Qualifies 66

    B. Special Rules in Court Proceedings 67

    C. Quick View of the Marriage-Based Green Card Application Process 68

    D. Detailed Instructions for the Marriage-Based Green Card Application Process 70

    E. Bringing Your Children 76

    F. If Your Marriage Is Less Than Two Years Old 78

    G. If You Marry Again 80

    H. Common Questions About Marriage and Immigration 80

8 Your Parents as Immigrants 83

    A. Who Qualifies to Petition for Parents 84

    B. Who Qualifies as Your Parent 85

    C. Quick View of the Application Process 86

    D. Detailed Instructions for the Application Process 87

9 Child Immigrants 91

   A. Who Qualifies 92

   B. Definition of "Child" 93

   C. Quick View of the Application Process 97

   D. Detailed Instructions for the Application Process 97

   E. Automatic Citizenship for Some Children 99

10 Orphan Immigrants in Non-Hague Convention Countries 101

   A. Who Qualifies as an Orphan Child 103

   B. Who Can Petition for an Orphan Child 103

   C. Preadoption Requirements 104

   D. Starting the Adoption Process 104

   E. After the Petition Is Approved 106

   F. Filing for a Visa 107

   G. Automatic Citizenship for Adopted Orphans 107

11 The Diversity Visa Lottery 109

   A. Who Qualifies for the DV Lottery 111

   B. How to Apply for the DV Lottery 112

   C. After You Win—The Green Card Application 114

   D. How to Bring Your Spouse and Children 116

12 Your Brothers and Sisters as Immigrants 119

   A. Who Counts as Your Brother or Sister 120

   B. Quick View of the Application Process 121

   C. Detailed Instructions for the Application Process 122

   D. What Happens After Filing Form I-130 123

13 Refugees and Asylees 125

   A. Who Qualifies 127

   B. Who Is Barred From Qualifying 129

   C. How to Apply for Refugee Status 131

   D. How to Apply for Asylum 132

   E. If Your Asylum Application Is Denied 137

   F. Asylees Can Bring Overseas Spouses and Children to the United States ... 138

   G. Getting a Green Card After Asylum Approval or Refugee Entry 139

   H. Revocation of Asylee Status 139

   I. Temporary Protected Status (TPS) 140

   J. Deferred Enforced Departure (DED) 142

14 **Military Veterans and Enlistees**..143

    A. Which Military Members Qualify to Apply for Citizenship Without a Green Card..144

    B. Which Military Members Qualify for U.S. Permanent Residence..........................145

15 **Cancellation of Removal: Do Ten Illegal Years Equal One Green Card?**......149

    A. Applying in Court Proceedings..150

    B. Who Qualifies for Cancellation of Removal..150

    C. Who Is Not Eligible for Cancellation..151

    D. Preparing a Convincing Case..151

    E. How to File..154

    F. Approving Your Application..155

    G. Additional Types of Cancellation of Removal..155

16 **Adjustment of Status**..157

    A. Who Is Allowed to Use the Adjustment of Status Procedure 158

    B. People Who Can't Adjust Status at All..162

    C. How to File..163

    D. After You Apply..167

    E. Interview and Approval..168

17 **Consular Processing**..173

    A. How Your Case Gets to the U.S. Consulate 175

    B. Forms and Documents You'll Need to Provide 177

    C. Attending Your Visa Interview..179

    D. Approval of Your Immigrant Visa 180

    E. Arriving in the United States 180

18 **Deferred Action for Childhood Arrivals**..181

    A. Who Are the DREAMers?..182

    B. How to Renew DACA 182

19 **U Visas for Crime Victims Assisting Law Enforcement**..187

    A. Who Is Eligible for a U Visa..188

    B. How to Apply for a U Visa..192

    C. Your Legal Status While U Visa Is Pending..195

    D. Green Card Possibilities After U Visa Approval..196

20 **Acquiring Citizenship Through U.S. Citizen Parents** 201

A. Who Qualifies for Acquisition of U.S. Citizenship 202

B. Obtaining Proof of U.S. Citizenship 205

C. Dual Citizenship 206

21 **Filling Out and Submitting Immigration Applications** 207

A. Don't Give False Answers 208

B. Get the Latest Forms and Fee Amounts 208

C. Tips for Filling Out Forms 209

D. When Additional Proof Is Required 210

E. Submitting Photographs for Identification 214

F. Fingerprinting Requirements 215

G. Keep Your Own File 215

H. Tips for Filing Applications 215

22 **Tracking Your Application Through the System** 219

A. Understanding U.S. Government Culture 220

B. How to Track Your Application Online 220

C. What to Do When Things Go Wrong 221

D. Inquiring About Delays 222

E. Speeding Up Processing in Emergencies 223

F. Reporting Wrongdoing 225

23 **Keeping, Renewing, and Replacing Your Green Card** 227

A. Renewing or Replacing Your Green Card 228

B. When U.S. Immigration Authorities Can Take Away Your Card 229

C. Planning to Apply for U.S. Citizenship 232

24 **How to Find and Work With a Lawyer** 233

A. Where to Look for a Lawyer 234

B. Deciding on a Particular Lawyer 235

C. Paying the Lawyer 236

D. Managing the Lawyer 237

E. Firing a Lawyer 238

Appendix

How to Access the Sample Filled-In Forms on the Nolo Website 241

List of Sample Immigration Forms Available on the Nolo Website 242

Index 245

Your Immigration Companion

A. Types of Green Cards We Cover...2

B. How Much You Can Do Without a Lawyer..2

C. Using This Book...3

Are you a foreign-born person who's interested in making your home in the United States? If so, this book might be just the ticket to finding out whether you're eligible for permanent U.S. residence, also known as a "green card." A green card gives you the right to live and work in the United States your whole life, travel in and out of the country without too much hassle, sponsor certain family members to join you, and, if all goes well for a few years, apply for U.S. citizenship.

This book will help you learn the application procedures, fill out the various forms, and pick up tips for dealing with often-difficult government officials. We try to give you a realistic view of your immigration possibilities and guide you along the path—which could be a long one—to reaching your goals. And unlike many government publications, we'll warn you about what could go wrong, and what steps to take to avoid delays and problems. Immigrants to the United States have to face a huge and often unfriendly government bureaucracy. Often, it's not the law itself that gives immigrants problems, but dealing with government delays, mistakes, and inattention. So, it helps to have a friend like this book by your side.

However, some people won't get the help they need from this book alone, so read this chapter carefully before you continue!

A. Types of Green Cards We Cover

This book was designed to help the "average" person—for example, someone who doesn't have a million dollars to invest, isn't internationally famous, and hasn't received a job offer from a U.S. employer. That's why we've focused our discussion on the following types of green card opportunities:

- family-based green cards, available to close relatives and adopted children of U.S. citizens and permanent residents

- political asylum and refugee status, available to people fleeing certain types of persecution
- the visa lottery ("diversity visa"), available to people from certain countries with a minimum level of education who win a random drawing, and
- opportunities for people who have lived in the United States for ten years or more and are in removal proceedings ("cancellation of removal").

This book does *not* cover green cards through employment, investment, the amnesty programs of the 1980s and the followup "NACARA" program, religious workers, or other, more obscure categories. Nor does it cover temporary visas (distinct from green cards in that they expire, usually in a few years). Examples of temporary visas include student, business visitor, H-1B specialty worker, and J-1 exchange visitor visas. (For a quick overview of these temporary visas, see Chapter 3.)

CAUTION
Don't confuse green cards with U.S. citizenship. The highest status you can obtain under U.S. immigration laws is citizenship. However, with only a very few exceptions, you must get a green card before you can apply for citizenship. For example, an immigrant who marries a U.S. citizen can gain the immediate right to apply for a green card, but not yet to apply for U.S. citizenship.

B. How Much You Can Do Without a Lawyer

The advice given in this book is for simple, straightforward cases. In other words, it's for people who clearly meet the immigration eligibility requirements and have the education and skills to understand and handle the application requirements.

Many key tasks you can do yourself, such as filling in forms, collecting documents, and attending interviews. Still, even filling out immigration forms can be a challenge. Minor mistakes or inconsistencies in the information you provide can lead to delays or denial. Hiring an attorney—who handles this type of paperwork every day and knows whom to call when things go wrong—can be well worth the expense, both for convenience and for your own peace of mind.

And if your case is more complex, you absolutely should hire a lawyer to advise or represent you. This might be the situation if any of the following are true:

- You have been ordered to appear before an Immigration Judge for what are called "removal" proceedings because U.S. immigration authorities do not believe that you have a legal reason to either enter or continue to stay in the United States.
- You have a criminal record.
- You have some other problems with your immigration paperwork; for example, you have submitted
- The paperwork and technical requirements are too heavy; for example, you plan to apply for asylum, are feeling traumatized, and need to assemble a lot of evidence about conditions in your home country; or you are appealing a negative decision made in your case by immigration authorities.

Of course, the key is to get a really good, experienced attorney. See Chapter 24 for guidance in hiring and working with a lawyer.

C. Using This Book

You need not read every chapter in this book—only those helpful to your specific situation. Here is some guidance.

Read **Chapter 1** if you're interested in a summary of immigration trends and laws throughout history.

Definitely read **Chapters 2, 3, and 4.** They describe the basic baseline requirements for obtaining legal permission to stay in the United States.

Also be sure to read **Chapter 5.** It explains the general forms and procedures required for obtaining a green card and the annual numbered limits or quotas that might apply.

 TIP

This book doesn't provide blank forms, for good reason. All the application forms you'll need—and we'll tell you exactly which ones they are—are either readily available for free (www.uscis.gov or www.state.gov) or will be mailed to you by the immigration authorities when the time is right. Some can be filled out online. The forms get revised frequently, so it's best for you to obtain the most up-to-date form straight from its source when ready to use it. We have, however, provided sample filled-in forms at www.nolo.com/back-of-book/GRN.html to illustrate what this book describes and show you what the form will actually look like.

Now you can choose and read the specific chapters that concern you. Look over the chapter headings for **Chapters 6 through 15, as well as 18 and 19**—and read the ones that make the most sense in your specific situation. For example, if you believe that you might qualify for a green card because you will be marrying or are already married to a U.S. citizen, read **Chapter 7.** It might refer you to other chapters you should read to get a more complete picture.

After reading about the various rules for specific types of immigrants, if you decide that you qualify to file for yourself or another person, read **Chapters 21 and 22.** These chapters will help you with filling out the necessary forms and getting them into the right hands.

If you lose your green card or need to renew or replace it, read **Chapter 23** to find out how to do so.

Some people will find that they don't qualify for U.S. immigration at all, or at least not yet—it's a complicated and narrow system. But the good news is that approximately one million people receive U.S. green cards every year.

 CAUTION

Green cards come with certain limitations. It's not a completely secure status. For example, you can lose your right to your green card if you:

- commit a crime
- don't make your primary home in the United States
- forget to report your change of address to the immigration authorities
- involve yourself in terrorist or subversive activities, or
- otherwise violate the immigration laws.

Steps You Must Take to Keep Up to Date

This book was as up to date as we could make it on the day it was printed. However, immigration laws change frequently, and USCIS changes its fees, rules, forms, and procedures even more often—at times without warning anyone.

That's why you must take certain steps on your own to protect your rights and interests. In particular, be sure to:

- Check the USCIS website before turning in any application, at www.uscis.gov/forms. Make sure the form you filled out is still the most up to date, and that the fee hasn't gone up.
- Check the companion page for this book at **www.nolo.com/back-of-book/GRN.html** Here, you'll find sample filled-in government forms, legal updates, and other useful information. Also see whether we've published a later edition of this book, in which case you'll probably want to obtain it.
- Listen to the news, particularly for changes by the U.S. Congress. But don't rush to USCIS to apply for something until you're sure it's final. A lot of laws in progress get reported on before the president has actually signed them.

America: A Nation of Immigrants

A. **America's Earliest Settlers** 6
   1. Forced Migration 6
   2. European Exodus 6
   3. Growth of the Continental U.S. 6

B. **Early Immigration Restrictions** 7

C. **Today's Immigration Laws** 8
   1. Preference for Skilled Workers 8
   2. Refugees and Political Asylum 8
   3. Amnesty for Undocumented Workers in the 1980s 9
   4. Immigration Acts From 1990 to the Present 9

D. **Looking Forward** 10

To understand current immigration policy, it helps to know how it came about.

A. America's Earliest Settlers

Long before Cristóbal Colón—the Spanish name for Christopher Columbus—opened the Americas to the Europeans in 1492, the area was inhabited by Native American Indians, including the Eskimos. Other early settlers included the Vikings, in the northernmost part of North America, and the ancestors of today's Hawaiians.

From the 15th century onward, the continent became a magnet for explorers and colonists from Spain, Holland, France, and England. In 1620, the pilgrims landed in Massachusetts and founded their new Zion, free from the interference of the English government. Quakers settled in Pennsylvania. Maryland provided refuge for Catholics who had been persecuted in England.

Spanish Jews, who had settled in Brazil after being expelled from Spain, arrived in New York when the Portuguese took over the former Spanish colony and started the Brazilian inquisition. After the Scottish rebellion was crushed, people from Scotland left for the colonies.

Other immigrants came in groups and provided special skills to the new cities and settlements: Austrians from Salzburg made silk; Poles and Germans made tar, glass, and tools and built homes. Later, Italians came and raised grapes. New Jersey was settled by the Swedes; northern Pennsylvania attracted a large number of Germans.

1. Forced Migration

Not everyone who came to the New World did so of their own free will. Many crossed the ocean as indentured servants for landowners in the English colonies.

In the South, cotton and other plantation owners turned to the inhuman trade of African people to create a huge and cheap workforce, while businesses of the North benefited indirectly.

By the time the first census of the new republic was taken in 1790, only two-thirds of its four million inhabitants were English-speaking.

Although the U.S. Congress amended the Constitution in 1808 to ban importing slaves, it took nearly half a century before the smuggling of human beings stopped.

2. European Exodus

Between 1820 and 1910, at least 38 million Europeans moved to the United States.

Several important events caused this migration: the Napoleonic Wars; political disturbances in Germany, Austria-Hungary, Greece, and Poland; the Potato Famine in Ireland; the religious persecutions of Protestants, Catholics, and Jews in Czarist Russia and other parts of Europe; and the Industrial Revolution, which produced thousands of unemployed workers and peasants.

3. Growth of the Continental U.S.

The United States didn't always have the shape and territory it does today. The country grew by purchase, such as the Louisiana Purchase from France's Napoleon I, which bought an expanse of land from the Mississippi to the Rocky Mountains; and the purchase of Florida from Spain. It grew by war, such as the one waged with Mexico over California and Texas, and the one with Britain in 1812, which ended with a treaty granting the United States parts of Canada. The nation also grew by possession of Native Americans' ancestral lands, sometimes by treaty, sometimes by purchase, and all too often by outright massacre.

B. Early Immigration Restrictions

In California, the Gold Rush of 1849 brought people not only from all over America but also the Chinese from across the Pacific Ocean. Chinese workers provided cheap labor for railroad construction. However, they were not granted the right to become American citizens.

By 1882, there were approximately 300,000 low-wage Chinese laborers in America. They became targets for antagonism and racial hatred. The Chinese Exclusion Act, passed in 1882, completely banned noncitizen Chinese from immigrating to the United States. This law remained in effect until 1943.

The Japanese then stepped in to handle low-wage jobs in agriculture, domestic work, lumber mills, and salmon fisheries. These workers also were targets of racial hatred. They were excluded from the United States in 1908 and prohibited from becoming U.S. citizens by the Immigration Act of 1924.

Also during this time, after America purchased the Philippines from Spain in 1898, Filipinos were able to immigrate. They concentrated mostly on the East Coast and Hawaii as laborers on farms and sugar plantations, and in fish canneries and logging camps. They too were excluded from citizenship, by immigration laws passed in 1924.

This great influx of people in the late 19th and early 20th centuries brought the passage of several restrictive immigration laws. At various times, the U.S. Congress forbade people it considered undesirable to enter—paupers, drunkards, anarchists, polygamists, and people of various specific national origins.

In 1917, Congress passed an Immigration Act to restrict the entry of immigrants, especially the flow of illiterate laborers from central and eastern Europe. No immigration was permitted to the United States from the Asiatic Barred Zone. In addition to China and Japan, this zone included India, Siam (Thailand), Indochina (Vietnam, Cambodia, and Laos), Afghanistan, parts of Siberia, Iran, and Arabia, and the islands of Java, Sumatra, Ceylon, Borneo, New Guinea, and Celebes.

After World War I, America faced economic depression and unemployment, and immigrants became the scapegoat. In 1921, a tight national-origins quota system was enacted as a temporary measure. Total immigration was limited to about 350,000 per year. Immigration from each country in a given year was limited to 3% of all nationals from that country who were living in the United States during the 1910 census.

This system was made permanent when the U.S. Congress approved the National Origins Act of 1924. Its purpose was "to arrest a trend toward a change in the fundamental composition of the American stock." Based on the ethnic composition of the United States as recorded in the 1920 census, it limited the entry of aliens from any one country to 2% of the number of their people living in the United States. In one stroke, the law reduced the total immigration of aliens from all countries to 150,000 per year.

The object was not simply to limit immigration but to favor certain kinds of immigrants. More were permitted from western Europe and fewer from southern and eastern Europe. The law totally excluded Asians.

After World War II, however, the door to immigration would again open—this time, to a few carefully selected groups of immigrants. A new category of naturalized Americans was admitted: thousands of alien soldiers who had served with the U.S. armed forces overseas.

Congress also passed the War Brides Act in 1945 to facilitate the reunion of 118,000 alien spouses and children with members of the U.S. armed forces who had fought and married overseas.

The Displaced Persons Act of 1948 allowed 400,000 refugees admission to the U.S. over the next two years. Most of them had been displaced from Poland, Romania, Hungary, the Baltic area, the Ukraine, and Yugoslavia.

When the Iron Curtain fell on Eastern Europe, the Refugee Relief Act of 1953 allowed 214,000 refugees from Communist countries to be admitted into the United States.

C. Today's Immigration Laws

When the Immigration and Nationality Act was passed in 1952, it wove all the existing immigration laws into one and formed a basic immigration law that's similar to the one we know now. (However, it was not until President Lyndon Johnson signed the 1965 amendments into law that the racially biased national origin quota was abolished.)

Where to Find U.S. Immigration Laws

The entire set of immigration laws is now available online and at law libraries, in Title 8 of the U.S. Code. Occasionally in this book, we'll tell you where you can read a certain piece of the immigration laws by referring to the code section—for example, 8 U.S.C. § 1101.

However, immigration lawyers and government officials tend to use a separate numbering system for the same codes, preceded by the letters I.N.A., for "Immigration and Nationality Act," so when we include citations here we'll also give you the I.N.A. section reference. The I.N.A. is available on the USCIS website (www.uscis.gov) under "Laws."

The amendments introduced two primary ways of becoming an immigrant: by family relationship and by the employment needs of the United States.

The legislation established a preference system—giving priority to some groups of immigrants over others. For example, spouses and children of U.S. citizens had higher priority than their brothers and sisters. The law also provided a separate category for refugees.

1. Preference for Skilled Workers

In 1965, the laws were amended to allow skilled workers to move more easily to the United States. The departure of doctors, lawyers, engineers, scientists, teachers, accountants, nurses, and other professionals caused a "brain drain" not only in Europe, but also in Asia, the Pacific Rim, and developing countries.

This preference for skilled workers remains in effect. Although the laws allow a few unskilled workers to immigrate, the numbers are so limited that the category is useless for many people.

2. Refugees and Political Asylum

The end of the Vietnam War resulted in a flow of refugees from the Indochinese peninsula.

In 1980, Fidel Castro declared that the Port of Mariel was open to anyone who wanted to leave. Cuban refugees arrived on the shores of Florida by the thousands. These included some criminals and mentally ill people who had been forced by Castro to leave the jails and mental hospitals.

In response, the U.S. Congress passed the Refugee Act of 1980, which defined a "refugee" as someone who fears persecution in his or her home country because of religious or political beliefs, race, national origin, or ethnic identity. Based on this law, the U.S. admits a limited number of refugees annually. In the past, it has been tens of thousands per year, but the Trump administration has sharply reduced those numbers.

The U.S. also grants asylum to many who have fled persecution and made it to the U.S. on their own.

3. Amnesty for Undocumented Workers in the 1980s

The Immigration Reform and Control Act of 1986, more commonly known as the "Amnesty Law," benefited many Mexicans and others who had entered and were living without legal status in the United States. Those who'd been resident here since January 1, 1982—more than two million— were, if they met various other requirements, granted legal residency. Their spouses and children were also entitled to the same benefits.

At the same time, the Amnesty Law attempted to control the future influx of undocumented persons—and those controls still exist today. Any employer who hires or recruits a foreign national who lacks statusor who, for a fee, refers one to another employer without first verifying the person's immigration status, is subject to a fine ranging from $200 to $10,000 per employee

4. Immigration Acts From 1990 to the Present

With the Immigration Act of 1990, the U.S. Congress approved a comprehensive overhaul.

This act provided for a huge increase of immigrants, up to 675,000 annually. It aimed to attract immigrants with the education, skills, or money to enhance U.S. economic life, while maintaining the policy of family reunification. The law made it easier for scientists, engineers, inventors, and other highly skilled professionals to enter the United States. Millionaire entrepreneurs received their own immigrant classification.

Citizens of nations that have had little immigration to the United States for the past five years were allocated 50,000 immigrant visas yearly under the diversity visa "lottery" system. Temporary protections were added for people fleeing war or natural disasters, such as earthquakes.

Such provisions made the Immigration Act of 1990 the most humane legislation for immigrants in a century. However, more recent changes again closed America's doors to many immigrants. These included 1996's Antiterrorism and Effective Death Penalty Act (AEDPA) and Illegal Immigration Reform and Immigrant Responsibility Act (IIRIRA).

A variety of legislative and regulatory changes were also added after the terrorist attacks of September 11, 2001, tightening controls on would-be immigrants as well as those already here.

The USA Patriot Act of 2002 expanded the definition of terrorism and increased the government's authority to detain and deport immigrants. Also in 2002, legislation established the new Department of Homeland Security (DHS), thus breaking the Immigration and Naturalization Service (INS) into three agencies under the DHS's control. These new agencies include U.S. Citizenship and Immigration Services (USCIS), which took over public INS functions such as deciding on applications for immigration benefits; Immigration and Customs Enforcement (ICE), which now handles enforcement of the immigration laws within the U.S. borders; and Customs and Border Protection (CBP), which handles U.S. border enforcement (including at land borders, airports, and seaports, and interior areas near the border).

It's also important to remember the important role that federal court decisions can play in interpreting or even nullifying portions of the immigration laws and related federal laws. So, for example, the Supreme Court's 2013 decision in *U.S. v. Windsor* was a groundbreaking moment for same-sex binational couples. By striking down portions of the federal Defense of Marriage Act (DOMA), it removed the primary obstacle blocking rights to a green card, a fiancé visa (which leads to a green card), or various nonimmigrant visas for accompanying spouses, based on a same-sex relationship with a U.S. citizen or permanent resident. The Supreme Court's 2015 decision in *Obergefell v. Hodges* further cemented these rights, with its ruling that the U.S. Constitution guarantees a nationwide right to same-sex marriage. These changes further illustrate how U.S. immigration policy shifts according to political will.

D. Looking Forward

Immigration law policies are a subject of ongoing congressional scrutiny. With every shift in presidential administration and the U.S. economy and sense of security (or insecurity), public attitudes toward immigrants shift as well.

By the time this book went to print in 2022, President Biden was in the process of undoing especially harsh measures instituted under the Trump administration. Although only Congress has the power to actually change U.S. immigration law (as opposed to interpreting or enforcing it), the Executive Branch sometimes steps in when Congress fails to act, as it has for years.

The opening lines of the Declaration of Independence of the United States, so eloquently written by Thomas Jefferson more than 200 years ago, remain both an inspiration and a challenge:

We hold these truths to be self-evident, that all men are created equal, that they are endowed by their Creator with certain unalienable Rights, that among these are Life, Liberty, and the pursuit of Happiness.

All Ways to Get a Green Card

A. Family-Based Relationships 12

    1. Related or Engaged to a U.S. Citizen 12

    2. Related to a Lawful Permanent Resident 12

    3. Other Relatives 13

B. Employment-Based Relationships 13

    1. Priority Workers 13

    2. Other Workers 13

C. Special Immigrants 14

D. Entrepreneur Immigrants 14

E. Asylum and Refugee Status 15

F. Diversity Visa Lottery 15

G. Amnesties 15

H. Private Bills 16

The official name for the green card is the Permanent Resident Card or Form I-551. It has been called a "green card" because, when it was first introduced in the 1940s, the color of the plastic identification card with the alien's photo, registration number, date of birth, and date and port of entry was green.

Over the years, the card's color has been, at various times, blue, white, and pink, but now it is green again.

Front of Green Card

Back of Green Card

There are several ways a person can obtain a green card—that is, become a lawful permanent resident. The most popular ones are through family and work. The other ways include proving that you're fleeing from persecution, making large investments in the United States, and a few more obscure bases.

This book covers the green card categories most readily available to ordinary people, with an emphasis on family categories. However, this chapter will tell you a little about the other major green card categories, and where to go next if you're interested in them.

A. Family-Based Relationships

Recognizing that the family is important in the life of the nation, the U.S. Congress created ways for family members to be reunited with their relatives who are U.S. citizens or lawful permanent residents.

1. Related or Engaged to a U.S. Citizen

If you are the spouse (opposite sex or same sex), child, brother, sister, or parent of, or are engaged to be married to, a U.S. citizen, you can become a lawful permanent resident. The person to whom you're related or engaged must start the process by filing a petition with USCIS or the U.S. embassy in your country of residence.

If you are the widow or widower of a U.S. citizen and it was a good-faith marriage (not a sham to get a green card), you can petition for a green card for yourself, provided you file the application (Form I-360) within two years of the death of your spouse (unless your spouse had already filed a Form I-130 for you), you weren't legally separated at the time of death, and you haven't remarried.

2. Related to a Lawful Permanent Resident

If you are the spouse or unmarried child of a lawful permanent resident, you can obtain a green card—someday. First, the relative who has the green card must file a petition with USCIS. But you'll have to wait several years, until you reach the top of a waiting list, to apply for the actual green card.

3. Other Relatives

If you are the aunt, uncle, niece, nephew, cousin, grandmother, or grandfather of a U.S. citizen, or if you are the brother, sister, parent, or fiancé of someone who holds a green card, you do not qualify for a green card based on a "family relationship." Understandably, the U.S. Congress had to draw the line on what constitutes a family for the purpose of immigration.

NEXT STEP

If you believe you qualify for a family-based green card, or are helping someone who does, here's where to go next: Readers who are engaged to U.S. citizens, see Chapter 6. Readers who are married to U.S. citizens or permanent residents, see Chapter 7. Readers who are parents of U.S. citizens, see Chapter 8. Readers who are children of U.S. citizens or permanent residents, see Chapter 9. For how to bring in an orphan child, see Chapter 10. Readers who are brothers or sisters of U.S. citizens, see Chapter 12.

B. Employment-Based Relationships

If you do not have a close family member who is a U.S. citizen or who holds a green card, you might be able to obtain a green card through a job offer from an employer in the United States—as either a priority or a nonpriority worker.

1. Priority Workers

Priority workers are people with extraordinary ability (such as an internationally known artist), outstanding professors and researchers, and multinational executives and managers. Another name for this category is "employment first preference."

Such highly skilled people have a relatively easy immigration process. Some do not even need a job offer, and none are required to go through the difficult labor certification process that other immigrating workers must pass, in which the Department of Labor determines that there are no qualified U.S. workers available and willing to do the same job.

2. Other Workers

Applicants who have been offered jobs that require graduate degrees in the arts or sciences or a profession (such as a law degree), or a master's degree in business administration (MBA), or a bachelor's degree plus five years of specialized experience are eligible for immigrant visas. This category is known as "employment second preference."

These applicants will first need certification from the Department of Labor saying that no qualified U.S. worker is available, willing, and able to do the job.

Also, ordinary professionals (without graduate degrees) and skilled or unskilled workers (factory workers, plumbers, domestic workers, carpenters, and the like) may apply for labor certification and a green card on the basis of a job offer. This category is known as "employment third preference."

SEE AN EXPERT

If you believe you qualify for any of these employment-based green cards, consult an experienced immigration attorney. As explained earlier, this book doesn't cover employment-based immigration. The employer who has offered you a job (and you must have a job offer in almost all categories described above) might have an attorney it works with regularly. In fact, the Department of Labor's labor certification rules require the employer to pay attorneys' fees and other costs.

Be Ready to Wait

It could take you a long time to become a permanent resident under some of the immigrant visa categories described in this chapter. Once you or your petitioner files the first petition form to set the process in motion, however, it might become difficult for you to come to the United States as a tourist or another nonimmigrant, or to have your status as a nonimmigrant extended. That's because, in order to obtain most nonimmigrant visas, you have to prove that you plan to return to your home country after your stay on the visa—and it's hard to prove permanent ties to your home country if you're simultaneously planning to leave it behind and get a U.S. green card.

The only groups who need not be concerned with this warning are diplomats (A visas), employees of international organizations (G visas), intra-company transferees (L-1 or L-2 visas), and workers in specialty occupations that require a bachelor's degree or its equivalent (H-1B visas).

- former employees of the Panama Canal Zone
- retired officers or employees of certain international organizations who have lived in the United States for a certain time, plus their spouses and unmarried children
- foreign workers who have been employees of the U.S. consulate in Hong Kong for at least three years
- foreign children who have been declared dependent in juvenile courts in the United States, and
- international broadcasting employees.

All these people fall into a green card category known as "employment-based fourth preference" or EB-4.

 SEE AN EXPERT

If you believe you fit one of these categories, consult an experienced immigration attorney. Special immigrants are not covered in this book. Your employer-petitioner might be willing to hire an attorney for you.

C. Special Immigrants

Certain categories of people may obtain a green card by special laws intended to benefit limited groups. These include, for example:

- priests, nuns, pastors, ministers, rabbis, imams, and other workers of recognized religious denominations
- former employees of the U.S. government, commended by the U.S. Secretary of State for having performed outstanding service to the government for at least 15 years
- medical doctors who have been licensed in the United States and have worked and lived in the United States since January 1978

D. Entrepreneur Immigrants

An alien entrepreneur from any country who invests at least $1.8 million in a business (or $900,000 if the business is in an economically depressed area) and who employs at least ten U.S. citizens or lawful permanent residents is eligible for a green card. Each year, 10,000 immigrant visas are set aside for this millionaire immigrant category, which is designed to create employment. This category is also known as "employment-based fifth preference" or "EB-5."

SEE AN EXPERT

Are you financially able to qualify for a green card based on investment? If so, it's well worth hiring an experienced immigration attorney to analyze the latest legal developments and help with your application.

E. Asylum and Refugee Status

People who can prove that they fled their country based on past persecution or out of fear of future persecution owing to their race, religion, nationality, membership in a particular social group, or political opinion may apply for legal status as refugees (if they're outside the U.S.) or asylees (if they're already inside the U.S.).

A person who gains U.S. government approval as a refugee or an asylee can apply for permanent residence status later (more specifically, one year after being admitted to the United States as a refugee or one year after asylee status is granted).

NEXT STEP

For more information on applying for refugee or asylee status, see Chapter 13.

F. Diversity Visa Lottery

The Immigration Act of 1990 created a green card category to benefit people from countries that in recent years have sent the fewest numbers of immigrants to the United States. You can enter the lottery if you are a native of one of those countries and meet certain educational and other requirements. Because the winners are selected through a random drawing, the program is popularly known as the "green card lottery." Its official name is the "Diversity Immigrant Visa Lottery."

There are 50,000 winners selected each year. They are chosen by dividing the world into regions and allocating no more than 7% of the total green cards to each region.

However, even if you win the lottery, you still have to make it through the green card application process—and many people fail, because they're inadmissible or the government can't process their applications by the deadlines set by law.

NEXT STEP

For more information on applying for the visa lottery, and what to do if you win, see Chapter 11.

G. Amnesties

Once in a while, Congress gives blanket green card eligibility to people who have been living in the United States illegally.

The most recent amnesty was offered in the early 1980s. Although anti-immigrant commentators regularly complain that every new law that benefits immigrants is an "amnesty," there has been no actual amnesty offered since that time.

Some lawmakers have proposed bills offering an amnesty-like path to a green card in recent years, at least for "DREAMers," or those who were brought to the U.S. when young. Keep your eyes on the news and the Nolo website for updates, and beware of the many scammers urging immigrants to pay to submit an application when no such application exists.

CAUTION

Interested in learning more about a past or upcoming amnesty? Consult an experienced immigration attorney or a local nonprofit. Do not go to a USCIS office unless you want to risk deportation.

H. Private Bills

You might have heard of people who became permanent residents by means of a private bill passed by the U.S. Congress. However, such cases are rare. You must have very special circumstances—and strong political ties—to get a private bill passed.

Look into the possibility of a private bill where the law is against you but your case has strong humanitarian factors. Private bills succeed when an injustice can be corrected only by a special act of the U.S. Congress.

The successful ones tend to be people in unusually tragic situations, such as a family that came to the U.S. seeking cancer treatment for a child, only to have the father and mother of the child killed in a car wreck.

A private bill must be sponsored by one or more members of the House of Representatives and one or more members of the Senate.

It must be introduced in both houses of Congress, then recommended favorably by the Judiciary Committee to which it has been assigned in both houses, after having been favorably reported on by the Subcommittee on Immigration of both houses.

Both houses of Congress must approve the bill during a regular session. The president of the United States must then sign it into law.

Thus, if you are a foreign-born person facing deportation, you will have to go through the eye of a needle before getting your private bill passed by Congress and signed by the president. In short, hiring the best immigration lawyer in town will likely give you a better chance to obtain a green card than will the private bill route. ●

Short-Term Alternatives to a Green Card

A. How Do Foreign Nationals Enter the United States?.. 18

B. Types of Visas 18

   1. Immigrant Visas.. 18

   2. Nonimmigrant Visas... 18

   3. Nonimmigrant Visa Classifications 19

   4. Deferred Action for Childhood Arrivals.. 21

   5. Nonimmigrant U Visa Can Lead to a Green Card.. 21

C. Tourists Who Can Visit Without a Visa 21

   1. What You'll Need for VWP Travel... 21

   2. VWP-Eligible Countries.. 22

D. The Importance of Staying Legal 23

E. How to Extend a Visitor Visa... 23

F. Changing Your Reason for Staying..24

G. What to Do If USCIS Denies Your Extension Application 24

H. Tips on Filling Out Form I-539.. 25

As you know, this book is only about green cards—or, in legal-speak, U.S. permanent residence. However, you probably also know that many people who want U.S. green cards will never be able to get one. The green card categories are very limited, and the application process is hard to get through successfully. That's why this chapter will briefly tell you about other —sometimes easier—ways to come to the United States, even if it's for a shorter time.

RESOURCE

Want to learn more about the ways to stay temporarily in the United States? See *U.S. Immigration Made Easy,* by Ilona Bray (Nolo).

A. How Do Foreign Nationals Enter the United States?

The basic rule is that most people may enter the United States only after receiving permission from the U.S. government, through the U.S. embassy or consulate in their own country. The permission or authority to enter the United States is called a "visa," and is stamped in your passport by the U.S. consul. A major exception is if you are eligible to enter under the Visa Waiver Program; see discussion in Section C, below.

If you enter the United States without permission, without a visa or a visa waiver, and without being examined by the immigration authorities, you are called "undocumented" within the immigration laws and an "illegal alien" by the general public.

B. Types of Visas

There are two kinds of visas an alien can receive from the U.S. embassy or consulate: an immigrant visa and a nonimmigrant visa.

1. Immigrant Visas

Just to avoid confusion, we should mention that even those people who are in the process of getting a green card, as discussed in the rest of this book, must get a physical visa first if they'll be arriving from another country. They receive what is called an "immigrant visa." They receive the actual green card only after they have arrived in the United States and claimed their permanent residency. People who apply for their green cards from within the United States must also be allocated a visa number, although they'll never see or receive a physical visa.

2. Nonimmigrant Visas

Nonimmigrant visas are the main topic we'll introduce you to in this short chapter. A nonimmigrant visa gives you the ability to stay in the United States temporarily with limited rights.

A visa that expires in a few years is probably your second choice, given that you're reading a book on green cards. However, a nonimmigrant visa might serve you in two ways. First, it might allow you to legally visit the United States in order to decide whether you really want a green card, or to make a decision that will lead to your getting a green card. For example, a person might come to the U.S. on a tourist (B-2) visa to visit a U.S. citizen boyfriend or girlfriend and find out whether getting married seems like a good idea.

Second, a nonimmigrant visa might be your only choice for the moment. If your research, using this book and other resources, leads you to believe that you don't qualify for a green card, then a nonimmigrant visa might allow you to at least live in the United States for a while, developing U.S. contacts or job skills, hoping that a green card opportunity will open up.

Unfortunately, nonimmigrant visas are not only short-term solutions, but they restrict your life in the United States in other ways. For example, a visitor visa (B-2) does not allow you to work. A student visa (F-1 or M-1) does not allow a student to stop studying in order to work. A temporary worker's visa (H-1B), given to a professional worker such as an accountant or engineer, does not authorize one to change employers without permission.

3. Nonimmigrant Visa Classifications

You will often hear visa classifications referred to in shorthand by a letter followed by a number. The following table summarizes the nonimmigrant visa classifications available.

Classification	Summary
A-1	Ambassadors, public ministers, consular officers, or career diplomats, and their immediate families
A-2	Other foreign government officials or employees, and their immediate families
A-3	Personal attendants, servants, or employees of A-1 and A-2 visa holders, and their immediate families
B-1	Temporary business visitors
B-2	Temporary pleasure visitors
C-1	Foreign travelers in immediate and continuous transit through the U.S.
D-1	Crewmembers (sea or air)
E-1	Treaty traders and their spouses or children
E-2	Treaty investors and their spouses or children
E-3	Australians who have at least a bachelor's degree or its equivalent, working in specialty occupations
F-1	Academic or language students
F-2	Spouses or children of F-1 visa holders
G-1	Designated principal resident representatives of foreign governments coming to the U.S. to work for an international organization, and their staff members and immediate families
G-2	Other representatives of foreign governments coming to the U.S. to work for an international organization, and their immediate families

Classification	Summary
G-3	Representatives of foreign governments and their immediate families, who would ordinarily qualify for G-1 or G-2 visas except that their governments are not members of an international organization
G-4	Officers or employees of international organizations, and their immediate families
G-5	Attendants, servants, and personal employees of G-1 through G-4 visa holders, and their immediate families
H-1B	Workers in specialty occupations requiring at least a bachelor's degree or its equivalent in on-the-job experience
H-2A	Temporary agricultural workers coming to the U.S. to fill positions for which a temporary shortage of American workers has been recognized by the U.S. Department of Agriculture
H-2B	Temporary workers of various kinds coming to the U.S. to perform temporary jobs for which there is a shortage of available qualified U.S. workers
H-3	Temporary trainees
H-4	Spouses or children of H-1A/B, H-2A/B, or rH-3 visa holders
I	Representatives of the foreign press, coming to the U.S. to work solely in that capacity, and their immediate families
J-1	Exchange visitors coming to the U.S. to study, work, or train as part of an exchange program officially recognized by the U.S. Department of State
J-2	Spouses or children of J-1 visa holders
K-1	Fiancés and fiancées of U.S. citizens coming to the U.S. for the purpose of getting married
K-2	Children of K-1 visa holders
K-3	Spouses of U.S. citizens awaiting approval of their immigrant visa petition or the availability of a green card
K-4	Children of K-3 visa holders
L-1	Intracompany transferees who work as managers, executives, or persons with specialized knowledge

Class-ification	Summary
L-2	Spouses or children of L-1 visa holders
M-1	Vocational or other nonacademic students
M-2	Immediate families of M-1 visa holders
N	Children and parents of certain special immigrants
NATO-1	Principal permanent representatives of member states to NATO and its subsidiary bodies, who are residents in the U.S., and resident official staff members, secretaries general, assistant secretaries general, and executive secretaries of NATO, other permanent NATO officials of similar rank, or their immediate families
NATO-2	Other representatives to member states to NATO and its subsidiary bodies, including its advisers and technical experts of delegations, members of Immediate Article 3, 4 UST 1796 families; dependents of members of forces entering in accordance with the Status-of-Forces Agreement or in accordance with the Protocol on Status of International Military Headquarters; members of such a force if issued visas
NATO-3	Official clerical staff accompanying representatives of member states to NATO and its subsidiary bodies, and their immediate families
NATO-4	Officials of NATO other than those who can be classified as NATO-1, and their immediate families
NATO-5	Experts other than officials who can be classified as NATO-1, employed in missions on behalf of NATO, and their dependents
NATO-6	Members of civilian components accompanying forces entering in accordance with provisions of the NATO Status-of-Forces Agreement; members of civilian components attached to or employed by allied headquarters under the Protocol on Status of International Military Headquarters set up pursuant to the North Atlantic Treaty; and their dependents
NATO-7	Attendants, servants, or personal employees of NATO-1 through NATO-6 classes, and their immediate families

Class-ification	Summary
O-1	People with extraordinary ability in the sciences, arts, education, business, or athletics
O-2	Support staff of O-1 visa holders
O-3	Spouses or children of O-1 or O-2 visa holders
P-1	Internationally recognized athletes and entertainers
P-2	Artists or entertainers in reciprocal exchange programs
P-3	Artists and entertainers coming to the U.S. to give culturally unique performances in a group
P-4	Spouses or children of P-1, P-2, or P-3 visa holders
Q-1	Participants in international cultural exchange programs
Q-2	Irish Peace Process Cultural and Training Program (Walsh Visas)
Q-3	Immediate family members of Q-1 visa holders
R-1	Workers in religious occupations
R-2	Spouses or children of R-1 visa holders
S-5	Certain people supplying critical information relating to a criminal organization or enterprise
S-6	Certain people supplying critical information relating to terrorism
S-7	Immediate family members of S-5 and S-6 visa holders
T	Women and children who are in the United States because they are victims of trafficking, who are cooperating with law enforcement, and who fear extreme hardship (such as retribution) if returned home
TN	NAFTA professionals from Canada or Mexico
TD	Spouses and children of NAFTA professionals
U	People who have been victims of crimes, have useful information about them, and have been helping U.S. law enforcement authorities with investigating and prosecuting these crimes.
V	Spouses and children of lawful permanent residents who have visa petitions that were filed for them prior to December 21, 2000, and who have been waiting for three years or more to qualify for a green card

4. Deferred Action for Childhood Arrivals

Another short-term alternative to a green card came not in the form of a visa, but as a special program to prevent deportation of people who came to the U.S. very young, and had attended school and otherwise made the U.S. their home. Instituted by President Obama, the Deferred Action for Childhood Arrivals or DACA program's future now is embroiled in lawsuits, following attempts by President Trump to cancel it. At the time this book went to print, current DACA holders could renew their status, but no new applications were being accepted. Congress also occasionally considers passing legislation to grant legal status to DACA recipients (also called "DREAMers," a name drawn from the title of long-promised Congressional legislation) but so far has still failed to come to any agreement.

5. Nonimmigrant U Visa Can Lead to a Green Card

One of the visas mentioned on our summary table bears further explanation. The U visa, for people who have been the victims of crimes in the U.S. and suffered as a result, and who are cooperating with law enforcement officials, can ultimately lead to a U.S. green card. For that reason, we cover it in Chapter 19 of this book.

C. Tourists Who Can Visit Without a Visa

The Visa Waiver Program (VWP) allows the citizens of certain countries—that the Department of State (DOS) chooses, based on low rates of visa overstays or abuse—to visit the United States for 90 days without first having a tourist visa stamped on their passports.

1. What You'll Need for VWP Travel

At the moment, 40 countries participate in the VWP. If you're from one of these countries, and wish to enter the U.S. without a B visa, you'll need to get these things first, before starting your trip:

- **A passport meeting U.S. government requirements.** This means an electronic passport with an integrated chip (e-passport) that is valid for six months past your expected stay in the United States.
- **A ticket for both your arrival to and departure from the United States.** Your arrival ticket needs to be with an airline or boat company that is authorized to carry VWP passengers. The exception is if you'll be entering via Canada or Mexico, in which case, no departure ticket is required.
- **Prior U.S. government authorization.** You'll do this through the Electronic System for Travel Authorization (ESTA), online at https://esta.cbp.dhs.gov. You can apply at any time prior to travel. There is an initial processing charge of $4 for electronic travel authorization. If your VWP application is approved, you'll need to pay an additional $10. The ESTA system requires use of a MasterCard, Visa, American Express, or Discover debit or credit card. You'll probably get an answer immediately, although it sometimes takes up to three days. Authorizations are generally valid for up to two years, or until your passport expires, whichever comes first. If you don't receive authorization, you'll need to apply for a nonimmigrant visa at a U.S. embassy or consulate.
- **Entry fee.** Travelers arriving at a land border (from Canada or Mexico) will be required to pay an entry fee.

! CAUTION
Nationals of or visitors to countries with ties to terrorism cannot use the VWP. Congress has prohibited its use by nationals of or recent visitors to "high-risk" countries with ties to terrorism. Nationals of a country on the terrorism watch list who carry the passport of another country that is on the VWP list would thus be excluded from VWP travel. There are minor exceptions, including for people performing military service in a country of concern, or based on law enforcement or national security interests. This isn't an outright prohibition on U.S. entry: People who cannot travel on the VWP can still apply for a visitor visa at the nearest U.S. embassy or consulate.

EXAMPLE: You want to visit the United States for two months. If you live in a country that is included in the VWP, you first make sure your passport meets U.S. requirements, then get authorization to travel by filling out the online ESTA application, and then buy your round-trip plane ticket to the United States. You do not need to visit a U.S. consulate to get a tourist visa. You may, however, upon arrival in the U.S., be asked to show your departure ticket as evidence that you are simply visiting and that you will return to your country within the 90-day limit.

2. VWP-Eligible Countries

Under the Visa Waiver Program, citizens of the following countries who can present a machine-readable passport are exempted from getting visas before entering the United States:

Andorra	Czech Republic
Australia	Denmark
Austria	Estonia
Belgium	Finland
Brunei	France
Chile	Germany
Croatia	Great Britain (United Kingdom)
Greece	New Zealand
Holland (Netherlands)	Norway
Hungary	Poland
Iceland	Portugal
Ireland	San Marino
Italy	Singapore
Japan	Slovakia
Latvia	Slovenia
Liechtenstein	South Korea
Lithuania	Spain
Luxembourg	Sweden
Malta	Switzerland
Monaco	Taiwan

To be included in the Visa Waiver Program, the country must have:

- a very low rate of refusals of tourist visa applications, and
- few violations of U.S. immigration laws.

In short, countries whose citizens are least likely to stay too long or work illegally in the United States are most likely to be included in the Visa Waiver Program.

Disadvantages of Entering Without a Visa

There could be disadvantages to entering the U.S. under the Visa Waiver Program.

You cannot change your tourist status to another nonimmigrant status, such as that of student or temporary worker, nor can you request an extension of your 90-day stay.

With few exceptions, you also cannot change your status to a lawful permanent resident while staying in the United States.

In addition, should U.S. border officials deny you entry into the United States for any reason, you have no right to appeal. Political refugees who are fleeing persecution and who apply for asylum in the United States are the sole exception. (See Chapter 13.)

D. The Importance of Staying Legal

If you enter the United States as a tourist, student, temporary worker, entertainer, or in any other nonimmigrant category, your chances at a future green card depend on your maintaining your legal status and not violating the conditions of your stay in the United States. Do not overstay the limits of your visa. Do not work when you are not authorized to work. Do not change schools or employers without first requesting and receiving permission from U.S. immigration authorities.

The consequences for breaking the rules controlling immigration can be quite serious: You could be detained in an immigration jail; removal proceedings could be started against you; and, if deported, you could be barred from returning to the United States for the next five years or more.

Even if you are not deported, if you overstay by 180 days (around six months) and then leave the United States, you will have to remain outside for three years before being admitted again. If you overstay by 12 months and then leave, the waiting period is ten years before you will be allowed to return. (See Chapter 4.)

More to the point, by obeying the law, you can make use of almost all the ways enumerated in this book to stay in the United States, as long as your current status is legal.

If you are running out of time on a permitted stay, one possibility is to apply to extend it (if you can show a good reason for needing more time) or to change your status, for example from tourist to temporary worker. You can apply for extensions or changes of status only (in most cases) if your current immigration status is legal, you are not overstaying a visa, and you have not worked illegally.

If, instead, you overstay, your visa will be automatically void—even if it is a multiple entry, indefinite visa. You will then be required to apply for a new visa at the U.S. consulate in your home country, unless you can prove "exceptional circumstances."

If there is some issue in your case, or if you need to change status, seek professional advice from an experienced immigration lawyer. (See Chapter 24.) Do not depend on advice from your friends or relatives, or worse, information on the Internet.

E. How to Extend a Visitor Visa

Temporary business or tourist visitors—those who hold B-1 or B-2 visas—once admitted to the United States, can apply for an extension of stay. The basis can be business circumstances, family reasons, or any other good reason consistent with your visa.

For example, a tourist who decides to visit different locations or to spend more time with relatives can seek an extension. (See the USCIS website at www.uscis.gov for filing details and addresses; you may file electronically on the USCIS website or by mail.)

The application must include the following:

- Form I-539, Application to Extend/Change Nonimmigrant Status
- a copy of your Form I-94, which you (unless you're one of the few people who received a paper I-94 card when entering the U.S.) will need to download from the U.S. Customs and Border Protection (CBP) website at https://i94.cbp.dhs.gov
- a filing fee (currently $370) and a biometrics fee (currently $85) for the required fingerprint/photo appointment; either personal check or money order will be accepted

- a company letter or other supporting documentation stating the reason for the extension request—for example, more business consultations, ongoing medical reasons, extended family visit with a complete itinerary, or another reason
- evidence to show that the visit is temporary—particularly, evidence of continued overseas employment or residence and a return plane ticket, and
- evidence of financial support, such as a bank letter including amounts in accounts. You can also have a family member promise to support you, by filling out USCIS Form I-134, available at www.uscis.gov.

Also attach an itinerary or a letter explaining your reasons for requesting the extension.

The extension might not give you as much time as you'd like. Extensions of more than six months are rare. However, you are legally allowed to stay until USCIS makes a decision on your extension.

USCIS recommends that you file for an extension at least 45 days before the expiration date of your stay, which is shown on your Form I-94. If you procrastinate, at least try to file the request for extension 15 days before the expiration date shown on your Form I-94.

F. Changing Your Reason for Staying

If you wish to request a change of status from one immigration category to another or apply for a green card, be aware that applying for the change within the first three months after arriving in America could lead to USCIS denying your application based on the theory of "preconceived intent." Preconceived intent simply means that you lied about your reasons for coming to the United States.

For example, if you attempt to change your status from B-2 tourist to H-1B specialty worker soon after arriving in the United States, USCIS could conclude that you had the preconceived intent of working in the United States when you applied for a tourist visa from the U.S. embassy or entered the United States. Your failure to reveal your actual reason for going to the United States could be considered fraud.

A similar problem can arise for people who want to study in the U.S., but sensibly want to visit some schools and see whether they like them before going through the hassle of filling out application forms. You might think the logical thing would be to come as a tourist and then, after choosing a school, apply for a change to student status.

However, logic and the immigration laws don't always match up. USCIS may deny this type of applicant's request to change status, saying that they lied about their intention to be a tourist (the real, secret intention having been to become a student).

Fortunately, this is one of the few immigration law traps that one can sometimes get around with advance planning. If, when applying for your tourist visa, you tell the U.S. consular official that you might wish to change to student status after looking around, then you can have a "prospective student" notation made in your tourist visa. After that, you'll be free to apply to change status without worrying that it will look like you lied.

G. What to Do If USCIS Denies Your Extension Application

If USCIS denies your request for an extension of your stay in the U.S., you could contest the denial. However, this will require help from an experienced immigration lawyer. (See Chapter 24.)

It might be easier to leave the U.S. and apply for a new visa from overseas. This is far safer than staying in the U.S. illegally.

H. Tips on Filling Out Form I-539

Most of Form I-539 is self-explanatory; see the filled-in sample at www.nolo.com/back-of-book/ GRN.html. However, on Part 4 of Form I-539, Additional Information, Questions 3 through 15 can act as time bombs if you answer "yes" to any one of them—that is, they could prove fatal to your application. (In the case of 14, however, you'll be okay if your employment was undertaken while you had a work permit (EAD) from USCIS.)

Do not lie and misrepresent your answer as no when the truthful answer is yes. But if you have to answer yes to any of these questions, it is best to consult with an immigration lawyer or another experienced immigration professional first.

> **EXAMPLE:** The third question on this part of Form I-539 is: Are you, or any other person included on the application, an applicant for an immigrant visa? Answering "yes" is problematic, because it raises the possibility that you don't have the "nonimmigrant intent" required for a temporary U.S. stay—that is, that you are secretly looking for a way to stay in the U.S. until your green card comes through. Do not answer "no" if your U.S. citizen brother filed a relative I-130 petition for you, even if it was ten years ago, and your immigrant visa is still pending. In all probability, USCIS would discover your fraudulent answer, and you might never get your green card as a result.

Do Not Bring This Book With You

Because this book tells you how to stay and work legally in the United States, you should not have it— or any other book about immigrating to the U.S. —with you when you enter the United States on a tourist or other nonimmigrant visa.

If the border officials suspect that you are not a bona fide tourist, they may detain and question you at the airport or border about your purpose in coming to the United States.

For the same reason, you should not board the plane with a wedding dress, a stack of resumes, or letters from your Aunt Mary or cousin John stating that employment has been arranged for you as soon as you arrive in the United States. Should the border officials find such things when you land, you will not be admitted as a tourist; you may, in fact, be sent back to your home country without being allowed to set foot outside the airport or other port of entry in the United States.

If this happens, you will be unable to return to the U.S. for five years.

4

Will Inadmissibility Bar You From Getting a Green Card?

A. What Is Inadmissibility? 28

B. The Possibility of Waiving Inadmissibility 28

C. Most Troublesome Grounds of Inadmissibility 34

    1. Being Unable to Show Family Financial Support 34

    2. Being Stopped at the U.S. Border 37

    3. Being Barred From Returning After Past Unlawful U.S. Presence 37

    4. Limitations on Who Can Adjust Status 37

    5. Inadmissibility for Having Committed Crimes Involving Alcohol or Drugs ... 38

    6. Inadmissibility Based on Suspected Terrorist Activity 38

D. Reversing an Inadmissibility Finding 39

    1. Correcting Grounds of Inadmissibility 39

    2. Proving That Inadmissibility Does Not Apply 39

    3. Proving That an Inadmissibility Finding Is Incorrect 40

    4. Applying for a Waiver 40

    5. Provisional Waiver for Applicants Facing Three- or Ten-Year Bar 41

    6. Remaining Outside the U.S. for the Required Amount of Time 43

The U.S. government has decided that foreign nationals with certain histories or conditions are a risk to others and therefore should not be allowed to enter the country. These people are called "inadmissible." This chapter explains the conditions that make a person inadmissible—and whether there is any way under the bar of inadmissibility.

A. What Is Inadmissibility?

The U.S. government keeps a list of reasons that make a person unwelcome in the United States. The list includes affliction with various physical and mental disorders, commission of crimes, participation in terrorist or subversive activity, and more.

You may be judged inadmissible any time after you have filed an application for a green card, nonimmigrant visa, or other immigration status. Even a permanent resident who departs the United States for more than 180 days or who commits a crime while abroad may be examined with regard to inadmissibility upon return.

If you are found inadmissible, your immigration application will probably be denied. Even if you manage to hide your inadmissibility long enough to receive a green card or visa and be admitted into the U.S., if the problem is discovered later—perhaps when you apply for naturalized U.S. citizenship—you can be removed or deported.

 CAUTION
The COVID-19 pandemic has created separate reasons that people can be barred from the United States. Through presidential proclamations, travelers are sometimes forbidden from entering the U.S. after having spent time in one of the countries with major outbreaks. Check the immigration legal updates at www.nolo.com for details on which countries and who is affected.

B. The Possibility of Waiving Inadmissibility

Not everyone who falls into one of the categories of inadmissibility is absolutely barred from getting a green card or otherwise entering the United States. Some grounds of inadmissibility may be legally excused, or "waived." Others may not.

Possible Changes to Public Charge Rule on the Way

The legal wording, "likely at any time to become a public charge," has always been difficult to understand or interpret. A proposed rule that DHS put forth in 2022 would define it as applying to a noncitizen who is likely at any time to become "primarily dependent on the government for subsistence," as demonstrated by either receiving public cash assistance for income maintenance or long-term institutionalization at government expense. Only the following public benefits would be taken into account:

- Supplemental Security Income (SSI)
- cash assistance for income maintenance under the Temporary Assistance for Needy Families (TANF) program
- state, Tribal, territorial, and local cash assistance for income maintenance, and

- long-term institutionalization at government expense.

That means DHS would not consider various non-cash benefits, such as food nutrition assistance programs such as Supplemental Nutrition Assistance Program (previously called "food stamps"), the Children's Health Insurance Program (CHIP), most Medicaid benefits (except for long-term institutionalization at government expense), housing benefits, and transportation vouchers. Additionally, DHS would not consider disaster assistance; benefits received via a tax credit or deduction; or Social Security, government pensions, or other earned benefits.

Keep an eye on the news and Nolo's website (the immigration legal updates) for word on whether this rule actually goes into effect.

Inadmissibility Summary

Ground of Inadmissibility	Waiver Available	Conditions of Waiver and/or Exceptions
Health Problems		
Communicable diseases, particularly clinically active tuberculosis. Note: HIV (AIDS) was once listed as a ground of inadmissibility, but no longer.	Yes	A waiver is available to a person who is an asylee or is the spouse, unmarried son or daughter, or the unmarried minor lawfully adopted child of a U.S. citizen or permanent resident, or of an alien who has been issued an immigrant visa; or to an individual who has a son or daughter who is a U.S. citizen; or to a permanent resident or an alien issued an immigrant visa, upon compliance with USCIS's terms and regulations.
Physical or mental disorders that threaten the property, welfare, or safety of the applicant or others.	Yes	Special conditions required by USCIS, at its discretion.
Drug abusers or addicts.	No	
Failure to show that the applicant has been vaccinated against certain vaccine-preventable diseases.	Yes	Applicants must show either that they subsequently received the vaccine, that the vaccine is medically inappropriate as certified by a civil surgeon, or that having the vaccine administered is contrary to their religious beliefs or moral convictions.
Criminal and Related Violations		
Commission of crimes involving moral turpitude.	Yes	Waivers are not available for commission of crimes such as attempted murder or conspiracy to commit murder, or for murder, torture, or drug crimes, or for people previously admitted as permanent residents, if they have been convicted of aggravated felony since such admission or if they have fewer than seven years of lawful continuous residence before deportation proceedings are initiated against them. Waivers for all other offenses are available only to applicants who are a spouse, parent, or child of a U.S. citizen or green cardholder; or the only criminal activity was prostitution; or the actions occurred more than 15 years before the application for a visa or green card is filed, and the applicant shows that they are rehabilitated and not a threat to U.S. security.
Convictions for two or more crimes.	Yes	
Prostitutes or procurers of prostitutes.	Yes	
Diplomats or others involved in serious criminal activity who have received immunity from prosecution.	Yes	
Human traffickers and their adult family members who benefited financially from trafficking in persons.	No	
Money launderers.	No	
Drug offenders.	No	However, exceptions are available for a first and only offense or for juvenile offenders. There's also a waiver for simple possession of less than 30 grams of marijuana.
Drug traffickers.	No	

	Waiver Available	
Inadmissibility Summary (continued)		
Ground of Inadmissibility	**Waiver Available**	**Conditions of Waiver and/or Exceptions**
Immediate family members of drug traffickers who knowingly benefited from their illicit money within the last five years.	No	But note that the problem "washes out" after five years.
National Security and Human Rights Related Violations		
Spies, governmental saboteurs, violators of export or technology transfer laws.	No	
People intending to overthrow the U.S. government.	No	
Terrorists and members or representatives of foreign terrorist organizations.	No	
People whose entry would have adverse consequences for U.S. foreign policy.	No	Exceptions exist if the applicant is an official of a foreign government, or the applicant's activities or beliefs would normally be lawful in the U.S., under the Constitution.
Foreign government officials who carried out particularly severe violations of religious freedom.	No	
Involvement in population control policies including forced abortion or sterilization.	Yes	Does not apply to heads of state, heads of government, or cabinet level ministers. Waiver available if important to the U.S. national interest, with written notification and justification to Congress.
Involvement with coercive transplantation of human organs or bodily tissue, unless the foreign national has discontinued his or her involvement with, and support for, such practices.	Yes	Does not apply to heads of state, heads of government, or cabinet level ministers. Waiver available if important to the U.S. national interest, with written notification and justification to Congress.
Members of totalitarian parties.	Yes	An exception is made if the membership was involuntary, or is or was when the applicant was younger than 16 years old, by operation of law, or for purposes of obtaining employment, food rations, or other "essentials" of living. An exception is also possible for past membership if the membership ended at least two years prior to the application (five years if the party in control of a foreign state is considered a totalitarian dictatorship). If neither applies, a waiver is available for applicants who are the parent, spouse, son, daughter, brother, or sister of a U.S. citizen, or a spouse, son, or daughter of a permanent resident.
Participants in Nazi persecution, genocide, torture, extrajudicial killings, or the recruitment or use of child soldiers.	No	

Inadmissibility Summary (continued)

Ground of Inadmissibility	Waiver Available	Conditions of Waiver and/or Exceptions
Economic Grounds		
Any person who, in the opinion of a USCIS or a border or consular official, is likely to become a "public charge," that is, receive public assistance or welfare in the United States. The official can consider factors such as the person's age, health, family and work history, and previous use of public benefits.	No	However, the applicant can cure the ground of inadmissibility by overcoming the reasons for it. Also, there's an exception for some applicant categories, most notably refugees or asylees, U visa holders, and VAWA self-petitioners who are adjusting status. (See I.N.A. § 209.)
Family-sponsored immigrants and employment-sponsored immigrants where a family member is the employment sponsor (or such a family member owns 5% of the petitioning business) and the sponsor has not executed an Affidavit of Support (Form I-864).	No	But an applicant can cure the ground of inadmissibility by subsequently satisfying affidavit of support requirements.
Nonimmigrant public benefit recipients (where the individual came as nonimmigrant and applied for benefits without being eligible or through fraud). Five-year bar to admissibility.	No	But ground of inadmissibility expires after five years.
Labor Certifications & Employment Qualifications		
People without approved labor certifications, if one is required in the category under which the green card application is made.	No	
Graduates of unaccredited medical schools, whether inside or outside of the U.S., immigrating to the U.S. in a second or third preference category based on their profession, who have not both passed the foreign medical graduates exam and shown proficiency in English.	No	Physicians qualifying as special immigrants who have been practicing medicine in the U.S. with a license since January 9, 1978, are not subject to this rule.
Uncertified foreign health care workers seeking entry based on clinical employment in their field (but not including physicians).	No	But applicant may show qualifications by submitting a certificate from the Commission on Graduates of Foreign Nursing Schools or the equivalent.
Immigration Violators		
People who entered in the U.S. without inspection by U.S. border authorities.	Yes	Available for certain battered women and children who came to the U.S. escaping such battery or who qualify as self-petitioners. Also available for some individuals who had visa petitions or labor certifications on file before January 14, 1998 or before April 30, 2001 if they were in the U.S. on December 21, 2000 ($1,000 penalty required for latter waiver). Does not apply to applicants outside of the U.S.; or to refugees and asylees adjusting status (see I.N.A. § 209).
People who were deported after a removal hearing and seek admission within ten years.	Yes	Discretionary with USCIS.

Inadmissibility Summary (continued)		
Ground of Inadmissibility	**Waiver Available**	**Conditions of Waiver and/or Exceptions**
People who have failed to attend removal (deportation) proceedings (unless they had reasonable cause for doing so). Five-year bar to reentry.	Yes	Discretionary with USCIS.
People who have been summarily excluded from the U.S. and again attempt to enter within five years.	Yes	Advance permission to apply for readmission. Discretionary with USCIS.
People who made misrepresentations during the immigration process.	Yes	The applicant must be the spouse or child of a U.S. citizen or green card holder. A waiver will be granted if the refusal of admission would cause extreme hardship to that relative. Discretionary with USCIS.
People who made a false claim to U.S. citizenship.	No	
Individuals subject to a final removal (deportation) order under the Immigration and Naturalization Act § 274C (Civil Document Fraud Proceedings).	Yes	Available to permanent residents who voluntarily left the U.S., and to those applying for permanent residence as immediate relatives or other family-based petitions if the fraud was committed solely to assist the person's spouse or child and provided that no fine was imposed as part of the previous civil proceeding.
Student visa abusers (persons who improperly obtain F-1 status to attend a public elementary school or adult education program, or transfer from a private to a public program except as permitted). Five-year bar to admissibility.	No	
Certain individuals twice removed (deported) or removed after aggravated felony. Twenty-year bar to admissibility for those twice deported.	Yes	Discretionary with USCIS (advance permission to apply for readmission).
Individuals unlawfully present (time counted only after April 1, 1997 and after the age of 18). Presence for 180–364 days results in three-year bar to admissibility. Presence for 365 or more days creates ten-year bar to admissibility. Bars kick in only when the individual departs the U.S. and seeks reentry.	Yes	A waiver is provided for an immigrant who has a U.S. citizen or permanent resident spouse or parent to whom refusal of the application would cause extreme hardship. There is also a complex body of law concerning when a person's presence will be considered "lawful," for example, if one has certain applications awaiting decisions by USCIS or is protected by battered spouse/child provisions of the immigration laws.
Individuals unlawfully present after previous immigration violations. (Applies to persons who were in the U.S. unlawfully for an aggregate period over one year, who subsequently reenter without being properly admitted. Also applies to anyone ordered removed who subsequently attempts entry without admission.)	No	A permanent ground of inadmissibility. However, after being gone for ten years, an applicant can apply for permission to reapply for admission.

Inadmissibility Summary (continued)		
Ground of Inadmissibility	**Waiver Available**	**Conditions of Waiver and/or Exceptions**
Stowaways.	No	
Smugglers of illegal aliens.	Yes	Waivable if the applicant was smuggling in people who were immediate family members at the time, and either is a permanent resident or is immigrating under a family-based visa petition as an immediate relative; the unmarried son or daughter of a U.S. citizen or permanent resident; or the spouse of a U.S. permanent resident.
Document Violations		
People without required current passports or visas.	No	Except for limited-circumstance waivers. Under "summary removal" procedures, border officials may quickly deport people for five years who arrive without proper documents or make misrepresentations during the inspection process.
Draft Evasion and Ineligibility for Citizenship		
People who are permanently ineligible for U.S. citizenship.	No	
People who are draft evaders, unless they were U.S. citizens at the time of evasion or desertion.	No	
Miscellaneous Grounds		
Practicing polygamists.	No	
Guardians accompanying excludable aliens.	No	
International child abductors. (The exclusion does not apply if the applicant is a national of a country that signed the Hague Convention on International Child Abduction.)	No	
Unlawful voters (voting in violation of any federal, state, or local law or regulation).	No	
Former U.S. citizens who renounced citizenship to avoid taxation.	No	

Above is a chart summarizing all the grounds of inadmissibility, whether or not a waiver is available, and the special conditions someone must meet to get a waiver. (For more details, see I.N.A. § 212, 8 U.S.C. § 1182.)

C. Most Troublesome Grounds of Inadmissibility

Some of the grounds that have the most significant impact on green card applicants are summarized here.

1. Being Unable to Show Family Financial Support

All family-based immigrants seeking permanent residence must include with their application an Affidavit of Support, on either Form I-864 or I-864-EZ, signed by their petitioner. This form helps satisfy the requirement that immigrants show they are not likely to become public charges (receive government assistance or welfare).

By filling out the form and attaching various documents, the petitioning U.S. citizen or permanent resident shows proof of earnings and savings, and promises to use that money to support the immigrant or to pay back any government agency that supplies need-based support to the immigrant. But not every petitioner earns enough to successfully show this.

The I-864-EZ is a shorter, easier version of the form, which can be used only if you are the only person your petitioner is sponsoring, and your petitioner can meet the sponsorship requirements based solely upon personal income (not including anyone else's).

SKIP AHEAD
For a sample, filled-out Form I-864, see www.nolo.com/back-of-book/GRN.html.

Exceptions. There are limited exceptions to the Affidavit of Support requirement. If the immigrant will qualify for automatic U.S. citizenship upon becoming a permanent resident (discussed in Chapter 9), the I-864 is not necessary. Also, if the immigrant has already worked in the U.S. for 40 or more work quarters as defined by Social Security (about ten years), Form I-864 is not required. Moreover, the immigrant can count time worked by either a parent, while the immigrant was younger than age 18, or by a U.S. petitioning spouse, toward these 40 quarters.

Others who don't need to submit a Form I-864 include self-petitioning widows or widowers of U.S. citizens, and self-petitioning battered spouses or children (explained in later chapters).

If you're exempt from the Affidavit of Support requirement due to one of these exceptions, you should fill out Form I-864W instead of the regular Form I-864.

Sponsor's responsibilities. The government can rely on the I-864 to hold the sponsor responsible if the immigrant receives public benefits. And it is also enforceable by the immigrant family member against the sponsor for support.

Finally, it requires that the sponsor show income for a similar household size (including family and dependents) that is at least 125% of the federal Poverty Guidelines level. It goes down to 100% for sponsors who are on active duty in the U.S. armed forces and petitioning for a spouse or child. These Poverty Guidelines are revised annually; see the table below.

Your sponsor's income will need to meet the guidelines for the year when your Affidavit of Support is filed. Don't worry if the required income levels get raised later—it probably won't affect you. Your sponsor should include a copy of the current Poverty Guidelines with your affidavit, in order to remind the immigration authorities of the then-current income requirements. Also, be aware that if more than a year passes since the affidavit was submitted, the immigration authorities can ask for proof of the sponsor's current income, in which case, they will judge it based on the most recent Poverty Guidelines.

2022 Poverty Guidelines Chart for Immigrants

For the 48 Contiguous States, the District of Columbia, Puerto Rico, the U.S. Virgin Islands, Guam, and the Commonwealth of the Northern Mariana Islands:		
Sponsor's Household Size	**100% of HHS Poverty Guidelines**	**125% of HHS Poverty Guidelines**
	For sponsors on active duty in the U.S. armed forces who are petitioning for their spouse or child	*For all other sponsors*
2	$18,310	$22,887
3	$23,030	$28,787
4	$27,750	$34,687
5	$32,470	$40,587
6	$37,190	$46,487
7	$41,910	$52,387
8	$46,630	$58,287
	Add $4,720 for each additional person	**Add $5,900 for each additional person**

Alaska		
Sponsor's Household Size	**100% of HHS Poverty Guidelines**	**125% of HHS Poverty Guidelines**
	For sponsors on active duty in the U.S. armed forces who are petitioning for their spouse or child	*For all other sponsors*
2	$22,890	$28,612
3	$28,790	$35,987
4	$34,690	$43,362
5	$40,590	$50,737
6	$46,490	$58,112
7	$52,390	$65,487
8	$58,290	$72,862
	Add $5,900 for each additional person	**Add $7,375 for each additional person**

Hawaii		
Sponsor's Household Size	**100% of HHS Poverty Guidelines**	**125% of HHS Poverty Guidelines**
	For sponsors on active duty in the U.S. armed forces who are petitioning for their spouse or child	*For all other sponsors*
2	$21,060	$26,325
3	$26,490	$33,112
4	$31,920	$39,900
5	$37,350	$46,687
6	$42,780	$53,475
7	$48,210	$60,262
8	$53,640	$67,050
	Add $5,430 for each additional person	**Add $6,787 for each additional person**

The immigrant's income can also be added to the mix to help reach the Poverty Guidelines minimum, if the immigrant is already living with the petitioner in the U.S. and working legally at a job that will continue after getting the green card.

Who fills out the Form I-864. Family-based immigrants who file adjustment of status or immigrant visa applications are required to have Form I-864 filed by the person who is sponsoring their immigrant petition. However, if that family petitioner's income isn't high enough, another person—a joint sponsor—may add income if theirs meets the 125% income requirement for the household and the person is:

- a U.S. legal permanent resident or citizen
- older than 18 years of age
- living in the United States, and
- willing to be jointly liable.

The joint sponsor files a separate Affidavit of Support. The principal immigrant can have only one joint sponsor. However, if the joint sponsor's income is not sufficient to cover all the derivative beneficiaries (such as children), a second joint sponsor may be added. Two joint sponsors is the limit, however.

What if the primary petitioner can't find a joint sponsor to make up for an insufficient income and assets? Other people who live in the U.S. petitioner's household may also add their income to that of the primary sponsor to help reach the 125% level, but only if they are age 18 or older and agree to be jointly liable, by filing Form I-864A, Contract Between Sponsor and Household Member. This is different than being a joint sponsor. It means that the person is literally living in the same house—perhaps is an older child or a parent—and is willing to have their own income counted toward the household total and support the immigrants.

Using assets to meet the requirements. Personal assets of either the sponsor or the immigrant—such as property, bank account deposits, and personal property, such as automobiles (minus any outstanding debts)—may also be used to supplement the sponsor's income if the primary sponsor's actual income does not add up to 125% of the federal Poverty Guidelines income levels.

The sponsor or immigrant must show assets worth five times the difference between the Poverty Guidelines level and actual household income (or three times the difference for immediate relatives, for example husband and wife). The assets must be readily convertible to cash within one year. If using assets owned by the sponsor's household members or the immigrant, those people must submit a Form I-864A.

Immigrant's Story: Compensating for a Low Salary

Here is how Daniel, a U.S. citizen, can deal with his low income in sponsoring his Norwegian wife, Liv, and her twin boys from a previous marriage.

Daniel works as a youth counselor at a Seattle nonprofit, earning $30,000 a year. However, according to the 2022 Poverty Guidelines, Daniel will need an income of $34,687 or more to support a family of four—meaning he's $4,687 short. Liv plans to work in the U.S., but she is currently living in Norway, so that doesn't help.

Daniel could pick up a weekend job, to raise his income until Liv gets her green card (at which time no one would stop him from quitting). However, an easier solution is for him to declare his assets when filling out Form I-864. Because the value of assets must be divided by three for U.S. citizens sponsoring their spouses, Daniel will need $14,061 in assets to make up the shortfall.

Fortunately, Daniel has $15,000 in a money market account, so declaring this on his Form I-864 will be enough to help Liv and her children get approved for a green card. He'll need to remember to include a copy of a bank statement showing how much is in the account when he prepares the Form I-864.

SEE AN EXPERT
The requirements and paperwork burden of the affidavit are complicated and substantial. If you have questions or are concerned that U.S. immigration authorities will conclude that you are a likely public charge, consult an experienced immigration attorney.

2. Being Stopped at the U.S. Border

Another law that has a drastic impact on individuals requesting to enter the United States is the summary exclusion law. This law empowers an inspector at the airport or other entry point to exclude and deport you at your attempted entry to the U.S. if either of the following are true:

- The inspector thinks you are making a misrepresentation (lying) about practically anything connected to your right to enter the U.S.—such as your purpose in coming, intent to return, prior immigration history, or use of false documents.
- You do not have the proper documentation to support your entry to the U.S. in the category you are requesting.

If the inspector excludes you, you may not request entry for five years, unless a special waiver is granted. For this reason, it is extremely important to understand the terms of your requested status and not make any misrepresentations.

If the inspector looks likely to summarily exclude you, you may request withdrawing your application to enter the U.S., which will prevent having the five-year order on your record. The inspector might allow you to do this in some cases.

3. Being Barred From Returning After Past Unlawful U.S. Presence

Relatively new grounds of inadmissibility apply to people who were unlawfully present in the United States for 180 days (approximately six months) after April 1, 1997, who subsequently left, and who now seek admission, for example through adjustment of status or by applying for an immigrant or nonimmigrant visa. Such people are subject to a three-year waiting period; the period is ten years if they were unlawfully present for 365 days after April 1, 1997. A waiver is available, as described in Section D4, below.

Some important exceptions help some applicants avoid this problem. For example, as long as you were younger than 18, your time in the U.S. doesn't count as unlawful presence. And people who have a bona fide pending asylum application or a pending application for adjustment of status are in the U.S. in perfectly lawful status. Battered spouses and children can get around the bars if they can show a substantial connection between their unlawful presence and the abuse.

The worst-case scenario is for people who have lived in the United States illegally for more than one year and who then left or were deported but returned to the United States illegally (or were caught trying to). They can never get a green card. This is usually referred to as the "permanent bar." (Check with a lawyer before concluding that you're subject to the permanent bar, however—recent case law has carved out a few exceptions.) No waiver is available to the permanent bar for the first ten years.

4. Limitations on Who Can Adjust Status

The rules concerning adjustment of status—or getting your green card in the U.S. rather than at a U.S. consulate—are somewhat complicated. In general, if you entered the U.S. properly—by being inspected by a border official—and maintained your nonimmigrant status, you can probably get your green card without leaving the United States.

In addition, a "grandfather clause" helps a few people who happened to be in the United States when certain laws were changed (in particular, a law known as § 245(i)"). Under the old laws, practically everyone had the right to stay in the

United States to adjust their status, simply by paying a $1,000 penalty fee. But under the newer laws, paying this fee is no longer an option except for those few people who had visa petitions filed on their behalf around two decades ago (see Chapter 16, Section A3 for details).

That means that many people who bypassed a U.S. border inspection are in a trap. If they stay in the United States, the fact that they entered illegally or committed certain other violations means they're not allowed to adjust their status to permanent resident within the United States. But if they leave the United States and attempt to apply for their green card through an overseas U.S. consulate, they might well face a three- or ten-year bar to returning to the United States, as punishment for their unlawful stay.

If you believe you're in this trap, consult a lawyer to make sure and to see if you might qualify for a waiver of the three- or ten-year bar. Since 2013, a "stateside" or "provisional" waiver has allowed some people to avoid the trap by submitting a waiver application and receiving an answer BEFORE leaving the U.S. for their consular interview (as described in Section D5 of this chapter).

Note: All refugees or political asylees can stay in the U.S. to adjust status.

5. Inadmissibility for Having Committed Crimes Involving Alcohol or Drugs

Criminal grounds of inadmissibility are the number one factor making temporary visa applicants inadmissible, and they affect a lot of green card applicants, too. If you've committed any sort of crime, you can be found inadmissible, and should consult an experienced immigration attorney. Some attorneys specialize in analyzing the significance of criminal convictions in the immigration context.

However, if you've been convicted of a crime involving alcohol, you've got double trouble. Even

if the crime itself doesn't make you inadmissible, USCIS can, and often does, argue that it's a sign that you have a physical or mental disorder associated with harmful behavior—in other words, that you're inadmissible on health, rather than criminal, grounds.

This is most often a problem for people with convictions for DUI or DWI (driving under the influence or driving while intoxicated). One DUI alone won't always create a problem, unless there were additional factors, such as someone having been injured, your license having been suspended, or your state treating the crime as a felony. But if USCIS sees a "significant criminal record of alcohol-related driving incidents," it will take a closer look. You could be required to undergo an additional examination by the doctor who filled out your medical report, or by more specialized doctors or psychiatrists.

DUIs aren't the only crime that can lead USCIS to find you inadmissible on health grounds. Crimes such as assaults or domestic violence where alcohol or drugs were contributing factors can lead to the same result. Again, see an attorney if this is an issue in your case—and remember that trying to hide crimes on your green card application will only get you in bigger trouble after the fingerprint or police report reveals them.

6. Inadmissibility Based on Suspected Terrorist Activity

No one will be surprised to hear that the U.S. forbids people who are linked to terrorism to enter the country, and takes an extra hard look at applications from anyone whose government is thought to support terrorism. (The U.S.'s current four suspected countries are Cuba, Iran, North Korea, and Syria.) However, the terrorism-based inadmissibility grounds are broader than you might expect, and have the potential to exclude some people who wouldn't ordinarily be thought of as terrorists.

The inadmissibility grounds cover being a member of a terrorist organization, inciting others to participate in terrorism, persuading others to support terrorism, endorsing terrorism, raising funds for an organization that the U.S. considers terrorist in nature, and more. The support and fundraising prohibitions can be especially problematic for people who have given money to organizations that serve a mix of purposes or that have become established political parties despite a terrorist or guerrilla past.

No hard proof or court conviction is necessary—the U.S. government can exclude someone based on having "reasonable grounds to believe" that the person falls into one of the categories described above.

Also, the spouse or child of any immigrant found inadmissible based on the above provisions can be excluded if the immigrant's activities took place within the last five years. To get around this, the spouse or child will need to show that they were not aware of, nor could reasonably have been expected to know of, the activity.

D. Reversing an Inadmissibility Finding

There are five ways to get past a finding that you are inadmissible:

- In the case of physical or mental illness only, you might be able to correct the condition.
- You can prove that you really don't fall into the category of inadmissibility USCIS believes you do.
- You can prove that the accusations of inadmissibility against you are false.
- You can apply for a waiver of inadmissibility.
- You can "wait out" the time period required by USCIS before reentering the United States.

Each of these is discussed in some detail below. However, you'll most likely need an attorney's help.

1. Correcting Grounds of Inadmissibility

If you have had a physical or mental illness that is a ground of inadmissibility and have been cured of the condition by the time you submit your green card application, or at least by the time a decision is made on it, you will no longer be considered inadmissible on that basis. For example, you might have been diagnosed with a clinically active and communicable case of tuberculosis ("TB") while awaiting a decision on your green card application. If you can show that you still test positive for TB on a skin test, but that the TB is latent and no longer infectious, you have "corrected" the ground of inadmissibility. If the condition is not cured by the time you apply, with certain illnesses you can still get a waiver of inadmissibility.

2. Proving That Inadmissibility Does Not Apply

Proving that inadmissibility does not apply in your case is a method used mainly to overcome criminal and ideological grounds of inadmissibility. When dealing with criminal grounds of inadmissibility, U.S. immigration authorities will consider both the type of crime committed and the nature of the punishment to see whether your criminal activity constitutes a ground of inadmissibility.

For example, with some criminal activity, only actual convictions are grounds of inadmissibility. If you have been charged with a crime and the charges were then dropped, you might not be inadmissible.

Another example involves crimes of moral turpitude; that is, crimes showing dishonest or basically immoral conduct. Committing a crime of moral turpitude can make you inadmissible, even if you have not actually been convicted.

Crimes with no element of moral turpitude, however, are often not considered grounds of inadmissibility. Opinions sometimes differ on which crimes are considered to involve moral turpitude and which are not.

Other factors that can work to your benefit are:

- expungement laws that remove the crime from your record (don't assume this will take care of the problem, however)
- the length of the prison term
- how long ago the crime was committed
- the number of convictions in your background
- conditions of plea bargaining, and
- available pardons.

Sometimes, a conviction can be erased or vacated if you can show it was unlawfully obtained or you were not advised of its immigration consequences. In either case, you still need to disclose the criminal charge on your immigration application or petition.

Proving that a criminal ground of inadmissibility does not apply in your case is a complicated business. You need to have a firm grasp not only of immigration law, but also the technicalities of criminal law. If you have a criminal problem in your past, you might still be able to get a green card, but likely not without the help of an experienced immigration lawyer. (See Chapter 24.)

3. Proving That an Inadmissibility Finding Is Incorrect

If your green card or nonimmigrant visa application is denied for inadmissibility, you can try to prove that the finding is incorrect. For example, if a USCIS medical examination shows that you have certain medical problems, you can present reports from other doctors stating that the first diagnosis was wrong and that you are free of the problem condition. If you are accused of lying on a visa application, you can present evidence proving you told the truth, or that any false statements were made unintentionally.

4. Applying for a Waiver

By obtaining a waiver, you don't eliminate or disprove the ground of inadmissibility. Instead, you ask USCIS to overlook the problem and give you a green card or visa anyway.

For example, you can apply for a waiver of unlawful presence if you can show that your being prevented from reentering the United States would cause extreme hardship to your U.S. citizen or permanent resident spouse or parent. (Note that having U.S. citizen children won't help here.)

The classic case of extreme hardship is if your spouse or parent is very ill, needs your care, and would suffer medically by joining you outside the United States. Note, however, that extreme hardship to you, the immigrant, does not count in this analysis.

All green card and visa application forms ask questions designed to find out whether any grounds of inadmissibility apply in your case. When the answers to the questions on these forms clearly show that you are inadmissible, you may be authorized to begin applying for a waiver immediately on filing your application. In most cases, however, the consulate or USCIS office insists on having your final visa or green card interview before ruling that you are inadmissible. If the USCIS office or consulate handling your case decides to wait until your final interview before finding you inadmissible, this will delay your ability to file for a waiver. This could delay your getting a green card or visa; waivers can take months to process.

Once it is determined that a waiver is necessary, you will need to complete Form I-601 and pay a filing fee (currently $930). Note that if you file this with a U.S. consulate abroad, you will have to wait for the consulate to send your application to a USCIS office. The consulate cannot approve the waiver.

Once again, many technical factors control whether or not a waiver of inadmissibility is granted. You stand the best chance of success by hiring a good immigration lawyer.

5. Provisional Waiver for Applicants Facing Three- or Ten-Year Bar

In 2013, green card seekers who are not eligible to adjust status in the U.S. and are afraid to leave for their consular interview because their past unlawful presence might block their return gained a new procedural option. Some can now submit a "provisional waiver" application, and hopefully have it approved, before leaving the United States. It's done on a different form than the usual one for waivers, called an "I-601A." We'll provide detailed information here on what's involved—but because of the complexities of the process, we urge you to get an attorney's help with this task.

a. Who Is Eligible to Submit a Provisional/Stateside Waiver Application

Not everyone is eligible to use this new option. Applicants must be:

- **The beneficiary of an immigrant petition**—that is, eligible for an immigrant visa on some basis, whether it's family based, employment based, or through the Diversity Visa (DV) lottery. If a Form I-130 or Form I-140 application has been approved on your behalf or you've been selected for the DV lottery, you likely fit this criterion.
- **At least 17 years of age.** This doesn't really hurt anyone, because you cannot accrue unlawful presence in the U.S., and therefore don't need a waiver, until you're at least 18.
- **Physically present in the U.S. at the time of applying.**
- **Otherwise admissible to the United States.** In other words, you cannot separately ask for a waiver of any criminal, fraud, or other grounds of inadmissibility (normally done on the old, standard waiver Form I-601). In fact, if USCIS has any reason to believe that you are inadmissible on some ground other than unlawful presence, it will deny the I-601A provisional waiver. Furthermore, if the consular

officer at your visa interview decides that you are otherwise inadmissible or are ineligible for the visa on some basis other than unlawful presence, the USCIS-approved provisional waiver will be automatically revoked.

- **Able to prove that, if not granted the waiver, their qualifying U.S. relatives will suffer extreme hardship as a result.** The list of qualifying relatives includes permanent resident and U.S. citizen's spouse or parents.

When the provisional waiver process was first implemented, denial rates were high, primarily due to criminal history issues. Applicants with even minor offenses on record, such as trespassing, shoplifting, or disorderly conduct were often denied the waiver. In response to protest by immigrant advocates, USCIS issued guidance to its officers in a January 2014 memo. It instructed officers not to deny a provisional waiver application if the criminal offense either 1) falls within the petty offense or youthful offender exception or 2) is not a crime of moral turpitude. (For definitions of "petty offense," "youthful offender exception," and "crime of moral turpitude," see I.N.A. § 212(a)(2).)

The provisional waiver process has gotten smoother since this memo, but applicants with arrests or convictions should take care to submit as much evidence as possible showing that their criminal past was relatively minor and would not render them inadmissible.

b. Timing of Filing a Provisional, Stateside Waiver Application

If the U.S. petitioner hasn't already submitted the Form I-130 petition that starts the immigration process for a family member, they should indicate in Part 4 Question 62 of that form that the immigrant will apply for an immigrant visa at a U.S. consulate abroad rather than adjusting status in the United States. (If the immigrant were legally allowed to adjust status in the U.S., you wouldn't have to bother with the provisional waiver.)

By doing so, you will alert USCIS that it needs to, upon approving the I-130, transfer the file to the National Visa Center (NVC) for further action, including transfer to the U.S. consulate. If the petitioner were to say on the I-130 that the immigrant will apply for adjustment of status in the U.S., you would then have to take extra steps to have the file transferred to the NVC. (This includes filing a Form I-824, paying a filing fee, then waiting months for action on the request.)

Only after USCIS approves the I-130 can you file your Provisional Waiver Application (on USCIS Form I-601A, available at www.uscis.gov/i-601a). You cannot submit the I-130 petition at the same time as ("concurrently" with) the waiver application.

USCIS will notify the National Visa Center (NVC) of the I-601A's approval. You will need to pay NVC any immigrant visa processing fee. (The NVC handles the case after USCIS approves the I-130 and schedules your immigrant visa interview at a U.S. embassy or consulate abroad.)

If NVC goes ahead and schedules your visa appointment before USCIS has acted on the waiver request, you must quickly ask the consulate at which your appointment is scheduled to postpone your interview until USCIS has made a decision on your waiver application.

The DOS tries to schedule applicants for an immigrant visa interview within about two or three months of USCIS approving the waiver request and the applicant filing all the necessary visa forms and documents. Applicants can remain in the U.S. during this time period.

c. Fee for Provisional Waiver Application

DHS has set the fee for Form I-601A at $630. In addition, applicants younger than age 79 will need to pay the biometrics (fingerprinting) fee, currently $85. No fee waiver requests will be considered.

The biometrics requirement means the immigrant will be fingerprinted and the name and prints run through an FBI database to check for a criminal and immigration enforcement record. If there's a chance this will turn up negative information, consult a lawyer before going any further.

d. What to File for a Provisional Waiver Request

In addition to Form I-601A and the fee, you will need to provide proof of your eligibility, and documents showing that you merit the waiver as a matter of discretion. USCIS requires that you provide:

- ☐ a copy of the USCIS approval notice of your Form I-130 or I-140 visa petition or DV Program Selection
- ☐ an EOIR Administrative Closure order (if applicable because your case was in removal proceedings)
- ☐ proof of the U.S. citizen or lawful permanent resident status of your qualifying relative IF it is not the same person who filed the immigrant visa petition for you
- ☐ proof of your relationship to your qualifying relative IF it is not the same person who filed the immigrant visa petition for you
- ☐ documents showing that your qualifying relative (U.S. spouse or parent) would suffer extreme hardship if you were denied the U.S. visa, and
- ☐ a receipt showing that you have paid the DOS-required immigrant visa processing fee.

Wondering what extreme hardship is? USCIS gives a number of examples, including health concerns, financial, educational, and personal considerations, and other special factors. For example, if your elderly U.S. citizen parent depends upon you for care and would be unable to receive medical treatment abroad, you should submit evidence of this. If you're the primary earner in your family and your spouse can't work full time, that would be excellent to submit proof of. Decisions about what qualifies as extreme hardship are highly discretionary, however, so your best bet is to seek an attorney's assistance in preparing a convincing waiver application—one demonstrating that the hardship your qualifying family members would suffer if you were denied a visa is greater than just the natural sadness of separation if you were forced to leave the United States.

USCIS will not, in most cases, call applicants in for an interview on their provisional waiver request, since it would then have to transfer the file from its National Benefits Center to a local office.

e. If USCIS Deems Your Waiver Application Incomplete

USCIS will not necessarily deny a provisional waiver application that's missing some materials. Instead, it routinely sends out Requests for Evidence (RFEs) for applications that lack critical information related to issues like the qualifying relatives' extreme hardship, whether the applicant merits a favorable exercise of discretion, or on some other relevant topic. But USCIS can also simply deny an application outright, so do your best to submit a complete one the first time around.

Also, if you don't pay the correct fee, sign your application, or provide certain key bits of eligibility information, USCIS will return your entire application to you and you will have to refile.

f. Options After Denial of Provisional Waiver

Although you cannot appeal USCIS's denial of your stateside waiver request, you have a couple of options.

You can file a new I-601A and waiver application with USCIS during the time that your case is still pending with the DOS. Of course, there is little point in doing this if you don't provide new or extra information to overcome USCIS's original reason for the denial. If you aren't already using an attorney, this would definitely be the time to consult one.

Another option is to go ahead and attend your consular interview, and then file the traditional waiver request on Form I-601 (Application for Waiver of Grounds of Inadmissibility) with USCIS. This, of course, risks your being unable to return to the U.S. for three or ten years if USCIS once again denies your waiver application, though it will be handled by a different USCIS officer this time around.

Should you worry that DHS agents will come knocking on your door in the U.S. to arrest you after an I-601A denial? According to U.S. government statements, "DHS also does not envision initiating removal proceedings against aliens whose Form I-601As are denied or withdrawn prior to final adjudication"—unless, that is, the person "has a criminal history, has committed fraud, or otherwise poses a threat to national security or public safety."

6. Remaining Outside the U.S. for the Required Amount of Time

If you're subject to a penalty requiring you to remain outside the U.S. for three or ten years before reentering—most likely because you stayed in the U.S. unlawfully—you don't have to wait for an immigration authority to tell you you're subject to the penalty to start the clock ticking on your time away.

For example, if you overstayed your tourist visa by more than 180 days but less than 365 days during a past visit to the U.S., you'll eventually be penalized by having to wait outside the U.S. for three years before reentering on any kind of visa. (That's the "three-year bar.") An unlawful stay of more than 365 days gets you a ten-year bar.

If you stay in the U.S. and wait to receive your visa interview notice before you leave—and then at your interview, the consulate denies your request for a waiver of your unlawful stay—you'll be stuck outside the U.S. for three or ten years following your interview. That's why some immigrants prefer to leave the U.S. sooner, in order to start counting up the three years as soon as possible. ●

How Long You'll Have to Wait

A. Immediate Relatives of U.S. Citizens: No Waiting for Eligibility 47

B. Relatives in Preference Categories: Longer Waits 47

C. Dealing With the Wait 48

D. Can You Predict How Long You'll Wait? 49

    1. The Priority Date 49

    2. Tracking Your Progress: Visa Cutoff Date 49

    3. Some People Can Switch Preference Categories 51

    4. Advise USCIS If You Can Upgrade 52

E. Revocation of a Petition or Application 53

Among the most common questions asked of immigration attorneys are ones concerning how long the immigration process takes, such as:

- "As a U.S. citizen, I filed the papers for my brother five years ago. Why is it taking so long for the U.S. Embassy in India to give him his immigrant visa?"

- "My ten-year-old daughter was born in Hawaii, where I was a graduate student. Since she is a U.S. citizen, when can I get a green card by having her claim me as her mother?"

- "Three years ago, based on my green card, I sponsored my wife, who comes from Mexico. She is still waiting for her green card. What is the problem?"

Such questions are often asked by people who might have expected some delay in getting their green cards, but who can't believe how many years it's taking.

There are numerous causes of common immigration delays. The first type of delay no one can escape. It's the operation of U.S. immigration law, defining when you become eligible for a green card. In the example of the mother of the U.S. citizen born in Hawaii, above, she'll need to wait until her child turns 21 to so much as start the immigration process.

Another common source of delay is simply the bureaucratic backup caused by overworked government agencies trying to deal with many thousands of applications every year. Even the amount of time you spend awaiting a decision on one application can be shocking—many months or years is normal. On top of that, the coronavirus pandemic has slowed processing considerably, even after most U.S. government offices reopened. Also, a fair number of people wait months only to discover that their application got misplaced or lost in the paperwork shuffle. Although USCIS is perpetually launching efforts to fix these problems, no one expects miracles. See Chapters 21 and 22 for tips on preventing and dealing with these delays.

Another type of delay is the security checks and double checks your name and fingerprints will be run through, sometimes more than once, during the application process. Although security checks were always part of the application process, they've become more rigorous since the terrorist attacks of September 11, 2001. For people with common names, this can create particular problems. Of course, if you've had any arrests or other history that you believe will raise questions in the immigration process, you should consult an attorney.

Then there is a type of delay that applies only to applicants in green card categories that have a yearly limit on how many are given out. For example, spouses of U.S. citizens don't have to worry, because as immediate relatives, the government can grant unlimited numbers of green cards to them, no matter how many people apply. But spouses of U.S. permanent residents are less lucky. Their annual limit is 87,934, and far more spouses than that typically apply every year. Spouses of permanent residents often (but not always) have to wait around two years or more, until all the people who applied before them have gotten their green cards. After that, in technical terms, a "visa number" is said to become available, and they can continue their application for a green card.

 TIP

"Visa" and "green card" can have similar meanings. When we're talking about numbers and quotas, the immigration laws always refer to "visas" rather than "green cards," for technical reasons. Part of the reason is that if you come from overseas, you don't become a permanent resident (green card holder) until you receive an "immigrant visa" and use it to enter the United States. But even if you're applying within the United States, you can't become a permanent resident until a "visa number" has been allotted to you. So, when you hear about numbers and limits on "visas" in this discussion, assume it means your right to a green card, no matter where you're coming from or whether you use an actual, physical entry visa.

You're likely to face delays based on limited numbers of visas if you apply for a green card in any of the so-called "preference" categories (which we'll explain below). All the preference categories come with limits, or "quotas," on how many visas or green cards can be passed out in a year.

To make matters more complicated, no country is allowed to send more than 7% of all preference-category immigrants (or 25,620 people) to the United States in a year. That means that for certain countries with high rates of immigration to the United States—like Mexico, India, China, and the Philippines—the U.S. government sometimes has to start a separate—and longer—waiting list. This isn't discrimination so much as it is mathematics.

A. Immediate Relatives of U.S. Citizens: No Waiting for Eligibility

Immigrant visas are immediately available for one group of eligible aliens: immediate relatives of U.S. citizens. They have the highest priority in immigration law because of the congressional intent to encourage families of U.S. citizens to live together and stay together.

Members of this group have to wait only for as long as it takes various government offices to handle their applications. This averages from two to twelve months, depending on various factors, such as whether the immigrant is coming from another country or already lives legally in the United States, and how backed up the office serving their region is.

For purposes of immigration law, you are an immediate relative and eligible for an immigrant visa without waiting if you are:

- the husband or wife of a U.S. citizen
- the parent of a U.S. citizen, if the citizen is at least 21 years of age
- the unmarried child younger than 21 years of age (including stepchildren and children adopted before they reach the age of 16) of a U.S. citizen, or

- the widow or widower of a U.S. citizen (assuming you weren't legally separated at the time of death and haven't remarried since).

Although children of U.S. citizens must remain unmarried until they receive their visa, those approaching 21 do get some protection from a law called the "Child Status Protection Act." As long as the initial I-130 petition was filed for them when they were younger than 21 years old, these immediate relative children never "age out," or lose their eligibility based on being too old. Previously, once an immediate relative child turned 21, they would automatically move into the less-favored preference category. Now, the child's age is frozen at whatever it was when the I-130 petition was filed, so the child stays in the immediate relative category.

> **EXAMPLE:** The U.S. citizen father of Yasmeen, a 20-year-old girl, files an I-130 petition for her along with an application for adjustment of status to permanent resident. By the time of the interview, however, Yasmeen is 22 years old. Fortunately, under the CSPA, Yasmeen's age of 20 years old was permanently frozen or "locked in" when the petition was filed, so she is considered 20 years old for as long as it takes USCIS to approve her green card.

B. Relatives in Preference Categories: Longer Waits

In all family-based preference categories, petitions from U.S. citizens generally have higher priority than those of lawful permanent residents.

Family first preference: unmarried sons or daughters of U.S. citizens. This category is for children who are 21 years old or older and not married—meaning either single, divorced, or widowed. (A son or daughter who is younger than 21 years and not married would be classified as an immediate relative.) A maximum of 23,400 immigrant visas are now available worldwide for the family first preference category. The current waiting period is approximately seven years, but 22 years if you're from Mexico and ten years from the Philippines.

Family second preference: spouses and unmarried children of permanent residents. This category is divided into two parts, including:

- husbands and wives of lawful permanent residents and their unmarried children who are younger than 21 years (Category 2A), and
- unmarried (meaning single, divorced, or widowed) sons or daughters (older than 21) of a lawful permanent resident (Category 2B, which waits somewhat longer than Category 2A).

A total of 114,200 immigrant visas worldwide are given to second preference immigrants. However, 77% (87,934) of the total is intended for the spouses and minor children of green card holders (2As), while 23% (26,266) of the total is meant for the unmarried children older than 21 years of age (2Bs).

The typical wait in Category 2A is approximately two to three years, though recently there's been no wait at all. In Category 2B, the current wait is approximately six years, except that applicants from Mexico wait about 21 years and applicants from the Philippines wait about ten years.

Family third preference: married sons and daughters of U.S. citizens. What if a U.S. citizen's unmarried son or daughter (in the family first preference category) gets married before entering the U.S. as a lawful permanent resident? Or what if the child is married already? Either way, the third preference category provides a solution, although the waits tend to be long. Only 23,400 visas worldwide are made available every year for married sons and daughters of U.S. citizens.

The current wait in the third preference category is approximately 13 years, except that applicants from Mexico wait around 24 years and applicants from the Philippines wait around 20 years.

Family fourth preference: brothers and sisters of U.S. citizens. The brother or sister of a U.S. citizen has to wait until the U.S. sibling turns 21 years of age before a petition can be filed for the alien brother or sister. A total of 65,000 visas worldwide are available each year for this category. The waiting list is always very long, from around 14 to 24 years.

C. Dealing With the Wait

If you belong to a preference category in which there are many hopeful immigrants waiting, it could be several years before your immigrant visa number becomes current.

If, during these years, you want to come to the United States as a nonimmigrant—as a tourist, businessperson, student, or other category—be prepared for it to be more difficult for you to get that visa. Once a visa petition has been filed for you by a family member, the U.S. government figures you intend to come to the U.S. and stay permanently— which disqualifies you from most short-term visas.

You might be able to convince the U.S. consul that you will not remain illegally in the United States waiting for your immigrant visa to come up by demonstrating your ties to your home country. You are more likely to be able to show that you will not remain in the U.S. illegally if you are in a category requiring a wait of ten years or more, rather than one or two.

There are only a few exceptions to the general rule that nonimmigrants must convince the U.S. consul that they do not intend to stay permanently in the United States. One is for people who qualify for certain temporary work statuses (H and L visas).

Although they might have an approved I-130 petition by reason of their U.S. citizen spouse, child, parent, brother, or sister, or a lawful permanent resident spouse or parent, the U.S. embassy is supposed to issue them an H or L visa if they qualify for that nonimmigrant visa while waiting for a visa number to become available. Another is for spouses of U.S. citizens who might qualify for the K-3 visa (see Chapter 7).

D. Can You Predict How Long You'll Wait?

No one can tell you for certain how long you'll wait for the U.S. government to process your visa or green card. If you're an immediate relative, you'll get your best estimate from asking people who work in the office you're dealing with what the current expected application processing times are. Processing times for certain applications are also posted on USCIS's website at www.uscis.gov. Click "Check Processing Times." You choose the type of application or petition and the office or service center at which your case is pending. You'll be given a range of months for that type of case at that office.

If you are not in the immediate relative category, pay careful attention to the U.S. State Department's *Visa Bulletin* to track how long you're likely to spend on the waitlist; see the information about the Visa Cutoff Date in Section 2, below.

1. The Priority Date

The Priority Date is the date on which your relative began the process by filing a petition for you with USCIS (or "INS," as it was formerly called).

The first notification of your Priority Date will be on the receipt notice that your relative gets, showing the date the petition was received and the fee paid to USCIS. That date will also be shown on your approval notice, which is the next piece of paper your relative will get from USCIS—and which is even more important to keep while you wait for your Priority Date to become current.

CAUTION

Your relative might wait several years for an answer on the initial I-130 petition. Instead of reviewing all petitions in the order received, USCIS sometimes prioritizes those filed on behalf of people whose visas will be available sooner. That means that if you're in a category with long waits, your U.S. citizen or resident relative could receive a receipt notice one year and the approval notice several years later, when it's almost time for you to immigrate. This practice won't add any delays to your overall wait—it's like having two sources of delay going on simultaneously. It will, however, add uncertainty to your life, since you won't know until the last minute whether the initial petition will be approved or denied.

The Department of State keeps careful count of how many immigrant visas are issued for each country in each preference category. If the quota has been reached in one category before the fiscal year is over (in October), the department will not issue any immigrant visas in that category for the rest of the fiscal year and will, in addition, state that visas are temporarily unavailable for that category, either for a particular country or worldwide.

October 1 of each year marks the beginning of another fiscal year for the federal government—and the count of the immigrant visas issued begins all over again for each country in each preference category.

2. Tracking Your Progress: Visa Cutoff Date

Each month, the Department of State issues a *Visa Bulletin,* which sets out the immigrant visa cutoff date of each visa preference, as a signal of who can move forward with their applications. See the sample below.

The State Department in fact publishes two charts each month: Final Action and Dates for Filing. The Final Action chart controls when you can actually receive your green card. The Dates for Filing chart controls when you can either submit an I-485 Application to Adjust Status from within the United States (see Chapter 16), if you already are here, or when you can start submitting your documents to the National Visa Center to prepare for consular processing (see Chapter 17). A layer of complexity on top of the two charts is that USCIS decides each month whether it will follow the Final Action or Dates for Filing chart and publishes

Family Sponsored	All Chargeability Areas Except Those Listed	CHINA-mainland born	INDIA	MEXICO	PHILIPPINES
F1	01DEC14	01DEC14	01DEC14	08SEP99	01MAR12
F2A	C	C	C	C	C
F2B	22SEP15	22SEP15	22SEP15	01SEP00	22OCT11
F3	22NOV08	22NOV08	22NOV08	15SEP97	08JUN02
F4	22MAR07	22MAR07	15SEP05	22APR99	22AUG02

Excerpt from *Visa Bulletin* for January 2022

the relevant chart in the Green Card section of its website (www.uscis.gov) under "Visa Availability & Priority Dates."

The bottom line is that these dates announce which Priority Dates in each category are receiving attention from the Department of State because people holding those numbers have become eligible or soon will be eligible for an immigrant visa. All applicants whose Priority Date falls before the applicable cutoff date will be given an appointment within a few months if they're overseas, or will be allowed to submit the next part of their application if they're in the U.S. and eligible to adjust status there. Anyone whose Priority Date falls after the cutoff date will have to wait.

EXAMPLE: You were born in Poland. Your brother, who is a naturalized U.S. citizen, filed a petition for you on February 21, 2007, which becomes your Priority Date. You are in the fourth preference category. The *Visa Bulletin* of January 2022 says the State Department is processing siblings with a Priority Date on or before March 22, 2007. Your appointment for your immigrant visa is currently available. It doesn't matter that the dates don't match exactly. The point is that people whose visa petitions were filed later than yours are receiving visas, so you should too.

However, if you were from another country, the waiting period could be longer, as you can see in the chart above.

The cutoff dates announced in the *Visa Bulletin* might not change much from one month to the next—sometimes one week for one preference and two weeks for another preference. Or the date might not move at all for several months in your category. Be prepared to wait.

Get the latest *Visa Bulletin* at https://travel.state.gov by clicking on "U.S. Visas" and then "Check the Visa Bulletin." Pay special attention to the Priority Date and the cutoff date that apply to your visa application. The *Visa Bulletin* is normally available in each embassy or consulate, or in USCIS offices. You can also call the Department of State in Washington, D.C., at 202-485-7699 for a recorded version.

As noted above, there's one more chart you will want to look at in order to move your application forward quickly, if you are not the immediate relative of a U.S. citizen and you are planning to adjust status while in the United States. It's called the "Adjustment of Status Filing Charts from the Visa Bulletin," found at www.uscis.gov/visabulletininfo. Here, you will find a date when you can submit your adjustment application and whether or not you can apply for a work permit in the meantime. That date might be BEFORE your Priority Date is actually current (though because you'll likely wait several months for an interview, it should be current by the time it matters). Only an immigrant legally in the U.S. on a valid, long-term visa (such as a student or employment visa) can obtain a green card through adjustment of status procedures, however. See Chapter 16 for more information about this process.

You can subscribe to an email service that will automatically send you the latest *Visa Bulletin* every month as it becomes available. Details about how to do this can be found at the bottom of the bulletin itself.

3. Some People Can Switch Preference Categories

A special rule applies to family-based immigrant visas, allowing you to hang onto your Priority Date if you change from one preference category to another.

If you belong to one family preference, and some event (marriage, divorce, death of spouse, or the simple passage of time) places you in a different preference category, your original Priority Date might remain unchanged. That means you won't lose much ground, because your place on the new waiting list will reflect the fact that your petition was filed long before many other people's.

The types of situations in which a family-based beneficiary who has undergone a change of circumstance can convert to another category without losing the original Priority Date include:

- Marriage of the son or daughter (older than 21) of U.S. citizen—moves down from first to third preference.
- Marriage of child (younger than 21) of U.S. citizen—moves down from immediate relative to third preference.

- Divorce of child or adult son or daughter—moves up from third preference to immediate relative or first preference, depending on child's age at divorce.
- Naturalization of legal resident petitioner—2A spouse and unmarried children younger than 21 move up from second preference to immediate relative and children age 21 or older move to first preference from category 2B.
- Child of lawful permanent resident reaching age 21 before Priority Date becomes current—drops from category 2A to category 2B of the second preference. However, if the child reaches age 21 after their Priority Date has become current but before actual approval for permanent residency, the child can retain 2A status as long as they apply within one year of the Priority Date having become current. (This represents a 2002 change in the law—formerly, such children would have also dropped into category 2B, simply by virtue of not having received approval on time, and therefore had to wait longer.)

CAUTION

Some life changes make you ineligible for any visa at all. Not everyone who marries, divorces, or whose petitioning family member dies can switch to another preference category. You can switch only if, at the time, an existing category fits your new situation. So, for example, the child of a U.S. citizen who marries can switch to the third preference category. But the child of a lawful permanent resident who marries is out of luck, because there's no category for married children of permanent residents. Such issues are explained further in Section E, below.

4. Advise USCIS If You Can Upgrade

If you can switch to a better (faster) visa category—most likely because the person petitioning for you has gone from being a permanent resident to being a U.S. citizen—you'll need to let USCIS know.

Sample Request for Upgrade to USCIS

123 Central Avenue
Treesbird, VT 14235
April 14, 2022

Department of Homeland Security
U.S. Citizenship and Immigration Services
P.O. Box 648005
Lee's Summit, MO 64064

RE: I-130 UPGRADE REQUEST
    Petitioner: Samuel Thornburgh
    Beneficiary: Junyi Cho

Dear Sir/Madam:

I filed an I-130 visa petition for the above-named beneficiary on February 11, 2022, during which time I was a U.S. permanent resident. That petition is still pending.

Since filing the petition, however, I have become a naturalized U.S. citizen. A copy of my naturalization certificate is attached.

Please continue processing this case, but as an immediate relative petition. Thank you for your attention to this matter.

Very truly yours,

Samuel Thornburgh

Enclosed: Copy of naturalization certificate
          USCIS Receipt Notice

How you do that depends first on where your file is located at the time of change. If, for example, your Form I-130 petition is still pending at a USCIS service center, you'll want to send a letter titled "I-130 UPGRADE REQUEST" identifying you and the petitioner and explaining the situation (see the sample above). Also be sure to include a copy (not the original) of the petitioner's signed naturalization certificate, and the receipt notice showing the Priority Date.

If the I-130 petition has already been approved, and the beneficiary is living outside the U.S., you'll need to contact the National Visa Center. Its online instructions for that say to submit a question through its online "Public Inquiry Form," but attorneys have found this doesn't always get results. Thus it's best to also send a letter, along with a copy of the petition approval notice (Form I-797) from USCIS, to:

National Visa Center
31 Rochester Avenue, Suite 100
Portsmouth, NH 03801-2915

Situations Where Children Are Protected From Switching Categories

The Child Status Protection Act of 2002 allows certain children of U.S. citizens and permanent residents to retain their original visa eligibility even if they turn 21 while they're waiting for the process to finish up. (Formerly, turning 21 would have automatically dropped them into a lower preference category and caused them to have to wait longer for their visa or green card.) Those who benefit include:

- Children of U.S. citizens—will retain immediate relative status even if they turn 21 at any time after a visa petition has been filed on their behalf.
- Children of lawful permanent residents—will retain 2A status if they turn 21 after their Priority Date has become current, so long as they file for a green card within one year of becoming current. (Technically, by filing for the green card the child "locks in" their age at 21 minus the number of days it took USCIS to approve the initial I-130 visa petition. However, given USCIS delays, that almost always shaves off enough months to keep the child's age, for immigration purposes, at less than 21.)

Immigrant Story: Uniting the Family

Here is how the quota system affected Giti and Meena, two young sisters from Afghanistan.

After waiting for more than ten years, their father was about to get a green card through his U.S. citizen brother. He planned to bring his wife and two children with him, as is allowed in this visa category (family fourth preference). What the family did not realize, however, was how their plans would be affected if either of the sisters married or turned 21 years old before they entered the U.S.

Just before the visa interview, Giti, who was 19 years old, married a man from their town in Afghanistan. Her eligibility for the green card was destroyed.

Meena, on the other hand, was unmarried but 21 years and 6 months old at the time of the family's interview. Her eligibility was not destroyed, because legal protections provided by the Child Status Protection Act allow her (and other children in the preference categories) to subtract from her age the amount of time it took USCIS to approve the visa petition. In this particular case, it had taken USCIS nine months to approve the petition (and then the family waited another ten years for the Priority Date to become current). So Meena is considered to have another three months before "aging out." Once her visa is approved, she needs to be sure that she enters the U.S. before she ages out.

What should the family do about Giti? Although it will take a long time, Giti's best bet is for one or both of her parents to learn English and become a U.S. citizen as soon as possible (this will normally take at least five years). Next, the parents will need to petition for her and her husband under the family third preference category. They'll wait approximately seven years before being allowed to immigrate to the United States.

Giti's father wonders whether Giti shouldn't just divorce the young man. However, that would be considered immigration fraud if done just to allow her to get a green card. If the immigration authorities found out about the fraud, it would destroy her eligibility for any green card in any category.

And if the beneficiary is living in the U.S. and is eligible to adjust status, you don't need to send a letter anywhere. You simply submit the full adjustment of status application (Form I-485, with supporting documents and fees) with a copy of the I-130 approval and the naturalization certificate to USCIS.

These rules might sound hard to follow, but because they can make a big difference in how quickly your application is processed, it is worth your time to understand them.

E. Revocation of a Petition or Application

Here is a bit of scary information, but it's better to know it than not to know: After a petition or application has been filed on behalf of an alien, it can be revoked or canceled—even if it has already been approved by the INS or USCIS.

One reason for revocation would be the potential immigrant's unintended "failure to prosecute" the petition. This can happen when your relative, the petitioner, has not informed USCIS about address changes, and so does not get notification that USCIS is ready for further processing of your case. If USCIS gets no response after repeated attempts to contact the petitioner, it will assume that you are no longer interested in going forward on the petition. USCIS then can revoke and cancel the petition! To avoid this, make sure USCIS always has the petitioner's updated address, and sign up for USCIS's automatic email/text alerts.

Another reason for revocation is a change in your circumstances that makes you no longer eligible for the visa. It can also be based on a discovery that you committed fraud, for example by pretending to be someone's relation when you really weren't.

USCIS will normally revoke a petition if, for example:

- The person who filed the petition decides to withdraw it and informs USCIS of this decision.

- The person who filed the petition dies; however, USCIS might decide not to revoke the petition if the law allows you to self petition (as it does for widows/widowers of U.S. citizens) or if it is convinced that there are "humanitarian reasons" not to do so.
- In a marriage case, the couple divorces or the marriage is annulled before the green card is approved.
- In a family second preference case, the unmarried son or daughter gets married before the green card is approved.

TIP

Don't let the NVC think you're no longer interested. The National Visa Center (NVC) has a one-year contact rule, which requires you to contact it within one year of notification that a visa has become available. If you do not, your visa application can be terminated. Avoid trouble by simply acting on your visa application and following the NVC instructions about steps to take before your interview is scheduled. If circumstances arise that require you to delay visa processing (for example, your parent is ill and requires you to provide home care before moving to the U.S.), contact the NVC explaining the delay.

Special Rules for Widows and Widowers

If the beneficiary is the spouse of a U.S. citizen, the petition will be granted as long as the widowed beneficiary was not legally separated or divorced from the citizen at the time of death, applies within two years of the spouse's death, and has not remarried.

Consider this scenario: A permanent resident mother has brought all her children to the United States except her eldest son, who marries before she could petition for him. After five years, she becomes a U.S. citizen and immediately files a petition for her married son, still living in the foreign country. The petition is approved, but before the son and his family come to the United States, the mother dies. The petition is automatically revoked, and the son remains separated from his brothers and sisters, who have been living in the United States since their mother received her green card.

That application of the regulations seems cruel. It is precisely for such cases that the regulations have been somewhat liberalized. The beneficiary of a petition filed by a U.S. citizen or by a permanent resident who dies before the foreign-born beneficiary could come to the United States is no longer in an entirely hopeless situation.

With a lawyer's help, you might be able to show the immigration authorities that for "humanitarian reasons" revocation would be inappropriate. There is, however, a catch: Because every immigrant to the United States must have a financial sponsor— that is, someone who promises to support an immigrant who is no longer able to be self-supporting—you will need to find a substitute sponsor for the person who died. Only certain people can fill this substitute role, including a spouse, parent, mother-in-law, father-in-law, sibling, son, daughter, son-in-law, or daughter-in-law. As in the case of other sponsors, this sponsor must maintain an annual income equal to at least 125% of the federal Poverty Guidelines. ●

Fiancé(e) Visas

A. Who Qualifies for a Fiancé Visa 56

   1. You Must Intend to Marry a U.S. Citizen 56

   2. You Must Have Met in Person Within the Last Two Years 56

   3. You Must Be Legally Able to Marry 57

B. Quick View of the Fiancé Visa Application Process 57

C. Detailed Instructions for the Fiancé Visa Application Process 58

   1. Documents Required for Fiancé Visa Petition 58

   2. Where and How to Send the Fiancé Petition 59

   3. Visa Petition Interviews 59

   4. U.S. Consulate Notified of Approval 60

   5. Interview at the Embassy 61

   6. At the Border 63

   7. Permission to Work in the U.S. 63

D. How to Bring Your Children on a Fiancé Visa 63

E. Marriage and After 64

The fiancé visa (K-1) was designed to allow people who've become engaged to—but haven't yet married—a U.S. citizen to travel to the U.S. for the wedding. Your minor children can go with you to the U.S. If you marry the U.S. citizen within 90 days, you and your children can apply for green cards. Otherwise, you must leave the U.S. before the date indicated on your passport.

Unfortunately, this visa isn't available to the fiancés of U.S. permanent residents (green card holders).

A. Who Qualifies for a Fiancé Visa

To qualify for a fiancé visa, you must:

- intend to marry a U.S. citizen (see Section 1, below)
- have met your intended spouse in person within the last two years (though this can be waived based on cultural customs or extreme hardship; see Section 2, below), and
- be legally able to marry (see Section 3, below).

It's important to realize that a fiancé visa is not a green card. It's only a temporary, 90-day right to be in the United States. However, it's included in this book because it's an important first step towards getting a green card. After the immigrant has arrived in the United States and gotten married, they can file for a green card—through a process called "adjustment of status"—at a U.S.-based USCIS office. (Or, an immigrant who has no desire for a U.S. green card can simply return home before the K-1 visa term runs out.)

1. You Must Intend to Marry a U.S. Citizen

As part of your application, you'll have to convince the U.S. government of your intention to get married. We'll talk more about how to do this in the sections that discuss paperwork.

TIP
Make your wedding plans flexible. You can't know exactly how long it will take to get a K-1 fiancé visa, but you'll have to hold your wedding within 90 days of entering the United States. Before you sign any contracts for catering, photographic, or other services, discuss the situation with the service providers and build flexibility into your contracts or agreements in case the date needs to change.

The person you plan to marry must be a citizen, not a permanent resident, of the United States. A U.S. citizen is someone who was either:

- born in the United States or its territories
- became a citizen through a process of application and testing (called "naturalization"), or
- acquired or derived citizenship through a family member (for more information, see www.nolo.com; search for the article entitled "U.S. Citizenship by Birth or Through Parents").

2. You Must Have Met in Person Within the Last Two Years

To protect against sham marriages, U.S. immigration law requires that you and your fiancé have met in person within the last two years. Even a brief meeting could be enough. Perhaps the immigrant can visit the United States on a tourist visa. However, getting approval for a tourist visa can be difficult, because the U.S. consulate might believe that the immigrant actually intends to get married and apply for the green card right away—which would be a misuse of the tourist visa, and could amount to visa fraud. It will probably be easier for the U.S. citizen to visit the immigrant overseas.

If, however, you're from a country where prospective husbands and wives don't meet before the wedding, for religious or cultural reasons, this meeting will obviously be a greater hardship. In such a case, you can ask the immigration authorities to "waive" (overlook) the meeting requirement.

To do so, you'll need letters from your religious leader, parents, or other relevant people, and other proof of the normal practices in your culture. Getting a lawyer's help would be a good idea here.

U.S. Citizen Petitioners Must Disclose Criminal Records

After Congressional concern that immigrating fiancés were particularly susceptible to domestic violence and abuse—particularly those whose engagements were arranged through marriage brokers (so-called "mail order brides")—Congress passed the International Marriage Brokers Regulation Act of 2005 (IMBRA).

As a result, the fiancé visa petition (Form I-129F) now asks *all* U.S. citizen petitioners whether they have a history of violent crime and crime relating to alcohol or controlled-substance abuse. In addition, Form I-129F now asks whether you and your fiancé or spouse met through an international marriage broker.

Many reputable online dating websites are exempt from IMBRA requirements and are not considered to be "mail order bride" services. A dating website or organization that does not serve mainly to provide international dating services between U.S. citizens and foreign residents and charges similar rates to both Americans and foreigners and men and women will not be considered "an international marriage broker" for IMBRA purposes. Nor will traditional nonprofit religious or cultural matchmaking services, as long as they otherwise comply with U.S. and local laws. If you did use a marriage broker, the immigrant will be asked, at the visa interview, whether the broker complied with legal requirements to collect information on the U.S. fiancé or spouse's criminal record and pass it to the immigrant.

---

3. You Must Be Legally Able to Marry

For most people, the requirement that you be legally able to marry won't pose any problems. However, if one of you is already married or too young to legally marry in the state or country where you plan to perform the wedding, or if the two of you are close relatives, such as cousins, and forbidden to marry in the state or country where you plan to hold the wedding, you might not qualify for a fiancé visa.

If possible, take steps to correct the problem— for example, obtain a divorce, figure out a different place to marry, or wait until you're older.

Same-sex couples saw a major hurdle removed when the U.S. Supreme Court issued its decision in *Obergefell v. Hodges*. As of 2015, same-sex couples can marry in any U.S. state or territory. (In the past, U.S. immigration law didn't recognize same-sex marriage at all, and it was permitted in only a minority of states.)

Keep in mind that a civil union or domestic partnership will not work for immigration purposes, and both opposite- and same-sex couples must legally marry in order for the foreign fiancé to eventually obtain a green card.

B. Quick View of the Fiancé Visa Application Process

Here's what to plan for on your path to a fiancé visa:
1. The U.S. citizen submits a fiancé petition to USCIS (on Form I-129F).
2. USCIS sends the U.S. citizen a receipt notice, after confirming that the application is complete, then (within months) a notice of its decision, hopefully approving the petition. (Occasionally, USCIS will call the U.S. citizen petitioner in for an interview before deciding on the petition.)

3. USCIS transfers the file to an intermediary called the National Visa Center (NVC), which then transfers it to the U.S. consulate serving the immigrant's country. The consulate instructs the immigrating fiancé on what documents to prepare.

4. The immigrating fiancé attends the visa interview, and if all goes well, is approved for a K-1 visa. The visa might need to be picked up on a separate day or might be mailed. The immigrant must use it to enter the U.S. within six months.

C. Detailed Instructions for the Fiancé Visa Application Process

Obtaining a fiancé or K-1 visa requires time, patience, and paperwork.

1. Documents Required for Fiancé Visa Petition

To start the process, the U.S. citizen must prepare or provide the following:

☐ Form I-129F, Petition for Alien Fiancé(e). (See the completed sample at www.nolo.com/back-of-book/GRN.html; get the latest version at www.uscis.gov/i-129f.)

☐ Separate passport-style color photographs of the U.S. citizen and the alien fiancé.

☐ Form G-1145 (optional, but useful so that you'll receive an email or text notification from USCIS when it has gotten your application; it's available at www.uscis.gov/g-1145).

☐ Proof of the U.S. fiancé's U.S. citizenship, such as a copy of a passport, birth certificate, or naturalization certificate (see Chapter 21, Section D3 for details).

☐ Proof that any previous marriages have been terminated by death, divorce, or annulment and proof of any name changes. Evidence of name changes can be found on a marriage certificate, divorce decree, or court order showing the name change.

Immigrant Story: Proving They'd Met

Doug, from Ireland, and Carol, a U.S. citizen, met online and exchanged emails for over a year before they decided to get married. However, Carol was living with her parents in Philadelphia while she finished her Ph.D. in medieval history, and her family was extremely protective. She knew they would have panicked at the idea of her so much as corresponding with a stranger online, much less marrying him.

So although Carol definitely wanted to meet Doug before the wedding, she decided a secret meeting would be best. When a history conference took her to Newark, New Jersey, she suggested to Doug that he meet her there. They stayed with friends of Carol's, had a great time, and reaffirmed their intention to marry.

Then came time to prove that they'd met the meeting requirement. Carol suddenly realized she had almost no proof of their meeting. She'd driven to Newark, hadn't paid for a hotel room, and had eaten either conference food or in her friends' kitchen the whole time. But after thinking harder, she realized she'd paid for gas with a credit card while in New Jersey, and registration materials from the conference. Plus, Carol's friends had taken a photo of the couple and posted it on social media during their trip. This, plus proof of Doug's plane ticket, was enough to satisfy the meeting requirement, and Doug was granted a fiancé visa.

☐ Proof that the U.S. citizen and the foreign-born fiancé have met each other within the past two years: photographs, plane tickets, letters, social media posts during the time you met, travel itineraries, hotel receipts, and so on. This evidence will also help show that your relationship is genuine.

☐ If the U.S. citizen has ever been convicted of any violent crime, or a crime involving domestic violence or substance abuse (a more complete list is provided in the Form I-129F instructions), certified copies of all police and court records showing the outcome (get a lawyer's help in this instance).

□ Proof that the two of you intend to marry within 90 days after the foreign-born fiancé arrives in the U.S.: for example, emails, letters, online chat logs, telephone records, letter from the religious or civil authority who will officiate at the wedding, receipts or contracts for the wedding location or wedding expenses, such as flowers, food, music, and formal wear, and engagement or wedding announcement or invitation. It used to be that both the U.S. citizen and foreign-born fiancé were required to submit signed statements about their relationship and intention to marry. Now, the U.S. citizen provides information about how the couple met in Form I-129F—but it's still advisable to provide additional statements about why you decided to marry (see a completed sample at www.nolo.com/back-of-book/GRN.html).

□ Filing fee (currently $535), either by credit card (fill out USCIS Form G-1450, Authorization for Credit Card Transactions), or by check or money order payable to the U.S. Department of Homeland Security. (You do not, however, have to pay the fee if you're already married and filing Form I-129F after filing a Form I-130 in order to obtain a K-3 visa, as described in Chapter 7.)

2. Where and How to Send the Fiancé Petition

Once the U.S. citizen petitioner has prepared everything on the above list, he or she should make two complete photocopies of everything, including the check or money order. This will be extremely important in the all-too-common event that USCIS misplaces the petition. Send one copy to the immigrating fiancé, for his or her records. The U.S. citizen should assemble the original package neatly, and preferably write a cover letter that lists, in bullet points, everything inside.

The petitioner should send the completed visa petition by certified mail, return receipt requested, to the appropriate USCIS lockbox. (See the USCIS website for contact details. As of this book's print date, all I-129F petitions were to be mailed to a Texas lockbox.) You *cannot* just walk the form into your local USCIS office.

It is also a good idea to file Form G-1145, asking USCIS to send you an email and/or text notification when your application has been accepted. (See a completed sample at www.nolo.com/back-of-book/GRN.html.)

Once you have a receipt from USCIS, you can use the receipt number to sign up to receive automatic email updates that let you know whenever mail is sent regarding your application. Go to the USCIS website at www.uscis.gov and click "Check Case Status." Here, you can also sign up for a USCIS account, so as to register for automatic case status updates by email or text message.

CAUTION

When's the most frustrating part of the process? Many K visa petitioners and beneficiaries report that it's the waiting period between when USCIS approves the Form I-129F petition and when the National Visa Center (NVC) takes further action and sends the case file to the U.S. embassy or consulate abroad. The NVC is notoriously slow and backlogged. If 30 days have elapsed with no word, contacting the NVC online via https://travel.state.gov (click "U.S. Visas" then "Immigrate" then " When and how to Contact NVC.")

3. Visa Petition Interviews

Although it does not happen often, it is possible that the U.S. citizen petitioner will be called in for an interview by a USCIS officer. The petitioner should bring all original documents to the interview. If the documents and the interview convince USCIS that true romance is behind the planned marriage, the petition will be approved and a Notice of Action, Form I-797, will be mailed to the U.S. citizen. The form will contain instructions for the next step to take—and might include a request for additional information or documentation.

What You'll Need for Your Consular Interview

It's never too early to begin gathering the necessary documents to bring with you to your scheduled interview at the U.S. embassy or consulate:

- [ ] the confirmation page and bar code, showing that you (and any accompanying family members) completed an online Form DS-160
- [ ] a current passport (unexpired for at least nine months after your intended entry to the U.S.) for yourself and for all of your unmarried children younger than 21 years of age, if they are coming with you or following you to the United States
- [ ] divorce or death certificates for any previous spouses of either you or the U.S. citizen, with English translations
- [ ] police clearance from all places you have lived for more than six months (except from the United States, where USCIS gathers the information)
- [ ] originals of all documents, copies of which were submitted by your U.S. citizen fiancé with Form I-129F (see the completed sample

at www.nolo.com/back-of-book/GRN.html) to confirm your relationship and show your eligibility for the visa
- [ ] two passport-style photographs of yourself and each of any children applying with you for a visa (see Chapter 21, Section E for detailed photo requirements)
- [ ] a report of your own medical examination and those of all children older than 14 years of age to verify that you've had all your vaccinations (including for COVID-19) and that no one has a communicable disease. You will need to get this medical exam from a designated panel physician. For a list of panel physicians near you, visit https://travel.state.gov.
- [ ] Form I-134, Affidavit of Support, filled out by your U.S. citizen fiancé. (See the completed sample at www.nolo.com/back-of-book/GRN.html.)

Some U.S. embassies and consulates require additional documents. Check the State Department website for details.

4. U.S. Consulate Notified of Approval

After USCIS approves the Form I-129F petition, it will advise a processing unit called the National Visa Center (NVC). The NVC will send you, the immigrating fiancé, a receipt number as well as information on what to do next.

You'll need to complete Form DS-160, Online Nonimmigrant Visa Application, prior to your visa interview. It's fairly straightforward, but you will need Internet access and at least some command of the English language. There is no paper version of the form (for which reason we do not supply a sample).

You can get translations of the questions into many languages from the drop-down menu in the

upper right corner of the form. You will, however, need to answer all questions in English. Each applicant for a K visa (including any accompanying children) will need to complete a separate Form DS-160, though you can complete the form for any of your children younger than age 16.

Make sure to record the Application ID that you receive upon beginning the online form. This will allow you to retrieve a saved DS-160 if you do not complete it or if the application "times out" due to issues such as a poor Internet connection.

You will be asked for personal information, such as any names used, date and place of birth, address, phone number and email, any national identification or other numbers, and passport information.

Also, you will need a recent and clear digital photograph of yourself to upload, and information on your U.S. travel plans. You will be asked for your expected date of U.S. arrival, names of any travel companions, previous U.S. travel history and contacts, family information, and work and educational history.

Although you don't need to print the application for submission, it's a good idea to keep a copy for your records. You WILL need a copy of the DS-160 confirmation page and bar code to bring to your interview at the U.S. embassy or consulate, which will allow the consular officer to upload your application.

While the procedure for interviewing for a K visa at a U.S. consulate or embassy is largely the same in all countries, some consulates do have slightly different requirements for people scheduling and attending interviews. For example, many require K visa applicants to pay the application fee (currently $265) before the appointment is scheduled. You can typically do so either by using a credit or debit card online or calling a telephone to provide banking information. Additionally, some consulates will permit the U.S. fiancé to attend the interview along with the immigrating fiancé, while others do not.

After the consulate or embassy nearest to you receives your case file from the NVC, it will send you instructions about how to proceed (including information about authorized medical examiners and how to obtain police records in your area). Many consulates will send an appointment letter. You will need to contact the consulate to reschedule if there is a conflict with the assigned interview date. However, some consulates will require you to schedule your own interview, using your receipt number and DS-160 bar code number. Check the consulate's website for its specific instructions about scheduling nonimmigrant or K visa interviews and any additional documentation required at the interview.

If you live far away from the consulate, you might want to arrive a couple of days before your actual interview. This will give you time to have the medical exam done and receive the results (if no doctors closer to your home were on the consulate's list). Also, check out the situation around the consulate itself. Often, there are long lines, so you'll need to arrive well before your appointment time and expect to be let in long after. Many prospective immigrants who have applied for a visa at a local consulate have posted their experiences online, so it's worth doing some homework.

5. Interview at the Embassy

On the date of your interview at the U.S. embassy or consulate, bring all the forms and documents listed in the consulate's instructions and under "What You'll Need for Your Consular Interview," above.

Form I-134. This form, called an "Affidavit of Support," is used to show that you will not become a public charge (dependent on government support) while in the U.S., because your petitioner/sponsor has sufficient income and/or assets to support you. See the completed sample Form I-134 at www.nolo.com/back-of-book/GRN.html (the latest is available at www.uscis.gov/i-134). Note that at one time, it was necessary to sign this form in front of a notary public, but no longer.

It's important to realize, however, that you'll need to prove you won't become a public charge at a later date, after you marry and apply for the green card in the United States. You will then need to submit a new Affidavit of Support on a different form, Form I-864, which comes with more demanding income requirements. For starters, Form I-134 sponsors need only show that their income is at least 100% of the federal Poverty Guidelines, while I-864 sponsors must show that it reaches 125%. In support of this form, the citizen should add copies (as appropriate) of their:

- ☐ bank statements
- ☐ recent tax returns and W-2s
- ☐ employment verification (make this an original letter from the employer detailing salary, hours, and whether the position is temporary or permanent), and
- ☐ if necessary to bring the citizen's income above the Poverty Guidelines levels, documents showing the value of any of the following property, if owned: bonds and stocks, real estate, and mortgage information or life insurance.

Medical exam. The immigrating fiancé will also need to have a medical exam done. The fiancé can't just go to the family doctor, but will have to go to a clinic specified by the consulate. The doctor will do an exam, ask questions about medical history and drug and alcohol use, take X-rays, and draw blood. Although vaccinations are not required for K visa issuance, they will be when you adjust your status to permanent resident. Embassies therefore encourage fiancés to fulfill the vaccination requirements at the time of the fiancé medical examination. The cost (including vaccines) is usually around $300, but varies by country.

Forms for accompanying children. Most of the forms and documents must be separately filled out for you and for any minor children who will also be going to the United States.

Security checks. Because of intense security procedures, you're unlikely to receive your visa on the same day as you attend your interview. It can take several weeks for the consulate to run security checks—even longer if you come from a country that the United States suspects of supporting terrorism.

Visa approval. If the U.S. consular official is ultimately convinced that you and your U.S. citizen fiancé are truly engaged to be married and will marry upon your arrival in the United States, and that you aren't barred from entry for any of the

reasons described in Chapter 4, your passport will be stamped with the K-1 visa. The passports of your accompanying minor children will be stamped with the K-2 visa, meaning that they are dependent upon you for their immigration status.

Questions to Expect at K-1 Visa Interview

At your interview, the U.S. consular officer will ask a few basic questions about you and your fiancé and about five to ten additional questions to test the validity of your relationship. On average, the entire K-1 visa interview takes 15 to 30 minutes.

Be prepared for questions about any previous marriages and about your or your fiancé's children. Make sure you know basic information about your fiancé including occupation, hometown, birthday, and names of close family members. Other sample questions about your relationship might include:

- "How long did you date before you got engaged?"
- "What types of activities do you like to do together?"
- "How many times have you met in person? Where and when?"
- "How are you communicating during the long-distance relationship? Is it difficult being apart?"
- Have you met your fiancé's family (or vice versa)?"
- "When and where will the wedding be held?"
- "Do you have any plans for a honeymoon?"

TIP

If you're already married but are applying for a K-3 fiancé visa, most of the advice in this section regarding the visa interview applies to you, too. However, you won't have to worry about convincing anyone that you plan to get married. Your main task will simply be to show that your paperwork is in order, with the understanding that you will complete the green card application after you've arrived in the United States.

The fiancé visa is considered a nonimmigrant visa because you are simply promising to marry a U.S. citizen. You are not yet a U.S. immigrant.

6. At the Border

Once you receive your fiancé visa, you'll have six months to use it to enter the United States. At the U.S. port of entry, the border officer will examine the contents of your visa envelope and ask you a few questions. Be careful with this—an officer who spots a reason that you should not have been given the fiancé visa, can deny your entry right there. You would have no choice but to find a flight or another means of transport home. And you might not be allowed back for five years (unless the officer allows you to withdraw the application before it's officially denied, which is entirely at the officer's discretion).

Assuming all goes well, the border officer will stamp your passport with your K-1 fiancé visa status, and indicate in your passport the 90-day duration of your status.

7. Permission to Work in the U.S.

When you arrive in the United States, you can, in theory, apply at once for an Employment Authorization card (EAD) that will enable you to work legally. The proper paperwork to complete for this is Form I-765. (See the USCIS website for the latest version, www.uscis.gov/i-765.)

However, you'll have to submit your application to a USCIS service center, and these are famous for months'-long delays. Submitting this application might not be worth the effort since the maximum time the EAD will be good for is three months (based on the length of your fiancé visa). You might be better off getting married, then submitting your green card application together with an I-765 application for a work permit.

This allows you more time to work before the card expires (it will last for approximately one year).

D. How to Bring Your Children on a Fiancé Visa

Your unmarried children younger than age 21 are eligible to accompany you on your fiancé visa and apply for green cards after you're in the United States and are married. This includes biological as well as adopted children. All you have to do at the beginning of the fiancé visa application process is to include your children's names in Part 2 of the fiancé petition (Form I-129F). You, as the parent, can complete a Form DS-160 for any accompanying child younger than age 16.

Your children will probably be asked to attend your consular interview with you, although some consulates let younger children stay home. The technical name of their visa will be K-2. For the visa interview, they'll normally be asked to bring:

- ☐ DS-160 confirmation receipt
- ☐ birth certificate (original and photocopy, with English translation)
- ☐ police record (if the child is older than age 16)
- ☐ passport (unless your country permits the child to be included on your passport)
- ☐ two photos, and
- ☐ medical exam results.

Even if your children don't accompany you when you first enter the U.S. as a fiancé, they can join you under the same visa for a year after yours was approved. Just make sure they remain unmarried and younger than age 21. They'll need to complete Forms DS-160 and schedule an interview. If they don't plan to immigrate with you, but want to attend your wedding, their other option is a visitor visa.

When it comes time to apply for green cards, you and your children will each have to submit a separate application, before each of your visas expires.

TIP

Don't let anyone tell you that your child needs to have been younger than 18 when you were married. Some USCIS officers get confused when dealing with K-2 applicants for adjustment of status, and expect them to meet the standards for stepchildren that apply to certain other applicants. But so long as your K-2 child is younger than 21 (and unmarried), and you've gotten married to your U.S. citizen petitioner, the child can apply to adjust status and get a green card.

E. Marriage and After

It's a good idea to marry as soon as possible after you arrive. That will give you enough time to prepare and submit your application for adjustment of status before your fiancé visa expires, so that you remain in lawful fiancé status the whole time. (See Chapter 16 for more about submitting your application for adjustment of status.) There could be delays in preparing the application that are out of your control. For example, your local government office could take several weeks to issue your official marriage certificate, which is a required document in your adjustment of status package—USCIS will not accept your application with just the initial "souvenir" certificate issued by civil and religious authorities.

Definitely try to marry within 90 days of entering the U.S., that is, before your fiancé visa expires. Even if you marry on day 90, you can legally wait until after the 90 days to submit your adjustment of status application, but you will be without any legal status during the gap.

If something happens and you even miss the 90-day deadline for getting married, you and your fiancé can still go ahead and get married and file for your adjustment of status. The difference is that you will have to also submit a Form I-130 petition along with its filing fee, currently $535.

CAUTION

What if, after coming to the U.S., you change your mind and decide not to get married? In that case, you should leave the U.S. before your 90 days on the fiancé visa are up.

If you fail to marry your U.S. citizen fiancé at all, USCIS can start removal (deportation) proceedings against you and all children who came with you on a fiancé visa.

If you enter the U.S. on a fiancé visa, you can adjust your status to permanent resident only if you marry your the U.S. citizen fiancé who petitioned you. If you marry someone else, you cannot adjust your status based on that other marriage—although you might be able to get a green card through consular processing. (Check Chapter 4 to see whether any grounds of inadmissibility might apply if you try to consular process, particularly the bar that is triggered if you were in the U.S. for more than 180 days after the expiration of your fiancé status.)

If you do marry your U.S. citizen fiancé within 90 days, there is one more important step you must take in order to get a green card: filing for adjustment of status (see Chapter 16), for yourself and all your minor children who came on the fiancé visa.

CAUTION

Beware of the two-year time limit. Going through the adjustment of status procedure will give you and your minor children conditional permanent residence status, and you will acquire a green card that is valid for only two years. To make it a permanent green card after the two years, follow the procedures for conditional permanent residents, laid out in Chapter 7.

Green Cards Through Marriage

A. Who Qualifies..66

B. Special Rules in Court Proceedings 67

C. Quick View of the Marriage-Based Green Card Application Process............................68

D. Detailed Instructions for the Marriage-Based Green Card Application Process.......70

   1. Beginning the Process: The I-130 Petition 70

   2. Option for Overseas Spouses of U.S. Citizens: The Fiancé Visa Petition (K-3)............72

   3. Moving the Process Forward...72

   4. Advice for Spouses of Permanent Residents...75

   5. Advice for People Who Entered the U.S. Without Inspection.................................75

   6. Documenting Your Bona Fide Marriage..76

E. Bringing Your Children...76

   1. If You're Marrying a U.S. Citizen...76

   2. If You're Marrying a U.S. Permanent Resident 77

   3. Final Phases of Children's Green Card Application 77

F. If Your Marriage Is Less Than Two Years Old..78

   1. Forms Required for Removal of Conditions...78

   2. If Your Spouse Does Not Sign the Joint Petition...79

   3. People Married Two Years or More 80

G. If You Marry Again...80

H. Common Questions About Marriage and Immigration..80

   1. Before Marriage...80

   2. After Marriage...81

Every year, thousands of immigrants fall in love with U.S. citizens or permanent residents. Some couples meet overseas, others meet when the foreign national is studying or traveling in the United States. In a few cases, both members of the couple are foreign born, but one becomes a U.S. citizen or permanent resident. No matter how the relationship came about, your topmost priority now might be to join up in the U.S. as soon as possible. This chapter will lay out the possibilities and help you decide the easiest, fastest way to achieve this.

CAUTION

We're assuming that you plan to live in the United States. If not, there's no point in applying for a green card now. You won't get one if the U.S. citizen or permanent resident can't show that he or she is, or soon will be, living and earning income in the U.S., and you'll lose the green card if you don't make the U.S. your home. If you're going to be living overseas for a while, wait until your plans change to apply for the green card.

A. Who Qualifies

You are eligible for a green card if you have entered into a bona fide (genuine), legal marriage with a U.S. citizen or lawful permanent resident. "Bona fide" means that the marriage is based on your desire to create a life together with your new spouse, not merely on your desire to obtain a green card. "Legal" means that it is valid and recognized by the laws of the state or country in which it took place. It doesn't matter whether the marriage ceremony took place in the United States or overseas, but you do need to abide by local laws—and obtain a document, such as a marriage certificate, to prove that you've done so.

Marriage to a U.S. citizen makes you an immediate relative and eligible to receive a green card just as soon as you can get through the application process.

Marriage to a U.S. permanent resident, unfortunately, will not yield such fast results. Your new spouse can file a visa petition for you right away, but you'll be placed in category 2A of the family visa preferences and quite possibly have to wait (the average is two or three years), before a green card becomes available to you. Only after that waiting period is over and you've applied for your green card will you be legally permitted to live in the United States.

The Inconveniences of Marriages of Convenience

In the early 1980s, the U.S. government came to believe that as many as half the petitions based on marriage were fraudulent—in other words, entered into for the purpose of obtaining a green card. In 1986, the U.S. Congress passed a law called the "Immigration Marriage Fraud Amendments," to eliminate as many "paper marriages" as possible.

U.S. citizens, permanent residents, and aliens who evade immigration laws by means of a fraudulent marriage can be charged with a federal crime. Those found guilty can be imprisoned for up to five years, fined up to $250,000, or both. In addition, permanent residents can be deported, as can those who are undocumented.

If you are even entertaining the idea of entering into a sham marriage, consider the following:

- Do you want to create the possibility of being blackmailed emotionally, psychologically, and financially?
- Do you want to be prosecuted for a federal crime with a penalty of five years in prison, a fine of up to $250,000, or both?

If USCIS discovers that you have entered into a marriage or even helped someone else enter into a marriage to evade the immigration laws—or if you have submitted papers to USCIS based on such a marriage—you will almost certainly forever lose the possibility of getting a green card, no matter what relationships you might have in the future.

!
CAUTION

If the U.S. petitioner has a criminal record, see an attorney. Under the Adam Walsh Child Protection and Safety Act of 2006, U.S. citizens and lawful permanent residents who have been convicted of any "specified offense against a minor" are prohibited from filing a family-based immigrant petition on behalf of any beneficiary (whether a child or not). USCIS will run security checks on all petitions and may call the petitioner in for fingerprinting. If the petitioner has a conviction for one of the specified offenses against a minor, then USCIS can't approve the petition unless it determines that the U.S. petitioner poses no risk to the beneficiary.

B. Special Rules in Court Proceedings

Suppose that removal—formerly called "deportation" or "exclusion"—proceedings have been started against you, perhaps because U.S. immigration authorities have found that you are out of status or that you entered the U.S. without the proper documentation. While the proceedings are pending, you marry a U.S. citizen. You are now potentially eligible to file your marriage-based petition and the application for adjustment of status with the judge.

However, because you married while removal proceedings were going on, your marital status is suspect. After all, you did get married with the "shotgun" of a possible removal order facing you. You, the newly married foreign national, will have to provide clear and convincing evidence showing that the marriage was entered into in good faith and not solely for the purpose of getting a green card, and that no fee or financial arrangements were given for filing the petition. (Don't worry about the money you might have paid an attorney or other person to help you prepare and submit the application, which doesn't count.)

You will have to clearly establish that you married to establish a life together—for love and with a real commitment—not simply to avoid removal from the United States. See Section D4, below, for more guidance on gathering this kind of evidence. Also seek help from an experienced immigration attorney.

Same-Sex Couples May Obtain Green Cards Through Marriage

On June 26, 2013, the U.S. Supreme Court in *U.S. v. Windsor* struck down major portions of the federal Defense of Marriage Act (DOMA), which had blocked U.S. spouses in same-sex marriages from filing immigration applications on behalf of their foreign spouses. Two years later, the Supreme Court went one step further in *Obergefell v. Hodges* and legalized same-sex marriage in all U.S. states and territories. As a result, it is now easier than ever for same-sex couples to get married in the U.S. and then apply for immigration benefits. The procedures for same-sex couples are exactly the same as described in this chapter and the rest of the book.

Same-sex couples who are not legally married (including in domestic partnerships and civil unions) will need to marry first in order for the foreign resident to receive a green card. This can be difficult if the foreign resident's country does not recognize same-sex marriage and international travel to the U.S. or another country where same-sex marriage is legal is expensive. The best way to get around this is to use the K-1 fiancé visa to bring your partner to the U.S. for the purpose of getting married (see Chapter 6 for information on fiancé visas).

C. Quick View of the Marriage-Based Green Card Application Process

Let's start with the general concept: To get a marriage-based green card, the U.S. citizen or permanent resident spouse must begin the process by submitting a "petition" on Form I-130. (By mail or online; you can't just walk this form into your local USCIS office.) This form serves to prove to U.S. immigration authorities that you're legally married. After USCIS approves that petition, you, the immigrant, complete your half of the process by submitting a green card application and attending an interview, usually with your spouse. Your application serves to prove not only that your marriage is technically legal, but that it's the "real thing," and that you're otherwise eligible for U.S. permanent residence.

However, the details of when and how all this happens depend on several things: first, whether you, the immigrant, are living overseas or in the United States; and second, whether your spouse is a U.S. citizen or a permanent resident. We'll briefly describe each possible situation separately. It will also depend on the procedures, practices, and scheduling backup at the embassy where you'll be receiving your visa eventually.

Immigrant living overseas, married to a U.S. citizen, option 1 (immigrant visa). Under the traditional method, the U.S. citizen submits the I-130 petition to USCIS. After USCIS approves it, the immigrant goes through consular processing (fully described in Chapter 17), which involves sending in fees and paperwork and ultimately attending a visa interview at a U.S. consulate in the immigrant's home country. At the interview (which only the immigrant is required to attend), the immigrant is approved for a visa. The immigrant must then use the visa to enter the United States within six months to claim U.S. permanent residence

(or "conditional" residence if the couple has been married less than two years at this time; see Section F for details). The entire process often takes a year or more.

Immigrant living overseas, married to a U.S. citizen, option 2 (K-3 visa). Years ago, obtaining a visa overseas based on marriage was took a lot longer than obtaining a fiancé visa. This was due to the amount of time it took USCIS to make a decision on the initial petitions (the I-130 and the I-129F). To address this unfair situation, a method was devised to allow the long-waiting spouses of U.S. citizens to enter the U.S. within the same time frame as a fiancé, by allowing spouses to enter the U.S. on a kind of fiancé visa for married people, called a "K-3" visa.

However, the K-3 visa process hasn't been worthwhile for many years, because it currently takes about the same amount of time to process it as entry on a regular immigrant visa; yet U.S. entry does not even represent the end of the green card application process. Someone who enters the U.S. using a K-3 will still have to submit paperwork to USCIS in order to receive a temporary work permit, permission to travel outside the U.S., and finally a green card. An immigration attorney can tell you the latest processing timelines, so it's worth consulting with one if you are considering applying for a K-3 visa; it might become beneficial after all.

If you decide to use the K-3 method, the U.S. citizen starts the process by mailing a petition (Form I-130) to USCIS. However, upon getting a receipt notice from USCIS, the citizen petitioner can submit a separate, fiancé petition (Form I-129F) to USCIS.

After USCIS approves the fiancé petition, the immigrant goes through consular processing (described later in this chapter), and attends an interview at a U.S. consulate. The consulate approves the immigrant for a K-3, or fiancé, visa. This does not mean that the immigrant has been approved for a green card; the K-3 visa simply allows the immigrant to enter the United States in order to apply for the green card there.

After entering the U.S., the immigrant can prepare and mail an adjustment of status application to USCIS. After several months, the immigrant and U.S. spouse must attend an interview, at which the immigrant will be approved for permanent residence (or conditional residence if they've been married for less than two years at that time; see Section F for details).

CAUTION

The traditional marriage visa procedure is certainly cheaper. At the time this book went to press, Option 1, the traditional consular processing method, cost $980 in filing fees, form review fees, and immigrant visa fees. In contrast, the K-3 visa and adjustment of status (Option 2) cost a total of $2,025 in filing fees and nonimmigrant visa fees. (Keep in mind, there are also other, miscellaneous expenses associated with all green card applications, such as fees for translating non-English documents, getting a medical exam from a USCIS-approved physician, and obtaining birth certificates and police records.)

Immigrant living overseas, married to a U.S. permanent resident. The U.S. permanent resident submits the I-130 petition to USCIS. It will stay there until close to the time the immigrant's Priority Date is current (see Chapter 5 for a discussion of Priority Dates). After it's approved, it will be sent to the National Visa Center for further processing, before being forwarded to the appropriate U.S. consulate.

At the U.S. consular interview (which the U.S. petitioner need not attend), the immigrant is approved for a visa and must enter the United States within six months to claim permanent residence.

Immigrant living in the United States, married to a U.S. citizen. Ideally, the U.S. citizen mails the I-130 petition together with the immigrant's green card application (adjustment of status packet complete with forms, photos, and the results of a medical exam; you also can submit the medical exam results later) to USCIS. The immigrant is sent a fingerprint appointment notice and later an interview appointment notice. Both spouses must attend the interview, which will be held at a local USCIS district office. At the interview, the immigrant is approved for permanent residence (or conditional residence, if they've been married less than two years at this time; see Section F for details). However, not all immigrants are eligible to use the adjustment of status procedure—in particular, those whose last entry into the U.S. was made without inspection and admission by a U.S. border official are not. See Chapter 16 for details. Also, applying within 90 days of arriving in the U.S. can raise questions about "preconceived intent" concerning your true plans when you came to this country. If you are in this situation, consult an immigration attorney.

Immigrant living in the United States, married to a U.S. permanent resident. The U.S. permanent resident submits the I-130 petition to USCIS. After it's approved, however, things can get complicated. The only way the immigrant can remain in the United States to adjust status (submit a green card application) is if they have either been living legally in the United States during all the intervening years up to the point when their Priority Date (discussed in Chapter 5) is current, in which case the immigrant can adjust status as described in this book, or started the process when previous laws were in effect. (See Chapter 16 for details on who can adjust status.) The immigrant's alternative is to continue with the case at an overseas U.S. consulate, but if the immigrant has been living illegally in the U.S., this could result in a three- or ten-year bar on reentry (as explained in Chapter 4). See an attorney for a full personal analysis.

Immigrant Story: Dealing With Entry Without Inspection

Carmela, from Costa Rica, won the green card lottery one year, and moved to San Diego, California. Her boyfriend Jorge, who missed Carmela terribly, made his way to Mexico and then crossed the border to join her. Jorge was unable to get a visa or another document allowing him to enter the U.S. legally, so he and some friends crossed the border at an unguarded spot—in immigration law lingo, without being "inspected and admitted."

Jorge and Carmela got married seven months later, and picked up a copy of this book. Carmela then filed a Form I-130 visa petition on Jorge's behalf. However, they also realized that Jorge would be ineligible to adjust status in the United States after his Priority Date became current (which they expected to take a few years).

What's more, Jorge realized, when it came time to get his green card at a U.S. consulate, he could be barred from returning for three years, because he'd already stayed in the U.S. unlawfully for more than 180 days—and that if he stayed another five months, he would be barred from returning for a whole ten years. (A waiver based on extreme hardship to family helps some people avoid this ten-year bar, but Jorge's situation presents no such extraordinary circumstances.)

Jorge decides to leave the United States before his unlawful presence has added up to one year. The good news is, he can work off the three-year bar on reentering as soon as he's out of the U.S. and while he's waiting for his Priority Date to become current.

CAUTION

Entering the U.S. without inspection causes problems. Except in rare circumstances (described in Chapter 16), people who entered the United States surreptitiously (for example, by crossing the border away from an inspection point) do not have the right to adjust status—that is, apply for a green card—in the United States. Attempting to turn your application in to USCIS could get you deported. Your best course is to get help from an experienced immigration attorney in evaluating and completing your application.

D. Detailed Instructions for the Marriage-Based Green Card Application Process

Now we'll break the application process down into individual procedures, some of which will be covered here and others in the next chapters—we'll tell you exactly where to turn to for your situation.

Note: The legal term for the U.S. citizen or permanent resident who is signing immigration papers for an alien spouse is "petitioner." The legal term for the immigrating spouse is "beneficiary."

1. Beginning the Process: The I-130 Petition

No matter what the circumstances, the U.S. citizen or permanent resident must prepare and collect the following items that make up the visa petition:

- ☐ Form I-130, Petition for Alien Relative. (Get the latest version at www.uscis.gov/i-130; and you can download a completed sample at www.nolo.com/back-of-book/GRN. html. If using the K-3 visa process, attach a statement indicating that you plan to file Form I-129F and adjust status in the United States. Form I-130 must be signed by the U.S. citizen or permanent resident spouse. It gives information about both the petitioner and beneficiary.)

☐ Form I-130A, Supplemental Information for Spouse Beneficiary. (Get the latest version at www.uscis.gov/i-130; and you can download a completed sample at www.nolo.com/back-of-book/GRN.html.)

☐ Form G-1145. This is optional, but filing it is a good idea, so that you'll receive an email and/or text notification from USCIS when your application has been accepted. Get it from www.uscis.gov/g-1145. Once USCIS sends you a receipt number, you can use that number to sign up to receive automatic email updates letting you know whenever mail is sent regarding your application.

TIP

How to sign up for automatic email updates: Go to www.uscis.gov and click "Check your case status" on the home page. Then under "Why sign up for an account?" look for "Click Here" and follow the prompts. Creating an account with USCIS will allow you to view your immigration application history in one place and to receive email or text message updates about your case.

☐ Photos of the immigrant and the spouse (one each). These must be passport style, in color, and taken within 30 days before the filing. See Chapter 21 for more detailed photo requirements. Write your name in pencil on the back of the photo, in case it gets separated from your file.

☐ Proof that the American half of the couple (the "petitioner") is either a U.S. citizen or permanent resident. If a citizen, the petitioner should provide a copy of their passport, birth certificate, naturalization certificate (don't worry, it's legal to photocopy it for this purpose), or copy of Form FS-240 (Report of Birth Abroad of a Citizen of the United States, issued by a U.S. consulate).

☐ If a permanent resident, the person should provide a copy of their green card (front and back), passport stamp, or USCIS approval notice.

☐ Documents to prove that there is a valid marriage, including copies of the documents listed below:

- **Marriage certificate.** Submit the civil registry certificate and not the marriage license or the church certificate, unless your country accepts a church marriage certificate as an official document. Marriage by proxy, a cultural practice in certain countries, is not acceptable to the immigration authorities.

- **Previous marriages.** If either of you was previously married, attach proof of the termination of the previous marriage—a divorce decree, an annulment decree, or a death certificate. Some foreign divorces might not be recognized by USCIS. The law provides that at least one of the parties must be living in the place where the divorce was granted. In addition, if the divorcing pair is living in the U.S., they should obtain a divorce in a local court, not at their embassy.

☐ Filing fee (currently $535) in the form of a check, money order, or certified check payable to the U.S. Department of Homeland Security. You may also pay by credit card, by filling out Form G-1450, Authorization for Credit Card Transaction (www.uscis.gov/g-1450). Place it on top of the stack of papers you send USCIS.

See Chapter 21 for more detailed instructions on preparing these documents.

When you've completed and assembled all these items, make two complete copies of the entire packet for yourself and your spouse. What you'll do with it next depends on where you are living, how you entered the U.S. and whether you're eligible to adjust status here, your spouse's status, and where your spouse is living, as detailed on the summary chart later in this chapter. Look under "Where to Mail the Application" for filing addresses.

2. Option for Overseas Spouses of U.S. Citizens: The Fiancé Visa Petition (K-3)

If you've elected to use the fiancé visa option to get you into the United States in order to adjust status there, the U.S. citizen will also need to submit a separate petition, consisting of:

☐ Form I-129F, Petition for Alien Fiancé(e). (Get it from www.uscis.gov/i-129f; and you can download a completed sample at www. nolo.com/back-of-book/GRN.html.) The most important thing to realize about this form is that it's usually used for people who haven't yet gotten married— who are, in fact, fiancés. Don't be thrown off by instructions or questions directed at people who aren't yet married.

☐ Proof that the U.S. half of the couple (the petitioner) is a U.S. citizen, such as a copy of their passport, birth certificate, naturalization certificate (don't worry, it's legal to photocopy it for this purpose), or copy of Form FS-240 (Report of Birth Abroad of a Citizen of the United

☐ Proof that the U.S. citizen spouse has already filed Form I-130, Petition for Alien Relative, with USCIS. Wait until USCIS sends a Form I-797 receipt notice, then photocopy this and send the copy.

☐ Photos of the immigrant and the spouse (one each). These must be in color, passport style, and taken within the 30 days before the filing.

As a K-3 applicant, your petitioner need not pay the usual fee for this petition.

When you've completed and assembled all these items, make two complete copies for each of your records. Then mail the completed package to the USCIS lockbox shown on the Form I-129F instructions.

3. Moving the Process Forward

After the U.S. citizen or permanent resident spouse has submitted Form I-130 (and possibly Form I-129F or an adjustment of status packet) to USCIS, it's time to start playing the waiting game.

See Chapter 5 for a full explanation of how long you're likely to wait, and why. Spouses of U.S. permanent residents should understand that years-long waits are caused by limitations on the number of green cards given out in their category every year.

The sooner the permanent resident spouses can apply for U.S. citizenship, the better. Once they become citizens, the immigrating spouses automatically become immediate relatives, and can proceed with the application for a green card. (You don't even have to file a new I-130 petition—it's enough to advise USCIS that the petitioner has become a citizen, by sending a letter, including a copy of his or her naturalization certificate, to the last USCIS office you corresponded with. See Chapter 5 for a sample letter.)

If you will be consular processing, and if your spouse is a U.S. citizen, the current (late-2019) processing time for a decision on the Form I-130 is approximately seven to 15 months.

If you will be consular processing, the current (early-2022) processing time for a decision on the Form I-130 is approximately four to 50 months. If you will not be consular processing, but instead will be filing to adjust status in the U.S., then as long as you send your I-485 and other documents for adjustment of status along with your I-130, you might get a decision sooner, because it will be handled by the same USCIS office as will handle your interview.

Summary Chart: From Petition to Green Card Application		
Your situation	**Where to mail the application**	**What's next**
You're living overseas, and your spouse is a U.S. citizen living in the United States.	**Option 1: Standard procedure.** The petitioner either submits the I-130 petition online at uscis.gov or sends it via Priority Mail with a return receipt requested to the USCIS lockbox in either Dallas or Phoenix, depending on where you live. This office will forward it to the service center that serves your spouse's geographic region. Find the correct address and post office box on the USCIS website at www.uscis.gov/i-130-addresses.	**Option 1: Standard procedure.** As soon as the petition is approved, you'll be able to apply for your immigrant visa and green card through an overseas U.S. consulate. (See Chapter 17.)
	Option 2: K-3 visa. Although you're married, you're allowed to use a special type of fiancé visa to get you into the United States, after which you must apply to adjust status in order to become a permanent resident. To take advantage of this option, send Form I-130 as detailed above, but as soon as you can prove that USCIS received it, also send Form I-129F to the USCIS office where the I-130 is pending.	**Option 2: K-3 fiancé visa procedure.** As soon as USCIS approves the Form I-129F fiancé petition, you will be able to apply for a nonimmigrant visa at an overseas consulate (see Chapter 6, Section C5 for instructions). (If your Form I-130 is approved before your consular interview for the K-3 visa, the consulate will prefer to continue processing your case so that you can enter the U.S. as a permanent resident rather than as a fiancé. You might need to make sure that the I-130 approval is forwarded to the consulate. After you enter the United States, it's time to apply for a green card through USCIS (see Chapter 16 for instructions on the adjustment of status application). To avoid USCIS confusion, you should, as soon as possible after entering the U.S., send a letter to the service center processing the Form I-130 saying that you are here and will be adjusting status. (Without such a letter, some service centers have been known to send the case to the overseas consulate for processing.)

Summary Chart: From Visa Petition To Green Card Application (continued)

Your situation	Where to mail the application	What's next
You're living overseas, and your spouse is a U.S. lawful permanent resident living in the United States.	The petitioner either submits the I-130 petition online at www.uscis.gov or sends it via Priority Mail with a return receipt requested to the USCIS lockbox in either Dallas or Phoenix, depending on where the petitioner lives. This office will forward it to the service center that serves this geographic region. Find the correct address and post office box at www.uscis.gov/i-130-addresses.	Approval of the I-130 petition will give you a Priority Date, but you'll potentially have to wait until that date is current to apply for your green card. You'll need to wait overseas during that time, after which you'll apply for your immigrant visa and green card through a U.S. consulate. (See Chapter 17.)
You're presently in the U.S., and your spouse is a lawful permanent resident.	The petitioner either submits the I-130 petition online at www.uscis.gov or sends it via Priority Mail with a return receipt requested to the USCIS lockbox in either Dallas or Phoenix, depending on where the petitioner lives. This office will forward it to the service center that serves this geographic region. Find the correct address and post office box at www.uscis.gov/i-130-addresses.	Approval of the I-130 petition will give you a Priority Date, but you'll potentially have to wait until that date is current to apply for your green card. Unless you have a separate visa to remain in the U.S. for those years, or will be eligible to adjust status in the U.S (see Chapter 16), you might have to leave soon to avoid the three- and ten-year time bars for having lived in the U.S. illegally.
You're presently in the U.S., and your spouse is a U.S. citizen. **Situation one:** You entered the U.S. without inspection.	See an immigration attorney for help—you might not be able to apply for a green card without leaving the United States, which could expose you to a three- or ten-year bar on returning; or you might qualify for a provisional waiver of unlawful presence, allowing you to safely leave for a consular interview and return.	
Situation two: You entered legally (with a visa or on a visa waiver, no matter if your expiration date passed), but did not misuse your visa to enter in order to get a green card.	You are eligible to adjust status in the United States. Submit your I-130 petition to USCIS in combination with the immigrant's adjustment of status application (Form I-485 and supporting documents, described in Chapter 16). See an attorney if you have already or plan to marry and/or submit your application within 90 days of arriving in the United States.	Await fingerprinting and, later, an interview at your local USCIS office.

Check current processing times by going to www.uscis.gov. Click "Check processing times." If you're proceeding with the consular processing method, select I-130 for case type and the service center where your I-130 is being processed (shown on your receipt notice). If using adjustment of status, select I-485 for case type and the Field Office where you will be interviewed and then review the processing time for the I-485 application (since your I-130 will be processed simultaneously with your I-485).

If your application seems to be held up due to a simple bureaucratic delay, see Chapter 21 for instructions on prodding USCIS into taking action.

> **TIP**
>
> **What if the U.S. petitioner dies?** If your U.S. citizen spouse submitted an I-130 on your behalf but then died before it was approved, all you need to do is submit proof of the death to USCIS, and it will automatically convert the I-130 to an I-360 "self-petition." You will then be able to proceed with processing your case. If the U.S. citizen did not submit the I-130 before dying, you can "self-petition" by submitting Form I-360. The requirements for this are that you and your U.S. citizen spouse were married (and not legally separated) at the time of death, that you file the self-petition within two years of the death, and that you have not remarried.

For the next step in the process, see the "What's next" column in the summary chart above. For most immigrants, the next step will involve either applying for a green card from outside the United States, through a process called "consular processing" (discussed in Chapter 17), or from inside the United States, through a process called "adjustment of status" (discussed in Chapter 16). However, a few unlucky immigrants will get stuck at this point, realizing that because of past illegal entries into the U.S. or other problems, their application cannot go forward. Such persons should consult with an experienced immigration attorney.

> **TIP**
>
> Regardless of whether you will be completing your application overseas or in the United States, come back to this chapter for a discussion of materials that only married couples need to prepare in advance of their interview. (See Section D.6, below.)

4. Advice for Spouses of Permanent Residents

You cannot apply for a green card as a second preference alien—that is, as the spouse of a green-card holder—until your Priority Date is current. The 2A category often has a wait of about two years, though it's been much shorter or even nonexistent recently. When there is a wait, U.S. permanent residents are usually eager to naturalize as soon as possible in order to speed up green card processing for their spouses and children.

Pay close attention to the *Visa Bulletin* (see Chapter 5 for a discussion on the *Visa Bulletin* and Priority Dates) when deciding whether the U.S. petitioner spouse should apply for U.S. citizenship before filing or proceeding with a pending Form I-130.

However, despite current favorable conditions for permanent resident spouses, keep in mind that if the date of your permitted stay in the U.S. expired or if you worked without authorization ("fell out of status"), you will not be able to apply for adjustment of status unless your U.S. spouse first becomes a U.S. citizen.

5. Advice for People Who Entered the U.S. Without Inspection

If you entered the U.S. without being met and inspected by an immigration officer ("EWI") you most likely won't be able to adjust status in the United States. There is a rare exception for people who are covered by an old law, the LIFE Act, which allowed otherwise ineligible applicants to adjust status by paying a $1,000 penalty. While most foreign citizens who EWI would love to simply pay a penalty to avoid leaving the U.S. and possibly facing a time bar before being allowed to return, it covers only people with a visa petition or labor certification on file before January 14, 1998; or those who were physically present in the U.S. on December 21, 2000 with a visa petition on file by April 30, 2001.

As time passes, fewer and fewer people are able to benefit from the provisions of the LIFE Act. The vast majority of people who EWI'd therefore cannot adjust status in the U.S. and will instead need to apply for a green card at a U.S. consulate abroad.

If you came to the U.S. as an EWI and your period of unlawful presence in the U.S. is less than 180 days, you should leave the U.S. immediately in order to avoid being barred from reentering for three years. If it's already too late and you've been time barred from applying for a U.S. immigration benefit, you might be able to benefit from a new waiver, the provisional waiver of unlawful presence. (For more on inadmissibility, and the provisional waiver, see Chapter 4.)

6. Documenting Your Bona Fide Marriage

Whether you are applying for adjustment of status or for an immigrant visa at a consulate abroad, start gathering documents for your green card interview. At the interview, you must present not only the standard information that every immigrant does, but also separate documents showing that you have a real, valid marriage. These might include:

- [ ] birth certificates for all children born to you and your U.S. spouse
- [ ] leases on apartments that you two have occupied, together with rent receipts or canceled checks
- [ ] hospital cards, union books, insurance policies, pay vouchers, joint bank account statements, utility bills, or charge cards containing both your names

- [ ] federal income tax returns, filed jointly, for the years that you have been married
- [ ] your wedding pictures, and
- [ ] any snapshots of the two of you together taken before the marriage and, more importantly, since the marriage, taken in different locations, and taken with different people or groups of people who might appear to know that the two of you are a couple.

Collect and make copies of as many of these documents as possible. If you and your spouse have married for love, you will eventually prevail. Nevertheless, you still have to present the required documentary proof.

E. Bringing Your Children

People immigrating through marriage are often allowed to bring their children with them, even if the children are from a previous marriage or relationship. For immigration purposes, your children must be unmarried and younger than age 21 to immigrate at the same time as you. (Options for older or married children are discussed in Chapter 9.)

However, the exact rules and procedures for having your children immigrate with you depend on whether your U.S. spouse is a permanent resident or a citizen.

1. If You're Marrying a U.S. Citizen

If you're marrying a U.S. citizen, each of your children must separately qualify as an "immediate relative" of your spouse in order to immigrate with you.

To qualify as an immediate relative, your child can either be:

- the natural child of the U.S. citizen (if born out of wedlock to a U.S. citizen father, the father must have either legitimated the child while the child was younger than 18 and living in his custody, or demonstrated a bona fide relationship, through financial or other support), or

- the stepchild of the U.S. citizen, meaning it's legally your (the immigrant's) child, whether by birth or adoption, and you married the U.S. citizen before the child reached the age of 18.

Your spouse will need to submit a separate petition (Form I-130) for each one of these immediate-relative children, preferably in the same packet as the petition for you, the immigrant. (If you have no choice but to submit the petitions separately, write a letter to accompany the later petitions, explaining that you'd like the cases joined together.)

If you're also using a fiancé visa for U.S. entry, your spouse must additionally fill out a separate Form I-129F fiancé petition for each child.

2. If You're Marrying a U.S. Permanent Resident

If you're marrying a permanent resident, your children (natural or adopted) who are unmarried and younger than age 21 are considered "derivative beneficiaries." As a practical matter, this means that, at least at the beginning, your children won't need a separate petition in order to be included in your immigration process—your spouse must simply fill in the blanks on Form I-130 where it asks for the children's names. Unlike many other applicants, your children won't need to prove that your spouse is their parent or stepparent.

Your children will be given the same Priority Date as you, and most likely get a visa at the same time (provided they remain unmarried and younger than age 21). If they marry, they lose their chance to immigrate as beneficiaries. If they turn 21 before the Priority Date becomes current, they risk dropping into a separate visa category (2B) and having to wait longer for their Priority Date to become current in that category. Under the Child

Status Protection Act, however, this situation is sometimes taken care of, because they get to subtract from their age the amount of time that they were waiting for USCIS to decide on the I-130.

EXAMPLE: Maria was 17 years old when her mother, Luisa, married a U.S. permanent resident, who immediately filed a petition for Luisa (which included Maria). Because USCIS knew that it would be approximately five years before the Priority Date became current in that category, USCIS waited three years and seven months to approve the petition. Under the old law, if the Priority Date was still not current when Maria turned 21 (four years after the petition was submitted), she would "age out" and immediately fall into the 2B category with a longer wait. Under the Child Status Protection Act, however, Maria gets to take into account the three years and seven months that she waited for the I-130 to be approved, so Maria will not "age out" until she is 24 years and seven months old. If her Priority Date still is not current at that point, she will drop into the 2B category. The U.S. petitioner should write a letter to the NVC or the USCIS office handling her case to request that her old Priority Date be retained.

3. Final Phases of Children's Green Card Application

After the I-130 petition has been approved and you and your children are ready to submit your paperwork for your green cards, each child must submit his or her own application, whether to the U.S. consulate overseas or to a U.S. immigration office. These applications are discussed in Chapters 16 and 17.

As a practical matter, however, you can help your child fill out the forms online, and even sign them if the child is too young (just write next to your signature, "by [*your name*], the child's [*mother or father*]").

F. If Your Marriage is Less Than Two Years Old

If you become a U.S. resident within two years of the date you were married, whether you were granted your green card through adjustment of status or consular processing, your green card is only conditional—in other words, it expires in another two years. You are considered a "conditional permanent resident."

It seems contradictory to be both "permanent" and "conditional" at the same time, but it actually makes sense in this situation. This is because once you remove the conditional basis, your two years of conditional residence will count as unconditional or permanent residence for naturalization (citizenship) and other purposes.

To receive a green card without conditions that will be valid for more than two years, you could wait until you have been married at least two years before becoming a permanent resident. In fact, if you're overseas, this might mean delaying your date of entry to the United States—because even after you get your immigrant visa from the consulate, you're not a permanent resident until you go through a U.S. port of entry. If your marriage is already two years old at the time your permanent residence is granted, you are a full-fledged permanent resident and do not need to file papers to remove any conditions.

However, most people go ahead and become permanent residents, then wait two years minus 90 days and request the removal of the conditional status. Your foreign-born sons or daughters who might have been petitioned by your spouse must likewise apply for removal of their conditional statuses.

> **CAUTION**
> **The timing of your request is crucial.** Mark on your calendar the third month before your second anniversary of becoming a conditional permanent resident, and get your application in before your residence expires. USCIS might send you a reminder, but keep track on your own, just in case (especially if you've changed addresses).

EXAMPLE: Your date of admission as a conditional permanent resident was December 7, 2021, the date printed on your conditional green card. The second anniversary of your conditional permanent residence is December 7, 2023. And 90 days (three months) before the second anniversary of December 7, 2023 is September 7, 2023. Therefore, you must file for the removal of the conditional status any time after September 7, 2023 and before December 7, 2023.

1. Forms Required for Removal of Conditions

Within the 90 days before the second anniversary of your conditional permanent residence, you must submit the following:

- ☐ Form I-751, Petition to Remove the Conditions on Residence, signed by both husband and wife (Get the latest version from www.uscis.gov/i-751; and you can download a completed sample at www.nolo.com/back-of-book/GRN.html), or by the alien spouse alone, if seeking a waiver, and
- ☐ the application fee (currently $590, which includes the biometrics fee) in the form of a money order or personal check, payable to U.S. Department of Homeland Security.

You must also present evidence of a true marriage. To do this, submit copies of as many of the following documents as possible (from within the past two years):

- ☐ your federal and state income taxes for the last two years (assuming they were filed as "married, filing jointly")
- ☐ title to house or condo or co-op, or any other real property showing joint ownership
- ☐ lease to your apartment showing joint tenancy since the time of marriage
- ☐ telephone or electric and gas bills showing both your names
- ☐ bank books or statements showing evidence of a joint checking or savings account; to prevent identity theft, you are allowed to partially black out the account numbers

- [ ] registration and title documents, with both names, of cars or any personal property
- [ ] insurance policies taken by husband or wife and showing the other as the beneficiary of any insurance benefits
- [ ] birth certificate of any child born of the marriage, showing both parents' names
- [ ] current letters from both husband and wife's employer on the company letterhead, stating present job and salary and the name of a person to be notified in case of emergency, if that person is your spouse
- [ ] current will showing one spouse as the beneficiary of the other's estate, and
- [ ] a minimum of two sworn statements from people who know that you are married. The letter writer could be your friend, relative, coworker, neighbor, or anyone else who knows that you are married. The person should give their own contact information—address and telephone number—and explain how he or she knows the two of you, and knows that you have a real marriage. It's helpful if the person can mention specific times and places at which you appeared as a married couple.

These documents should be to a USCIS lockbox, which will forward it to the service center that serves your geographic region. (See the USCIS website for the address and P.O. box.) You might receive a notice for an interview, or your petition might be approved without one. If you receive a notice for an interview, we recommend that you have an attorney review your case prior to the interview.

While you're waiting for a decision, however, the receipt notice that you get from the USCIS service center will be your only proof that you are legally in the United States. Your stay will remain legal until a decision is made on your Form I-751, but the receipt notice normally expires in 18 months. As long as your receipt notice has not expired, you can use it in combination with your expired green card to prove your right to work and to return from foreign travel. If you travel, however, the border officials will likely take your expired green card and put a stamp in your passport.

In any case, with or without an interview, your green card becomes permanent only when UCIS decides to approve your joint petition.

TIP

What if 18 months have gone by and you still haven't gotten a USCIS decision on your I-751 application? Although you're technically still legal, it will be hard to prove that to anyone. The best thing to do is call the USCIS Contact Center at 800-375-5283. They might be able to find out what's happening, and make an appointment at a local office, where you can get a stamp in your passport showing your conditional resident status.

2. If Your Spouse Does Not Sign the Joint Petition

If your spouse will not or cannot sign the joint petition, do not despair. Where certain circumstances are beyond your control, USCIS allows you, as the conditional permanent resident alien, to file without your spouse's signature.

You must fill out the same form, Form I-751, Petition to Remove the Conditions on Residence, and mail it with the same fee. However, you must also request one of the waivers described on the form. These waivers cover situations where:

- your spouse died
- you were the victim of battery or domestic abuse
- your marriage was valid when it occurred but is now legally terminated (you divorced or got an annulment), or
- you would suffer extreme hardship if removed.

These waivers require the assistance of an experienced immigration attorney. (See Chapter 24 for tips on finding a good one.)

3. People Married Two Years or More

If the original date of your admission as a permanent resident is more than two years after your marriage, you are not considered a conditional permanent resident. You are a full-fledged permanent resident and not subject to the conditions on residence.

> **EXAMPLE:** You married a permanent resident on February 14, 2015, and a petition was filed on your behalf shortly thereafter in the second preference category. However, your visa number was not immediately available, and you had to wait a few years. You finally received your green card and were admitted as a permanent—not conditional—resident on July 4, 2019, more than two years after your date of marriage.

G. If You Marry Again

If your marriage ends in divorce or annulment after you receive your permanent green card, and then you marry another foreign-born person, it will be difficult for you to sponsor your new spouse for a green card.

To obtain permanent residence for your foreign-born spouse during the first five years after you received your green card through marriage, you'll have to show by "clear and convincing evidence" that your first marriage—the one by which you got your green card—was not fraudulent and was entered into in good faith. (See I.N.A. § 204(a)(2)(A); 8 U.S.C. § 1154(a)(2)(A).) Again, this means showing you got married because you wanted to establish a life together, not just to get a green card.

In addition to the other proof required (see Section D, above), you will be asked to explain:

- why and when you got the previous divorce
- how long you lived with your first spouse
- how, when, and where you met your intended spouse, and
- facts about your courtship.

However, after you have been a green card holder for five years—the number of years required for naturalization—you can file a petition for your second spouse without providing such evidence.

Again, Congress provided this restriction because a number of binational couples had obtained green cards fraudulently. One of them would marry either a U.S. citizen or a permanent resident. After getting the immigrant visa, the marriage to the citizen or permanent resident would be ended by divorce or annulment. The immigrant, then in possession of a valid green card, would then marry the original boyfriend, girlfriend, or spouse to give that person a green card, too.

H. Common Questions About Marriage and Immigration

The answers to most immigration questions depend on timing and the specific history of those involved, so it is difficult to give one correct response in solving a problem. There are, however, a number of questions that are asked over and over.

1. Before Marriage

Q: My boyfriend, who is a U.S. citizen, is getting a divorce soon. Can he file a petition now for me to get a green card?

A: No—because he has not yet legally ended his previous marriage, he cannot marry you now. He can marry you as soon as his previous divorce petition is finalized and file a petition once you receive a marriage certificate.

Q: I intend to marry a U.S. citizen, but because work obligations will require us to live in different states for a while, we will not be living together for the first six months or so after we're married. Can she file for me to get a green card?

A: Yes. But you will have to prove to the USCIS examiner that your marriage is true and not a sham. Good evidence of that would be ticket stubs from visits to one another; telephone bills, emails, texts, and instant messages showing frequent contact; stubs from social events you attended together such as movies, theater performances, and meals; copies of joint bank accounts; and bills bearing both of your names.

2. After Marriage

Q: I entered the U.S. with another name. Now I am married to a U.S. citizen using my real name. Can I get my green card?

A: Yes. But you might need to request that the misrepresentation be waived, or forgiven, before USCIS will approve your case. You should see a lawyer in this case.

Q: I have a minor child living with me in the U.S. and two more young children now living outside the U.S. Can I get green cards for all of them?

A: Yes—if your U.S. citizen spouse files separate petitions for them. If your spouse is a permanent resident, not a citizen, he or she can simply include the children on your visa petition.

Q: What will happen if my marriage legally ends before the conditional status of my green card is removed?

A: A conditional resident can file an application for a waiver with USCIS. However, because there are complicated matters of proof, it is best to consult an experienced immigration lawyer for help. ●

Your Parents as Immigrants

A. Who Qualifies to Petition for Parents...84

   1. You Must Be a U.S. Citizen...84

   2. You Must Be at Least 21 Years Old..84

B. Who Qualifies as Your Parent..85

   1. Natural Mother..85

   2. Natural Father...85

   3. Stepmother or Stepfather 86

   4. Adoptive Parents..86

C. Quick View of the Application Process...86

D. Detailed Instructions for the Application Process..87

   1. The I-130 Petition 87

   2. The Green Card Application..88

f you are a U.S. citizen age 21 or over, and your parents are citizens of another country, your parents are your "immediate relatives" and you may request U.S. green cards for them. They must separately meet the other criteria for green card approval, however.

Another important issue is whether your parents really want to come to the United States. Many are interested in family togetherness, but don't really want to permanently leave the life they've made for themselves elsewhere. Remember that a green card is not just an easy travel pass—unless your parents are ready to settle down in the U.S. permanently, they could lose the green card by spending too much time overseas (and all your hard work could go down the drain).

However, one reason that some parents agree to come to the U.S. is that they can help other family members get green cards; see "Family Immigration Strategies After Your Parents Get Green Cards," below.

A. Who Qualifies to Petition for Parents

To petition to get a green card for your foreign-born parents, you must meet a couple of basic requirements

CAUTION

If the U.S. petitioner has a criminal record, see an attorney. Under the Adam Walsh Child Protection and Safety Act of 2006, U.S. citizens and lawful permanent residents who have been convicted of any "specified offense against a minor" are prohibited from filing a family-based immigrant petition on behalf of any beneficiary (whether a child or not). USCIS will run security checks on all petitions and may call the petitioner in for fingerprinting. If the petitioner has a conviction for one of the specified offenses against a minor, then the petition will not be approved unless USCIS determines that the U.S. petitioner poses no risk to the beneficiary.

1. You Must Be a U.S. Citizen

You must be a U.S. citizen to file a petition on behalf of your parents. You are a citizen of the United States if you were:

- naturalized (after you held a green card for a number of years, then applied and passed an exam)
- born in any of the 50 states of the United States or its territories—U.S. Virgin Islands, Puerto Rico, or Guam, or
- born outside the United States or its territories, if one of your parents was a U.S. citizen when you were born. See Chapter 20 for details or contact the U.S. Embassy; if you are not satisfied, consult a lawyer or another experienced naturalization professional. (See Chapter 24.)

2. You Must Be at Least 21 Years Old

As a U.S. citizen, you must be 21 years old or older to bestow the immigration benefit of a green card on your mother and your father as your immediate relatives.

If you were born in the United States to parents who live there illegally, 21 years will be a frustratingly long time to wait. In fact, because your parents might be ineligible to apply for green cards within the U.S. using the procedure called "adjustment of status" (see Chapter 16) but might instead have to leave the U.S. and apply through a U.S. consulate (see Chapter 17), your citizenship could turn out not to be much help to them.

The reason is that too much time spent in the U.S. illegally can result in bars on returning to the U.S. after they leave (for three or ten years, based on illegal stays of six months or one year or more).

In rare circumstances, your parents might be able to successfully apply for "provisional waiver of unlawful presence," which would allow them to have their unlawful time in the U.S. forgiven before leaving the U.S. for their consular interview. The major difficulty, however, is that your parents will not be able to get a waiver based on any hardship their ban would cause to you, the child petitioner.

They would need a "qualifying relative" who is either their U.S. citizen or lawful permanent resident spouse or a parent, and who would suffer extreme hardship if they were denied the green card. This is a tricky area of law, so you'd do best to consult with an attorney before applying for a waiver. See Chapter 4 for more about the provisional waiver.

B. Who Qualifies as Your Parent

If you're from a traditional family—that is, you were born and raised by a married couple—you should have little trouble petitioning for your parents to immigrate. However, U.S. immigration law also recognizes some variations on the traditional family. Under certain circumstances, you can also petition for unmarried parents, stepparents, and adoptive parents, as described further below. You'll usually have to provide additional documents to prove the relationship, as also described below.

1. Natural Mother

If your mother was not married to your father when you were born, so that your mother's maiden name appears on your birth certificate, you can prove your relationship by presenting a copy of your birth certificate when you file the petition for your mother.

If your mother has changed her name because she has married someone else, then also present her marriage certificate to show her change of name.

2. Natural Father

If your biological father did not marry your mother either before or after you were born, you can still petition for him as your immediate relative. You must also provide some evidence of your relationship: Make a copy of your birth certificate, baptismal certificate, or other religious records showing his name as your father. USCIS may require both you and your father to take a blood test as proof of your relationship.

If you and your father did not live together before you turned 18, you must present proof that, up to the time you turned 21 years of age, he maintained a father-child relationship with you by providing financial support, writing to you or your mother about your well-being, sending you birthday cards, holiday cards, and photographs, or perhaps naming you as a beneficiary to his life insurance.

If you lived with your father before your 18th birthday, you must present proof that there was a father-child relationship, as evidenced by school records, photographs, letters, civil records, or written statements from friends and relatives.

If You, the U.S. Petitioner, Have Changed Names

If you are a married U.S. citizen petitioning for your parents, you might have changed your name after marriage. Therefore, in addition to your birth certificate to prove the parent-child relationship when you send the Petition for Alien Relative, Form I-130, for your mother or father, you must also attach your marriage certificate to show your name change.

If you have changed your name by petitioning the court, you must attach a final court judgment as proof of that change.

3. Stepmother or Stepfather

If your father or mother marries somebody other than your biological parent before you turn 18 years of age, the person they married becomes your stepmother or stepfather.

When you file a petition for your stepparent as your immediate relative (by submitting the usual petition Form I-130), add to it the following documents:

- your birth certificate showing the name of your remarried parent, and
- the marriage certificate of your remarried parent to show the name of the new spouse (your stepparent).

For you to petition for a stepparent, the marriage must have occurred before your 18th birthday. If the marriage happened after your 18th birthday, then you'll have to explain, "Much as I love you, I cannot claim you as my immediate relative for immigration into the United States."

But all is not lost.

Immigrant Story: Petitioning for a Surviving Stepparent

Luzmaria, originally from El Salvador, married a U.S. citizen at age 25, and became a U.S. citizen herself at age 29. She then filed I-130 petitions for her father and stepmother, whom her father married when Luzmaria was 14.

Sadly, Luzmaria's father died a few months later. Luzmaria was doubly heartbroken, thinking that now her stepmother would not be eligible to immigrate.

However, because the stepmother continues to fit the criteria for immediate relative of a U.S. citizen (having married Luzmaria's father when Luzmaria was younger than 18), she is able to continue with her application and eventually receive a U.S. green card.

Your natural mother or father, after qualifying as your immediate relative and obtaining a green card, can petition for your stepparent who is now the spouse of a permanent resident in category 2A, second preference. Unfortunately, the stepparent might have to wait a few years until a visa becomes available in this category.

4. Adoptive Parents

Suppose you were adopted by a non-U.S. citizen before your 16th birthday. If you are now a U.S. citizen and are 21 years or older, you can petition for your adoptive parents as your immediate relatives.

When filing the I-130 petition, you must also submit:

- the court decree of your adoption
- your birth certificate showing the name of your adopting parents as your father and mother, and
- a statement showing the dates and places you have lived together.

 CAUTION

Adopted children cannot petition for their natural parents. When you were adopted, your natural parents gave up all parental ties with you. Therefore, you will never be able to petition for your natural parents as your immediate relatives. The adoption decree cuts off all legal ties between you and them.

C. Quick View of the Application Process

To get a green card for a parent, you must begin the by preparing a petition (Form I-130, together with certain documents). This serves to prove to U.S. immigration authorities that your parents are truly and legally yours. After that petition is approved (in most cases), your parents must complete their half of the process by submitting an immigrant visa application and attending an interview, sometimes but not necessarily with you accompanying them. Their application serves to prove that not only do they qualify as parents of a U.S. citizen, but that they're otherwise eligible for U.S. permanent residence.

However, the details of when and how your parents complete their half of the process depend on whether they are living overseas or in the United States, as described next.

D. Detailed Instructions for the Application Process

Now we'll break the application process down into steps, some of which will be covered in this chapter and others in later chapters—we'll tell you exactly where to turn for your situation.

1. The I-130 Petition

Let's start with the initial petition that all people seeking to sponsor parents for U.S. immigration must prepare, so as to begin the process. You'll need to assemble:

- ☐ Form I-130, Petition for Alien Relative (from www.uscis.gov/i-130; and you can download a completed sample at www.nolo. com/back-of-book/GRN.html)
- ☐ documents showing your U.S. citizenship
- ☐ a copy of your birth certificate, showing your name as well as your mother's name, if filing for your mother, and the names of both parents, if filing for your father
- ☐ a copy of the marriage certificate of your parents if you are filing for your father; your stepparents' marriage certificate, if you are filing for either stepparent

- ☐ a copy of your adoption decree, if you are filing for your adoptive parent
- ☐ the filing fee, currently $535 in a personal check or money order payable to the Department of Homeland Security. You may also pay by credit card, by filling out and submitting Form G-1450, Authorization for Credit Card Transaction (www.uscis. gov/g-1450) with your application. Place this on top of the other forms and documents you send to USCIS, if you apply by mail. (Online filing is also an option.) Don't send cash.
- ☐ Form G-1145. This is optional, but filing it is a good idea, so that you'll receive an email and/or text notification when USCIS accepts your application for processing. (Get it from www.uscis.gov/g-1145.) Once USCIS sends you a receipt number, you can use that to sign up to receive automatic email updates letting you know whenever mail is sent regarding your application.

TIP
How to sign up for automatic email updates: Go to www.uscis.gov and click "Check your case status." Then under "Why sign up for an account?" select "Click here." After accepting the terms and conditions, you can register as an applicant/petitioner.

Once you've assembled all these items, make a copy of everything (including the check or money order) for your records. It's also a good idea to write a cover letter, explaining what type of petition it is (for example, saying "I am a U.S. citizen, filing the enclosed I-130 petition on behalf of my mother"). The letter should include a bulleted list, much like the checklist above, of everything you're sending. This will help USCIS see that you're organized. It will help you, too, to make sure that nothing has been forgotten.

If your parents are not in the United States, apply online at www.uscis.gov by creating an account, or mail all these documents and the fee by Priority Mail to the USCIS Dallas or Phoenix lockbox, which will forward it to the appropriate USCIS office. (See the USCIS website for contact details.) If your parents are in the United States, they might be able to file directly for adjustment of status (see Chapter 16) in which case, you may choose to mail the I-130 along with the required forms and documents.

2. The Green Card Application

The next step in your parents' immigration process depends on where they're located. If they're in the United States, you need to start by figuring out whether they are eligible to adjust status (apply for their green card) here. See Chapter 16, Section A, to determine this. (If they entered on valid visas, then they are probably eligible, even if they remained in the U.S. past the date they were allowed to stay.)

> **CAUTION**
> **Traveling outside the U.S. might trigger penalties.** Even though remaining in the U.S. past the date allowed by USCIS will not prevent your parents' applications from being granted, if they travel outside the U.S. before that time—either with or without USCIS permission—they could trigger a penalty for their unlawful presence and might not be granted permanent residence for three to ten years, depending on the length of their unlawful stay.
>
> Your parents should also know that if they obtained a tourist or another visa with the secret intention of applying for a green card after getting here, that could be visa fraud. They can be denied the green card on this basis.

Be Kind to the Elderly

If your mother or father is elderly, take some time to help them get acquainted with U.S. customs and cultural habits.

Introduce them to the nearest senior citizen center. Teach them how to use the public transport system. Alert them to precautions to be taken if you live in a high-crime area. Bring them to cultural or popular entertainment activities. It's a chance to share your expertise at U.S. life!

NEXT STEP
If your parents are allowed to adjust status in the U.S. You can mail the I-130 petition in combination with an adjustment of status application to a USCIS office, as also described in Chapter 16. Eventually, they will be fingerprinted at a "biometrics" appointment, called in for an interview at a local USCIS office, and hopefully approved for U.S. residency. In straightforward cases, where all required paperwork is properly submitted with the application, USCIS may opt to approve the application without an interview.

NEXT STEP
If your parents still live in their home country. Their next step is to await USCIS approval of the I-130 petition and then go through consular processing, as described in Chapter 17. Eventually, they will be called in for an interview at their local U.S. consulate, at which time they will hopefully be approved for an immigrant visa with which to enter the United States and claim permanent residency.

NEXT STEP

If your parents do not qualify to adjust status but are currently in the U.S. With limited exceptions, if your parents entered the U.S. without inspection, they are not eligible to apply for adjustment of status. If they leave the U.S., however, to apply for a visa at a U.S. consulate, their departure after unlawful presence could result in a bar on reentering for three or ten years, depending on the length of their unlawful stay. The "provisional waiver of unlawful presence" allows certain immediate relatives who are in this situation to learn whether or not USCIS will grant them a waiver of the time bar BEFORE they leave the United States. (See Chapter 4 for more on this.) The provisional waiver is difficult to get, however, and they would need a qualifying U.S. citizen spouse or parent who would experience "extreme hardship," in order to apply. Seek the advice of an immigration attorney before applying.

RELATED TOPIC

See Chapter 23 for important information on how your parents can protect their right to keep the green card.

Family Immigration Strategies After Parents Get Green Cards

By becoming U.S. permanent residents, your parents can petition for all their unmarried children—in the family second preference, either Category 2A or 2B. If they become naturalized U.S. citizens, they can petition even for married children—in the family third preference category.

Although as a U.S. citizen you might have filed I-130s for your brothers and sisters (family fourth preference), your mother or father, after becoming U.S. citizens, could secure a green card for them more quickly.

It's okay to have different people file visa petitions for the same beneficiary. (You can wait to see which Priority Date becomes current first.)

However, your parents must be aware that getting a green card does not automatically mean that their children can get their own green cards. Your parents would also have to live (maintain residence) in the United States until their other children obtain their green cards, which will take years.

The rules on maintaining U.S. residency are complicated and require that the person make the United States his or her home. While the law allows travel overseas, most important family and business ties should be in the United States, and your parents should compile evidence of these, such as:

- a lease, rental agreement, or title to property in the United States
- utility bills
- a driver's license or car registration, or
- state and federal tax returns.

And that's just the minimum for maintaining permanent resident status. The rules for amount of time spent in the U.S. before applying for U.S. citizenship are even stricter. If you or your parents have questions about whether you are properly maintaining permanent residence, consult an immigration attorney.

Child Immigrants

A. Who Qualifies... 92

B. Definition of "Child" 93

    1. Child of Married Parents.. 93

    2. Child of Unmarried Parents... 93

    3. Legitimated Child of Recently Married Parents 94

    4. Stepchild 94

    5. Adopted Child 94

C. Quick View of the Application Process 97

D. Detailed Instructions for the Application Process.. 97

    1. Preparing the Form I-130 Petition.. 97

    2. Where to Submit the I-130 Petition 98

E. Automatic Citizenship for Some Children 99

    1. Children Living in the United States.. 99

    2. Children Living Overseas.. 100

When Congress writes laws regulating immigration, it aims to keep families together. Foreign-born children of U.S. citizens or permanent residents are potentially eligible to get a green card after a parent files a petition for them. However, you need to look carefully at who qualifies as a "child."

Note: This chapter addresses only children whose parents have already immigrated to the United States. The situation of children accompanying an immigrating parent is covered in other chapters of this book.

A. Who Qualifies

A person is eligible for a green card as the child of:

- a U.S. citizen, and is younger than 21 years of age (immediate relative)
- a U.S. citizen, if the child is older than 21 and not married (family first preference category)
- a U.S. citizen, if the child is married (family third preference category)
- a lawful permanent resident, if the child is not married and is younger than 21 (family second/2A preference), or
- a lawful permanent resident, if the child is older than 21 years of age and not married (family second/2B preference). If the child was formerly married, but is now divorced or a widow or widower, or if the marriage has been annulled, the child can still immigrate in the 2B category.

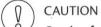

CAUTION

If the U.S. petitioner has a criminal record, see an attorney. Under the Adam Walsh Child Protection and Safety Act of 2006, U.S. citizens and lawful permanent residents who have been convicted of any "specified offense against a minor" are prohibited from filing a family-based immigrant petition on behalf of any beneficiary (whether a child or not). USCIS will run security checks on all petitions and may call the petitioner in for fingerprinting. If the petitioner has a conviction for one of the specified offenses against a minor, then USCIS will deny the petition, unless it determines that the U.S. petitioner poses no risk to the beneficiary.

Adult Children of Permanent Residents Wait Longer

Around 88,000 immigrant visas are allowed to be given out each year to the spouses and unmarried children younger than 21 years of age of green card holders. But only around 26,000 visas per year can go to their unmarried children older than 21 years of age. The law places no time limits on processing the applications.

The waiting period for a spouse and unmarried children younger than the age of 21 (Category 2A) is often up to about two years (though in recent years there's been no wait at all). Children older than 21 (Category 2B) should, however, be prepared to wait six years or more for immigrant visas.

The green-card holding parent or spouse might be able to hurry the process along by becoming a U.S. citizen.

CAUTION

Caution for children who get married or turn 21 before receiving green cards. As a broad rule, the visa categories described above must fit the children not only when the visa application process is begun, but at the very end. This end might be years later, when the child attends an interview at which they're approved for the green card, and also, if coming from overseas, when the child actually enters the United States.

There are exceptions to this rule, however, added by the Child Status Protection Act (CSPA). The exceptions depend on whether the child is an immediate relative or is in a preference category. For immediate relatives, as long as the I-130 petition was submitted when the child was less than 21 years old, that child remains an immediate relative child regardless of age at the time of actual immigration. Children in the 2A preference category, however, only get to add to their age the time that it took USCIS to make a decision on their I-130 petition. For details, see Chapter 5. Although CSPA exceptions will prevent some children from "aging out" after their 21st birthday, they won't protect children who marry. If, for example, the child of a permanent resident gets married, their green card eligibility will be destroyed (at least until the parent becomes a U.S. citizen and starts the petition process all over again). If you are a permanent resident, explain to your children that if they get married, it could nullify their right to immigrate with you.

B. Definition of "Child"

Immigration law recognizes many different meanings of the word "child" as it relates to obtaining a green card. This definition is important because it determines what kind of documents USCIS will require when the I-130 visa petition is filed.

1. Child of Married Parents

When a child is born to a couple who are married to each other, the child is, in legal terms, their legitimate child. If the mother will be filing the I-130 petition, the only document necessary to establish their relationship is the birth certificate showing the name of the mother and of the child.

If the father will be filing the I-130 petition, to show the relationship of father and child, two documents are necessary:

- the birth certificate, which shows the name of the father and the child, and
- the marriage certificate, which shows that the mother and the father were married before the birth of the child.

2. Child of Unmarried Parents

A woman and a man who conceive a child are that child's natural parents. Proving this relationship for immigration purposes requires extra steps if the woman and man are not married to one another.

Proving through mother. When a child is born of a woman who is not married to the child's father, the child is her natural child.

To establish the relationship of mother and child, the only document necessary is the birth certificate showing the name of the mother and the name of the child.

If the mother's maiden name as shown on the birth certificate of her child differs from her present name, the mother must present the document showing that her name was changed. Often, she has changed her name after marrying. The marriage certificate will then verify that the mother named on the birth certificate and the mother on the immigration form are the same person.

Proving through father. Even if the father of the child is not married to the mother when the child is born, the father can petition for the child to immigrate into the United States.

But proving the father-child relationship can get complicated. First, the father must establish that he is really the biological father of the child. The birth certificate is the best proof, if his name appears as the father of the child.

If his name is not on the birth certificate, the father should apply to his civil registry requesting that his name be added as the child's father. He should do this before the child turns 18.

In some countries, the father might have to acknowledge before a civil court, government agency, or civil registry that he is the father of the child. Doing this "legitimates" the child for purposes of U.S. immigration law. Again, such acknowledgment must occur before the child turns 18 years old.

If none of this is available, a blood test, accompanied by an affidavit from the mother stating that the man is the father of the child, might be acceptable to prove paternity, although it doesn't "legitimate" the child.

In cases where the father did not legitimate the child before the child turned 18, the father must show that he was not simply the biological father, but that a father-child relationship existed before the child turned 21. He must provide documents to prove that either:

- the father and child lived together before the child turned 21, or
- there was a true father-child relationship before the child turned 21 or got married.

This relationship can be shown by things like letters written by one to the other; canceled checks or other proof of money sent regularly to support the child; photos of both of them together; school records showing the father's name; sworn statements from at least two people who know of the father-child relationship;

U.S. income tax returns showing the child listed as a dependent; birthday cards; or holiday cards sent and received.

In short, almost any evidence can help show that the father did not abandon the child, but kept up paternal ties before the child turned 21 years old.

Some Countries Require No Proof of Paternity

The governments in some countries, such as China, Haiti, Trinidad and Tobago, and Jamaica, have passed laws erasing the legal distinction between children born to parents who are married to one another and those whose parents are not married.

But if these laws were recently passed, the father has to show USCIS that the law was changed before the child turned 18. If he can show this, he need not submit all those letters, sworn statements, school records, and other proof mentioned above.

---

3. Legitimated Child of Recently Married Parents

When a child is born to a man and a woman who are not married to each other but who marry each other before the child turns 18 years of age, the child is considered to be legitimated.

To prove the relationship of mother and child, only the birth certificate is necessary.

To prove the relationship of father and child, two documents are needed: the birth certificate and the marriage certificate.

4. Stepchild

When the mother or the father of a child marries a person who is not the biological parent of that child, a step-relationship is created between the new parent and the child.

For there to be any immigration benefit, the marriage between the child's parent and stepparent must occur before the child turns 18 years of age. A U.S. citizen or green card–holding spouse can petition for a foreign-born spouse's children (as stepchildren) at any time, as long as the children were younger than 18 years of age at the time of the marriage.

In addition to the birth certificate of the child, a marriage certificate is necessary to show that the step-relationship was created by a marriage that occurred before the child's 18th birthday.

5. Adopted Child

The first thing to know about adopting an immigrant child is that the adoption usually must be finalized before the child turns 16 years of age. An adoption after the age of 16 might benefit the child in ways unrelated to immigration—for example, making inheritance simpler—but it will not usually help the child get a green card.

The next thing to find out is whether the child you wish to adopt lives in a country that has signed onto the Hague Convention on the Protection of Children. You can find details about all of the countries on the U.S. Department of State's adoption website at http://adoption.state.gov. To find out which countries are included, click "For adoption professionals," then "Status Table of Adoption Convention Countries." At time of publication, 104 countries were listed.

Some of these, however, place restrictions on whether U.S. citizens can adopt from them.

When the child lives in a Hague Convention country. The Hague Convention entered into force in the U.S. in April of 2008, and has significantly changed the rules and procedures for immigrating adopted children. Each country that is a party to the Convention must have an officially designated central authority to safeguard the adoption process, which in the U.S. is the Department of State (DOS).

Only U.S. citizens may petition. The petition must be filed before the child's 16th birthday (no exceptions), and the child must be adopted abroad. One thing that is easier in Hague Convention cases is that, unlike in other cases, there's no requirement that you have two years' legal custody of and joint residence with the child.

CAUTION

Adoptions from Hague Convention countries must be completed in the exact order specified by the Convention, step by step. Even if you otherwise meet all the requirements, failing to meet them in the specified order can result in the child's being unable to immigrate based upon the adoption.

Here are the basic steps for nonorphan adoptions of children from Hague Convention countries:

1. **Choose an adoption service provider (ASP).** The ASP must be authorized to provide adoption services in connection with a Hague adoption, so ask about this before hiring or paying any money to a provider.

2. **Obtain a home study report.** This must come from someone authorized to complete a Hague adoption home study.

3. **File Form I-800A with USCIS.** This form must be filed before you are matched with the child to be adopted. To file this form, you must be a U.S. citizen and habitually reside in the United States. If you are married, your spouse must also sign your Form I-800A and must also intend to adopt any child whom you adopt. If you are not married, you must be at least 24 years of age when filing your Form I-800A, and you must be at least 25 years of age when you later file Form I-800.

4. **Once USCIS approves your Form I-800A, work with the ASP to obtain a proposed adoption placement.**

5. **File Form I-800.** This serves to determine the child's eligibility as a Convention adoptee.

6. **Adopt the child.** Or, you can obtain custody in order to adopt the child in the United States.

7. **Obtain an immigrant visa for the child.**

8. **Bring the child to the United States.** The filing fee for Form I-800A is $775. An $85 fee for biometrics is also required, not only for the applicant but also for each person 18 years of age or older who is living with the applicant. There is no fee required for the first Form I-800 filed for a child on the basis of an approved Form I-800A. If more than one Form I-800 is filed during the approval period for different children, the fee is $775 for the second and each subsequent Form I-800, except that if the children were siblings before the adoption, no additional filing fee is required. See the form instructions for where to file.

Adopting a child from a Hague Convention country is complicated. We recommend that you consult an attorney who is experienced in immigration and adoptions.

When the child does not live in a Hague Convention country. An adopted immigrant child from a non-Hague convention country will be considered the child (or adult son or daughter) of the adopting parent as long as there was a full and final adoption before the child's 16th birthday.

There is one exception to this age limit, which applies to a child between the ages of 16 and 18, if the older child is the natural sibling of a younger child you have already adopted or are adopting at the same time as the older one. "Natural sibling" means the children share at least one biological parent. Unlike an orphan child (discussed in Chapter 10), the adopted child is neither orphaned nor abandoned by his or her natural parents.

Additional requirements under this process are that the parent must have had legal and physical custody of the child for at least two years while the child was a minor, and the child must have lived with the adopting parents at least two years before the petition was filed.

When these two periods have occurred, either at the same time or one after the other, the immigrant petition can be filed.

Because of these requirements, the most practical way the adopted child can get an immigrant visa is, in most cases, for one or both of the adopting parents to live in the foreign country with the alien child. But this is, as a practical matter, impossible for lawful permanent resident parents, who must maintain their U.S. residences in order to keep their green cards.

What if you're a U.S. citizen and the child you want to adopt is already living in the United States? This gets complicated, and you'll probably want to get an immigration lawyer's help. But let's take a look at the three main possibilities, after first reviewing one bit of good news: A child younger than 18 can't rack up "unlawful presence" in the U.S., and therefore you probably won't have to worry about the three- and ten-year bars (described in Chapter 4) being used to block the child from returning to the U.S. after, for example, leaving the United States for a visa interview at a U.S. consulate. (But watch the timing carefully if adopting a child who's already close to 16.)

However, a child who is staying in the U.S. without a visa or other permission from U.S. immigration authorities can still be arrested and removed (deported).

The child entered the U.S. illegally. If the child entered illegally, you can petition a court for legal custody, but that just makes you the rightful parent. It doesn't make the child's U.S. stay legal for immigration purposes. At the end of the two years of legal custody and having the child live with you, you can file the visa petition, but will ultimately have to take the child to a U.S. consulate abroad for the visa interview (which completes the green card application process).

The child entered the U.S. legally but has overstayed. If the child originally came to the U.S. on a visa, but has stayed past the expiration date on the I-94 card (either a small white card tucked into the passport or the online I-94), you can petition a court for legal custody. However, being granted custody just makes you the rightful parent. It doesn't make the child's U.S. stay legal for immigration purposes. At the end of the two years' custody and residence, you can file a petition and an adjustment of status application with USCIS. (This is a different procedure than for the child who entered illegally; the combination of your U.S. citizenship and the child's legal entry saves this child from having to do part of the green card application through a U.S. consulate in another country.) However, don't interpret this section to mean that you should go to another country, adopt a child, then use a tourist visa to bring the child back to the U.S. in hopes of completing the application process here. That could probably be interpreted as visa fraud, and destroy the child's chances of immigrating.

The child entered the U.S. legally and is still legal. If the child originally came to the U.S. on a visa, and the expiration date on the I-94 card (either a small white card tucked into the passport or the online I-94), hasn't passed, you're in relatively good shape. You can petition a court for legal custody, making you the child's rightful parent. Then the question becomes, when does the I-94 run out? If the child is on a student visa, it might easily run for the two years you'll need before submitting the I-130 petition and green card application (without leaving the U.S.). If not, see the paragraph above this one—and talk to a lawyer. Though certain visa stays can be extended, you wouldn't want to ruin the entire plan by lying about the reasons for the extension.

Another alternative might be to process the immigration papers required for an orphan child. (See Chapter 10.)

C. Quick View of the Application Process

With the exception of children adopted from Hague Convention countries, the standard process for someone to get a green card as a child (whether biological, stepchild, or adopted) is as follows. The U.S. citizen or permanent resident parent must begin the process by submitting a petition (Form I-130) to USCIS. We're going to assume that the person reading this is the parent.

Form I-130 serves to prove to the immigration authorities that your children are truly and legally yours. After that petition is approved (in most cases), your children complete their half of the process (with your help, of course) by submitting an immigrant visa application and attending an interview, most likely with you or a close relative accompanying them. Their application serves to prove that not only do they qualify as children of a U.S. citizen or permanent resident, but that they're otherwise eligible for U.S. permanent residence.

However, the details of when and how your children complete their half of the process depend on whether they are living overseas or in the United States, as described next.

D. Detailed Instructions for the Application Process

Now we'll break the application process down into individual procedures, some of which will be covered in this chapter, and others in later chapters—we'll tell you exactly where to turn to for your situation.

1. Preparing the Form I-130 Petition

All U.S. parents of immigrating children must prepare Form I-130 and supporting documents to begin the process. You'll need to assemble:

☐ Form I-130, Petition for Alien Relative (get the latest version from www.uscis.gov/i-130;and you can download a completed sample at www.nolo.com/back-of-book/GRN.html)

☐ birth certificate of child

☐ parents' marriage certificate (if any) and proof that any prior marriages ended. If you are the father petitioning for your child born out of wedlock, provide evidence as described in Section B, above.

☐ documents proving the parent's U.S. citizenship or permanent residence (see Chapter 20)

☐ filing fee for Form I-130, currently $535, payable by check or money order to the U.S. Department of Homeland Security, and

☐ Form G-1145 (www.uscis.gov/g-1145). This is optional, but filing it is a good idea, so that USCIS will send an email and/or text notification when it accepts your petition for processing. Once USCIS sends you a receipt number, you can use it to sign up for automatic email updates letting you know whenever mail is sent regarding your case.

TIP

How to sign up for automatic email updates: Go to www.uscis.gov. Click "Check your case status," then under "Why sign up for an account?" choose "Click Here." After accepting the terms and conditions, you can register as an applicant/petitioner.

In cases where the child is adopted from a non–Hague Convention country, the following documents must also be presented (remember that if the child is from a Hague Convention country, Forms I-800A and I-800 are used instead of Form I-130, and that the legal and procedural requirements are different):

- ☐ the adoption decree showing adoption prior to 16 years of age
- ☐ documents showing legal custody for at least two years
- ☐ documents proving that the adopted child has resided with the adopting parent or parents for at least two years (such as school and medical records)
- ☐ a birth certificate of the child showing the adopting parent as mother or father by reason of the adoption decree, and
- ☐ documents showing the marital status of the petitioning parent.

Once you've assembled all these items, make a copy for your records. It's also a good idea to write a cover letter, explaining what type of petition it is (for example, saying "I am a U.S. citizen, filing the enclosed I-130 petition on behalf of my married daughter"). The letter should include a bulleted list, much like the checklist above, of everything you're sending. This will help USCIS see that you're organized. It will help you, too, to make sure that nothing has been forgotten.

2. Where to Submit the I-130 Petition

Once you've assembled and copied everything, your next step will be applying online or by mail, as detailed below.

NEXT STEP

Next step for unmarried children younger than age 21 of U.S. citizens (immediate relatives) if the children live overseas. The parent can create an account and file online at www.uscis.gov or mail the visa petition to the USCIS lockbox (indicated on the USCIS web page that offers the form). The lockbox facility will forward it to a USCIS office appropriate for the parent's geographical area. Soon after the visa petition is approved, the U.S. consulate serving the country where the child lives will take over. The child will apply for the immigrant visa and green card through consular processing, described in Chapter 17.

NEXT STEP

Next step for unmarried children younger than age 21 of U.S. citizens (immediate relatives) if the children live in the United States. If the child is eligible for adjustment of status (as explained in Chapter 16), then the parent shouldn't file the I-130 petition by itself, but should combine it with the adjustment of status application, and then mail it according to the instructions in Chapter 16. If, however, the child is not eligible to adjust status, and has spent any time in the U.S. illegally or out of status, consult an experienced immigration attorney.

NEXT STEP

Next step for all children of U.S. permanent residents, and married or older-than-21 children of U.S. citizens (preference relatives) if the children live overseas. The parent can create an account and file online at www.uscis.gov or mail the I-130 petition to a USCIS lockbox (the one indicated at www.uscis.gov/i-130; the exact one depends on where the U.S. petitioner lives). The lockbox facility will forward it to the appropriate USCIS office. After the petition is approved, the child will be put on a waiting list, based on Priority Date. When the Priority Date becomes "current," the U.S. consulate serving the country where the child lives will take over. The child will apply for the immigrant visa and green card through consular processing, described in Chapter 17.

Immigrant Story: Children Nearing Age 21

Rajiv, a U.S. permanent resident, petitioned for his wife and three children to come to the United States from India. When he first filed the I-130 petition, the children were younger than 21. But with people in Category 2A then having to wait about two years for their Priority Dates to become current, the family rightly worried that the children would "age out" before they could be issued their green cards.

When the Priority Date finally became current, the oldest child, Sandip, was already 22 years old and eight months. The middle child, Ayanna, turned 21 years old that month, and the youngest child, Iqbal, was then 19 years old.

Can Sandip and Ayanna immigrate to the U.S. even though they're both now older than 21? Under the Child Status Protection Act, the children get to subtract from their age the amount of time it took USCIS to approve the I-130. Although the family waited two years for the Priority Date to become current, they waited only eight months for USCIS to approve the I-130. Unfortunately, eight months is not enough to help Sandip. Eight months will help Ayanna, however, by making her—for purposes of getting a visa—20 years and three months old. To take advantage of this protection, Ayanna will have to file her green card application within one year of the Priority Date becoming current. So long as she acts soon, she doesn't have to worry about turning 21.

The last child, Iqbal, is still only 19 years old, so he does not need to worry (unless he ruins his eligibility by getting married).

NEXT STEP

Next step for all children of U.S. permanent residents and married or older-than-21 children of U.S. citizens (preference relatives) if the children live in the United States. The parent can create an account and file online at www.uscis.gov or mail the I-130 petition to the USCIS lockbox serving the area where the U.S. petitioner lives). The lockbox facility will forward it to the appropriate USCIS office for the parent's geographical area. After the petition is approved, the child will be put on a waiting list, based on Priority Date. It could be years before the Priority Date becomes current, during which time the mere filing of an I-130 petition gives the child no rights to remain in the United States (though many do, illegally). After the child's Priority Date becomes current, then:

- If the child is still living in the U.S. and is eligible for adjustment of status (unlikely), see Chapter 16 for instructions.
- If the child is living in the U.S. and is not eligible for adjustment of status, or has left the U.S. but spent more than six months here illegally before leaving, see an experienced immigration attorney for help.
- If the child left the U.S. without having spent too much time there illegally, you can safely continue the process, and the U.S. consulate serving the country where the child lives will take over. The child will apply for the immigrant visa and green card through consular processing, described in Chapter 17.

E. Automatic Citizenship for Some Children

In 2000, Congress passed important legislation allowing many children living in the U.S. with green cards to become citizens automatically if they have at least one U.S. citizen parent. Natural-born as well as adopted children can benefit from these laws.

The law is slightly less helpful for children living overseas, who must go through an application process in order to claim their U.S. citizenship.

1. Children Living in the United States

For natural-born children to qualify for automatic citizenship, one parent needs to be a U.S. citizen, the child must have a green card and be living in the legal and physical custody of the U.S. citizen parent, and the child must still be younger than age 18 when all of these conditions are fulfilled.

For adopted children to qualify, one of the parents must be a U.S. citizen, a full and final adoption must have occurred, the child must be living in the United States after having entered on an immigrant visa (meaning the child is a green card holder), and the child must still be younger than age 18 at the time that all these things become true.

Though the process is automatic—and USCIS tries to send such children certificates of citizenship within six weeks of when they get their green cards —it's an excellent idea for such children to also apply for U.S. passports as proof of their U.S. citizen status.

> **EXAMPLE:** Lorna is 16 years old and living in Mexico. Some years ago, her father, a U.S. permanent resident, petitioned for her to immigrate. Even before her Priority Date became current, however, he became a U.S. citizen, so the process was speeded up. Lorna successfully applies for an immigrant visa through consular processing, and enters the United States to live with her father.
>
> Almost as soon as Lorna enters the U.S., she automatically becomes a U.S. citizen, because she (1) has a U.S. citizen parent, (2) has a green card, (3) is living in the citizen parent's legal and physical custody, and (4) was still younger than 18 when the first three things became true. USCIS should, recognizing her status, automatically send her a citizenship certificate. (Note: If Lorna's father had become a citizen after she got her green card and came to the U.S., but before she turned 18, USCIS wouldn't realize she'd become an automatic citizen, and Lorna would have to request a certificate to prove it.)

Children living in the U.S. can also, if USCIS fails to send a certificate, file for a certificate of citizenship on Form N-600. This form is used for biological and adopted children. For further instructions, see www.uscis.gov/n-600.

2. Children Living Overseas

For children who are living overseas, the process is somewhat more complex. Either natural-born or adopted children may qualify for automatic citizenship, but they need to have one U.S. citizen parent; that parent or the parent's parent must have been physically present in the U.S. for five years, two of which were after the age of 14; the child must be visiting the U.S. on a temporary visa or other lawful means of entry; the child must live in the legal and physical custody of the U.S. citizen parent in their overseas home; and the child must remain younger than the age of 18 and in valid visa status until USCIS makes its decision on the citizenship application.

In practice, these conditions are hard to meet. You might wish to consult with a lawyer. The application is made on Form N-600K for biological and adopted children. For further instructions and to download the form, see the USCIS website at www.uscis.gov/n-600K; and download a completed sample at www.nolo.com/back-of-book/GRN.html. You can file online or by mail. ●

Orphan Immigrants in Non-Hague Convention Countries

A. Who Qualifies as an Orphan Child 103

B. Who Can Petition for an Orphan Child 103

C. Preadoption Requirements 104

D. Starting the Adoption Process 104

    1. When the Child Is Not Yet Identified 105

    2. When the Child Is Identified 106

E. After the Petition Is Approved 106

F. Filing for a Visa 107

G. Automatic Citizenship for Adopted Orphans 107

f you're considering adopting a child, and that child might be an orphan, you might not need to read this chapter—it depends entirely on what country the child is from. That's because some but not all countries have signed on to the Hague Convention on the Protection of Children and Cooperation in Respect of Intercountry Adoption. This took effect in the United States in 2008. If you plan to adopt from a country that has signed onto the Hague Convention, it doesn't matter whether the child is an orphan or not—the procedures will essentially be the same as those covered in Chapter 9, rather than this one.

If, however, you plan to adopt from a country that has not signed onto the Hague Convention, keep reading. This chapter describes the special process for adopting orphans who live in countries that have not signed the Hague Convention.

To check whether a country is a party to the Hague Convention, go to the Department of State's website at https://travel.state.gov and click "Intercountry Adoption" then "Country Information," then enter the country you're interested in adopting from in the search box. You'll find not only information about U.S. immigration requirements, but about each country's individual requirements for adoptive parents.

The requirements for adopting and immigrating a non-Hague child who is an orphan are less difficult than the requirements for adopting and immigrating a non-Hague non-orphan. In particular, you need not live with an orphan child for two years before the adoption. That is why many U.S. citizens who adopt from overseas choose orphans.

There are two types of orphan immigrant visas:

- an IR-3 visa classification, for orphans who have met the U.S. parents and whose adoptions were completed abroad, and

- an IR-4 classification, for orphans who, although in the legal custody of the U.S. citizen parent or parents, still need to be legally adopted after reaching the United States, or who need to be readopted because the U.S. parents haven't yet seen the child.

In either case, the application process includes a number of complexities. If you're like many Americans, you might find it easiest to use an agency that specializes in international adoptions, although direct adoption is also possible. Even with help from an agency, expect the process to take at least six to twelve months.

A nonprofit called the Intercountry Adoption Accreditation and Maintenance Entity, Inc. (IAAME) collects information on accredited adoption agencies. See www.iaame.net.

Look for an agency that has been doing adoptions for a number of years, successfully completes a comparatively large number per year, serves the countries in which you're interested, and is happy to show you evidence that it's licensed and comes with good references.

CAUTION

If the U.S. petitioner has a criminal record, see an attorney. Under the Adam Walsh Child Protection and Safety Act of 2006, U.S. citizens and lawful permanent residents who have been convicted of any "specified offense against a minor" are prohibited from filing a family-based immigrant petition on behalf of any beneficiary (whether a child or not). USCIS will run security checks on all petitions and may call the petitioner in for fingerprinting. If the petitioner has a conviction for one of the specified offenses against a minor, then USCIS will deny the unless it determines that the U.S. petitioner poses no risk to the beneficiary.

ⓘ **CAUTION**
You'll also need to follow the rules of the country you're adopting from. Not every country allows international adoptions, and those that do usually impose various requirements on the parents. For example, some countries refuse to allow single-parent adoptions, or require that adopting parents be of a certain age. This chapter covers only the U.S. requirements; you'll need to research the international requirements with the help of your adoption agency or on the DOS website.

A. Who Qualifies as an Orphan Child

A child younger than 16 years of age (or younger than 18, if being adopted along with a brother or sister younger than 16) is considered an orphan if the child meets any of these conditions:

- Both parents have died or have disappeared.
- The sole or surviving parent is incapable of providing the proper child care and has, in writing, released the child for adoption and emigration.
- Both father and mother have abandoned the child, or have become separated or lost from the child—and the legal authorities in the child's country, recognizing the child as abandoned, have granted legal custody of the child to an orphanage.

However, if the child has been placed with other people or temporarily in the orphanage, or if one or both parents continue to maintain contact—for example, sending gifts, writing letters, or showing that they have not ended their parental obligations to the child—the child will not be considered an orphan by the U.S. government.

You can't get around these requirements by having the overseas parent or parents "abandon" the child into the hands of the adopting U.S. couple or person.

B. Who Can Petition for an Orphan Child

Only U.S. citizens are allowed to file a visa petition for an orphan child; lawful permanent residents may not do so. A number of other regulations also apply:

- If a married couple is adopting, only one of them need be a U.S. citizen (but both have to be age 21 or over and sign the petition).
- A U.S. citizen who is not married must be at least 25 years of age before filing the petition. If the citizen is younger than 25 when a foreign adoption takes place, that adoption will be considered invalid, and the citizen will have to readopt the child after the child reaches the United States (if allowed in their state of residence).
- The orphan child must be less than 16 years of age when the petition is filed (or younger than 18, if the parents are also petitioning for the child's brother or sister who is younger than 16).
- The adopting married couple, or single person, must have completed certain preadoption requirements, such as a home study, before filing the petition. (See Section C, below.)
- The adopting married couple, or single person, must have seen the child in the orphan's country before or during the adoption proceedings, or show that they'll be able to "readopt" the child in the United States.

ⓘ **CAUTION**
Beware of lawbreakers. In some developing countries, kidnapping poor children and then selling them for adoption to childless couples in the United States and Europe has become rampant.

Your search for a child of your own should not cause the kidnapping or sale of another person's child. Before signing up with any adoption organization, check its references with friends who have worked with the organization—or ask for the names of some former clients, and then call them. Above all, avoid direct arrangements with the surviving parent or private individuals acting as brokers for a fee.

International Adoption for Lesbians and Gays

Many countries prohibit adoption by an openly gay person or a same-sex couple.

People have found ways to adopt from some of these countries nonetheless. If you are proceeding with a foreign adoption, you might opt to keep your sexual orientation—and your relationship with your partner—hidden from the host country. It is a judgment call as to whether to tell the agency helping you with the adoption. Some will find ways to get around the barrier, such as by referring to one partner as a "roommate" in reports to the host country, and ignoring the issue of sexual orientation.

For more about adoption and parenting for same-sex couples, check out *A Legal Guide for Lesbian & Gay Couples,* by Emily Doskow and Frederick Hertz (Nolo).

C. Preadoption Requirements

To protect the child and to ensure that the adopting parent or parents will care for the child properly, U.S. immigration laws require what's called a "home study" before an adoption decree is finalized or before a petition for an orphan child will be approved. Many couples take care of this first, as part of an advance processing application, described below in Section D1.

The purpose of the home study is to allow the state agency handling adoptions to investigate the future home of the child (and any adult living in it) and verify whether the adopting couple, or the single person, is psychologically and economically fit. Most home studies take about three months.

The home study must result in a favorable report recommending the proposed adoption. The report must be signed by an official of a state agency, or an agency licensed by the state in which the child will live with the adopting parent or parents. The home study should be submitted to USCIS within six months of its completion date.

This report must cover:

- the financial ability of the parent or parents to raise and educate the child
- a discussion of possible negative factors, such as a history of substance abuse, child abuse, sexual abuse, domestic violence, criminal behavior, or past denials of adoptions or unfavorable home study reports
- a detailed description of the living accommodations, including any special accommodations for a child with disabilities or medical issues, and
- a factual evaluation of the physical, mental, and moral ability of the adopting parent or parents, including observations made during personal interviews.

In addition to the home study, other preadoption conditions may be required by some states before an adoption petition can be filed with local courts. Therefore, if you are planning to adopt the orphan child in the United States, you must first comply with these state rules.

D. Starting the Adoption Process

The first steps toward adoption depend in part on whether or not the orphan child has been identified (chosen).

1. When the Child Is Not Yet Identified

If a particular child has not yet been singled out and the parents are going abroad to locate an orphan child for adoption, or for adoption after arrival in the United States, they should file an advance processing application, as follows:

☐ Form I-600A, Application for Advance Processing of Orphan Petition, signed by the U.S. citizen and, if married, the spouse. (Download the form from www.uscis.gov/i-600a; and you can download a completed sample at www.nolo.com/back-of-book/GRN.html.)

☐ Proof of applicant's U.S. citizenship. (See Chapter 21.)

☐ If married, evidence of the spouse's U.S. citizenship or lawful legal status in the United States and citizenship in another country.

☐ Marriage certificate, divorce or annulment decree, or death certificate, as evidence of present and previous marital status.

☐ Fees for biometrics (fingerprints and so on) of the U.S. citizen and, if married, of the spouse, plus for any other adults aged 18 years or older who live in your household. ($85 per person.) If paying by check or money order, make it out to the U.S. Department of Homeland Security. Your other option is to pay by credit card, using Form G-1450, Authorization for Credit Card Transactions.

☐ Evidence of petitioner's age, if unmarried, and if not already shown on other documents.

☐ A favorable home study report. If the home study report is not yet available, it must be submitted within one year from the date of filing the advance application. Otherwise, the application will be considered to have been abandoned.

☐ Proof of compliance with any preadoption requirements of the state in which the child will live if the adoption is to be completed in the United States (see Section C).

☐ A filing fee (currently $775).

After USCIS approves the advance processing application, you have 18 months in which to locate an orphan child and continue with the process. If you're not having any luck finding an orphan child within the one year, you can ask USCIS for a onetime extension. Do so within the 90 days before the USCIS approval notice expires—don't wait until it has already expired. You must make the request in writing, to the same office that approved your Form I-600A. With your letter, you must include an updated or amended home study report. You'll probably also need to request a onetime re-fingerprinting, since the original fingerprints are valid for only 15 months.

If you miss the deadline to ask for an extension, or you still can't find a child even after an extension, you basically need to start over. That means you'll have to submit a new advance processing application (with a new filing fee) if the child has not yet been identified, or a petition as described below (which also requires the filing fee of $775) if the child has been identified.

When you look at the sample I-600A, you'll notice that it assumes you've already figured out which country you plan to adopt a child from, and asks questions about your travel plans. But what if you end up being unable to find a child in that country? If you're still within the 18-month approval period, you can request a onetime change of country, at no extra charge. To do so, send a letter to the same USCIS office that approved the I-600A petition. However, if you later want to change the country of adoption a second time, you'll need to file USCIS Form I-824, Application for Action on an Approved Application or Petition, along with a filing fee (currently $465). The reason for all this paperwork is that by now, USCIS will have notified the U.S. consulate in the country you originally planned to adopt from, and now needs to notify a different consulate instead (you'll specify which one in Part 2 of Form I-824).

Can You Bring the Child to the U.S. First?

It's frustrating for parents eager to bring an orphan child into their home to have to wait for all the immigration procedures to be completed. In light of this, the U.S. government gives high priority to orphan petitions. However, the government doesn't smile upon efforts by parents to get around the U.S. immigration laws, for example by bringing the child in on a tourist or student visa, and attempting to complete the adoption and immigration processes afterward. Basically, this won't work. In rare cases, however, USCIS will grant humanitarian parole to allow an orphan into the U.S. even before the immigration procedures have been finished—most often because of a medical or similar emergency. You're best off consulting an experienced immigration attorney for help in requesting humanitarian parole.

---

2. When the Child Is Identified

When the adopting parent or parents have identified the orphan child they wish to adopt, they can immediately file a petition for the child at the appropriate USCIS service center. (See www.uscis.gov for the exact address.) Or, if the U.S. citizen will be overseas to adopt or locate the orphan, you can file the petition with the U.S. consulate in the country of the child's residence.

This can be done even if the advance processing application has not yet been approved or has not yet been filed. If the advance processing application has

been filed but not approved, include a copy of the filing receipt with the petition. If it has already been approved, include a copy of the approval notice.

You must file all the documents listed in Section D1, above (except Form I-600A), as well as:

- ☐ Form I-600, Petition to Classify Orphan as an Immediate Relative
- ☐ birth certificate of the orphan child, who must be younger than 16 years of age when the petition is filed
- ☐ death certificates of the parents of the child or proof of legal abandonment by both the father and mother
- ☐ the adoption decree or evidence that you have legal custody of the orphan and are working toward adoption, and
- ☐ filing fee (currently $775) unless you're filing based on an approved I-600A filed within the previous 18 months, in which case you don't need to pay the fee.

E. After the Petition Is Approved

If the petition is filed and approved by USCIS in the United States, the entire file is sent to the U.S. consulate in the country in which the child lives.

The consular officer then investigates the child. This can take months. The investigation aims to confirm that the child:

- meets the legal definition of an orphan, and
- does not have an illness or disability that was not described in the orphan petition.

A long delay in the adoption process of an orphan child can cause would-be parents much anxiety. However, keep in mind that the investigation is performed as a service to protect adopting parents from the heartbreaking situation that could develop if the child later proved not to be available for adoption.

Meeting Face-to-Face

The American individual or couple who wishes to adopt need not have seen the child personally before filing the petition if the adoption is to be done in the United States. However, if you are going to adopt a child to raise as your own for the rest of your life, you will likely want to find out what the child looks like, how you react to each other, what the child's physical condition is, and other imperceptible factors that only a face-to-face encounter can provide. Most people prefer to visit the child abroad before beginning adoption proceedings.

F. Filing for a Visa

When the petition is approved, the case will be transferred to the U.S. consulate in the orphan child's country of residence, for immigrant visa processing. (See Chapter 17 for advice and instructions on consular processing.)

In addition to the documents ordinarily required for consular processing, you'll need to bring the child's final adoption decree or proof of custody from the foreign government.

After receiving an immigrant visa, the orphan child can then enter the United States as a permanent resident. If the child has not yet been adopted in the foreign country, the U.S. citizen or couple can proceed to adopt the child according to the laws of the state in which they live.

G. Automatic Citizenship for Adopted Orphans

Under the Child Citizenship Act of 2000, orphans who enter on IR-3 visas (meaning the adoption is legally complete before they enter the U.S.) become citizens as soon as they enter the United States, and should receive a citizenship certificate by mail from USCIS within about six weeks.

Orphans who enter the U.S. on IR-4 visas will become U.S. citizens as soon as their adoptions are complete. To obtain proof of their citizenship, the parents will need to apply to their local USCIS office, using Form N-600K. ●

The Diversity Visa Lottery

A. **Who Qualifies for the DV Lottery**.. 111

   1. What Country—or Countries—You're a Native Of 111

   2. The Educational Requirements.. 112

B. **How to Apply for the DV Lottery**.. 112

   1. The DV Lottery Application... 112

   2. Notification of Winners 114

C. **After You Win—The Green Card Application** 114

D. **How to Bring Your Spouse and Children**.. 116

In 1990, Congress created a green card category to help balance out the numbers of immigrants coming from different countries, by opening up green card opportunities for people from countries that don't send many immigrants to the United States. Although the official name for this category is the "diversity visa" ("DV"), most people know it as the "visa lottery," because winners—50,000 in total—are selected through a random drawing. (The drawing is done by a computer.)

The visa lottery is held once a year. Every year the U.S. government looks to see which countries have sent the fewest immigrants to the United States in the last five years, and accordingly adds to or subtracts from the list of countries whose natives are allowed to put their names into the drawing. Diversity visas are divided among six geographic regions. No one country can receive more than 7% of the available diversity visas in any year.

You can enter the lottery if you are a native of one of the listed countries and meet certain other requirements. One of the requirements is some technological savvy—all applicants must submit their applications through the Internet and attach a digital photo. Also, the main applicant must possess a valid passport from the home country.

If you win the lottery, you've won the right to apply for green cards for yourself, your spouse, and your unmarried children younger than age 21—but no more than the right to apply. You can still be refused a green card for many reasons, including because of delays by the U.S. government causing you to miss the deadline, or because you've failed to meet the educational, health, or financial criteria for the diversity visa and green card.

Certain risks come with applying for the lottery. For example, if you win the lottery but are ultimately refused a green card, you've announced to the U.S. government that you're hoping to get a green card. That can make it more difficult to obtain or extend short-term visas to the United States—such as student or visitor visas. (Most short-term visas require you to assure the U.S. government that you have every intention of returning home afterward.) Even entering the lottery and losing is something you must declare on any later applications for U.S. visas, and it could be taken into account in considering whether you'll really return home on time.

Details of the Lottery That Began in 2021

At the time this book went to print, the most recent lottery had begun in 2021 (which the government calls "DV-2023"). Applications were accepted between noon on October 6, 2021 and noon on November 9, 2021. Entrants could check the status of their entries from May 2, 2022 through September 30, 2022, at https://dvprogram.state.gov/ESC. Natives of the following countries were not eligible (meaning that people who were natives of any other country in the world were allowed to enter):

Bangladesh	Jamaica
Brazil	Mexico
Canada	Nigeria
China (mainland-born, not including Macau, Taiwan, or Hong Kong)	Pakistan
	Philippines
	South Korea
Colombia	United Kingdom (except Northern Ireland) and its dependent territories
Dominican Republic	
El Salvador	
Haiti	Venezuela
Honduras	Vietnam
India	

CAUTION
The lottery changes every year and could disappear entirely. It is an annual event, with a slightly different set of rules, including qualifying countries, every year. The U.S. Senate often discusses eliminating the diversity lottery altogether and instead allocating visas using a points-based system, in which potential immigrants could better their chances of obtaining a visa by demonstrating their education and income levels, English language fluency, existing job offer, and other factors. Keep your eyes on the Legal Updates on Nolo's website, and double-check with the U.S. State Department during the year in which you'll be applying. The rules are usually announced around September, and posted on the State Department website at https://dvprogram.state.gov.

CAUTION
Beware of lottery scams. Every year, fraudulent emails and letters are sent to DV applicants. The scammers pose as the U.S. government—with increasingly sophisticated methods, such as including official-looking images of the U.S. flag, Capitol building, or White House—then attempt to get money from DV applicants. Don't be fooled! The U.S. government does not personally contact winners. Information about your DV entry will be available only through the official government website. To double-check that it's really a government website look for the ".gov" suffix on the URL. The same goes for any visa-related emails you receive. If they're not from an address ending with ".gov," be suspicious.

A. Who Qualifies for the DV Lottery

Whether or not you're allowed to enter the lottery depends on whether you:

- are a passport-holding native of one of the countries that is eligible that year, and
- meet the educational or work requirements.

It doesn't matter if you've already got an application for a green card underway in another category, for example through a family member or an employee—you can still enter the diversity visa lottery.

1. What Country—or Countries— You're a Native Of

Lottery applicants should make sure that they can actually claim what the law describes as "nativity" in an eligible country. Nativity is usually based on having been born in the country. Living in a country is not enough, even if you have residence rights there.

You might, however, be a native of more than one country. This can be helpful for lottery purposes if you were born in one of the ineligible countries, or if your native country has a lot of people applying for the lottery from it. There are two ways to gain nativity in a country other than having been born there:

- If your spouse was born in an eligible country, you can claim your spouse's country of birth for lottery purposes.
- If neither of your parents was born in your birth country or made a home there at the time of your birth, you might be able to claim nativity in one of your parents' countries of birth.

And remember, the list of eligible countries usually changes slightly every year, so check the State Department's instructions before you apply.

Immigrant Story: Applying Based on Spouse's Country

Azu was born and lives in Nigeria. Although in past years he's been able to enter the visa lottery, he has never won—and Nigeria was recently dropped from the list of eligible countries.

However, Azu's wife Marie is a native of Cameroon. So he submits a lottery application based on her country—and wins!

Assuming the U.S. consulate in Nigeria can process his case quickly enough, Azu, his wife, and their two unmarried children can become U.S. permanent residents.

CAUTION

You must choose on which country to base your application. Even if you're a native of more than one eligible country, you can't apply for the lottery more than once within a single year.

2. The Educational Requirements

Applicants from qualifying countries must have either:

- a high school diploma or its equivalent, meaning a successfully completed twelve-year course of elementary plus secondary education that would qualify you to enter a U.S. college or university, or
- a minimum of two years' work experience (within the last five years) in a job that normally requires at least two years' training or experience. American job offers are not necessary. However, you won't be allowed to argue about how much experience your job requires—this judgment will be made based on a list of job titles and descriptions kept by the U.S. government in an online database called O*NET, at www.onetonline.org. (To check this out yourself, go to the website and click "Find Occupations.")

You won't be asked to prove your educational qualifications on the lottery application—but that doesn't mean you can puff up the truth. If you win the lottery, you will have to come up with proof of your education as part of the green card application.

B. How to Apply for the DV Lottery

A new application period starts every year, usually in early October. You can submit one application—and only one. People who try to apply more than once will have all their lottery visa applications tossed out of the running. Husbands, wives, and children in the same family can, however, submit separate applications if each one who applies separately meets the educational and other eligibility criteria.

No fee is charged for applying, so watch out for websites and consultants who claim that there is, or who charge you a lot of money for supposed "special" handling. The application is fairly simple, and most find it can be done with minimal or no help from another person.

CAUTION

DV registrations submitted one year are not held over to the next. So if you are not selected one year, you need to reapply the next year to be considered.

1. The DV Lottery Application

We can't give you a sample application, because the one and only way to apply is online at https://dvprogram.state.gov. It doesn't matter what country you're in when you submit the online application. You can start the application and then stop without submitting it, for example if you realize you're missing a piece of information—but you cannot save or download your work. And if you try to submit an application and the system rejects it, you can try again until you succeed.

Once you start your application, the system will give you only an hour in which to submit it before it erases all the information you've entered, forcing you to start over. So, you'll need to assemble all the needed information ahead of time, and plan for a time when you can complete the entire application within that hour.

Here's what you'll probably be asked when you go to the State Department website to apply:

1. Full name—last name (family or surname), first name, middle name
2. Date of birth—day, month, year
3. Gender—"male" or "female" are so far the only choices, though the U.S. government has been moving toward recognizing nonbinary possibilities.
4. City where you were born
5. Country where you were born (use your country's current name, even if it had a different name when you were born there—for example, "Myanmar" instead of "Burma")
6. Country of eligibility or chargeability—normally, your country of birth. However, if you were born in a country that is not eligible for the DV lottery, you might be able to claim your spouse's or your parents' country of birth, if different from your own. See "What Country—or Countries—You're a Native Of," above.
7. Your passport number, along with its country of issuance and expiration date. It must be a valid, unexpired international travel passport. You can skip this, however, if you don't have or cannot get a passport because you are stateless or a national of a Communist-controlled country; or if you've received an individual waiver from the U.S. government.
8. Entry photograph(s)—you'll need to submit digital photographs of you, your spouse, and all your children (unmarried, younger than age 21), if you have any.

! CAUTION

Get the digital photographs right. Your entry will be rejected—or your visa later refused—if you don't submit all the required photographs or the photographs are not recent, have been manipulated, or fail to meet the specifications on the Department of State website at https://travel.state.gov (search for "visa photo requirements").

---

9. Mailing address—in care of, address, city/town, district/county/province/state, postal code/zip code, country; country where you live today
10. Phone number (optional)
11. Email address (required); be sure to triple-check this, because it's where you will receive follow-up communication from the Department of State.
12. What is the highest level of education you have achieved, as of today? (You don't need to list all your schooling, just the last type of school you completed, for example high school, vocational school, university, or graduate school.)
13. Spouse information—name, date of birth, gender, city/town of birth, country of birth, photograph
14. Number of and information about children who are unmarried and younger than 21 years of age (no need to mention children who are ineligible either because they are

U.S. legal permanent residents or U.S. citizens or are older than 21 years of age or married). Include adopted and step-children. You'll also need to add information about your children—name, date of birth, gender, city/town of birth, country of birth, photograph.

15. Marital status—unmarried, married, divorced, widowed, or legally separated. Do not choose "unmarried" if you were divorced or widowed.

CAUTION
If you are legally married and/or have children, be sure to say so. This is important even if your spouse or children do not plan to become permanent residents. If you fail to include them on your original DV lottery entry, and they later try to apply for permanent residence based on your DV winning, your entire case will be disqualified. This applies only to people who were family members at the time the original application was submitted, not those acquired at a later date.

After you've successfully completed and submitted your online application, you'll get a confirmation screen, showing your name, other personal information, and a date/time stamp. It can take several minutes before you receive this screen. The confirmation doesn't mean you've won, it simply means your application went through okay.

Be extra careful not to make typing errors. If your application contains a typing error, particularly in the spelling of your name, the State Department might throw it out. This is because it believes that people try to cheat the system by submitting more than one application with their name spelled slightly differently.

CAUTION
Don't sign off without writing down your confirmation number. You'll need this in order to find out whether or not you are selected as a winner. If you forget, the way to retrieve a confirmation number is at the entrant status check page at https://dvprogram.state.gov. Click "Forgot Confirmation Number," select the lottery year, and enter your name (spelled exactly the same as on your lottery entry), your date of birth, and your email address.

2. Notification of Winners

DV lottery winners are not notified by mail. The only way to find out whether or not you have been picked is to check the State Department website at https://dvprogram.state.gov. All entrants, including those not selected, will be able to check the status of their entries through this website. Be ready with the confirmation number that was given you when you made your online entry.

C. After You Win—The Green Card Application

Unfortunately, winning the lottery doesn't guarantee you a green card. The government always declares more than 50,000 winners—but gives out only 50,000 green cards. This means if you don't follow up quickly or receive your interview on time, the supply of green cards could run out. You'll have to complete the process and have received your visa or green card by September 30th of the year following your selection. (For example, applicants in 2021, who will be notified in 2022, will lose their chance if they can't complete the process by September 30, 2023.)

This can be a serious problem. You want to be ready to access the Entrant Status Check as soon as winners are posted. Even before learning whether you are a winner, it's worth taking a look at Chapter 16 (if you are already in the U.S. and eligible to adjust your status by filing an application with USCIS) or Chapter 17 (if you are outside the U.S. and will apply for your green card using consular processing) to see what types of documents you will need to collect, prepare, and ultimately submit with your application.

If you are among the lucky winners, you will receive a receipt number for the geographic location of your country, as well as instructions on how to apply for your lawful permanent residence. Winners will be instructed to check the *Visa Bulletin* to learn when their cutoff numbers appear under the appropriate region (or in some instances, country). If you are not immediately eligible to apply, keep checking the *Visa Bulletin* each month.

If you will be consular processing, use your DV case number to fill out Form DS-260, Online Immigrant Visa and Alien Registration Application. This alerts the Kentucky Consular Center (KCC) that your application is time-sensitive. You can also contact the KCC via email at KCCDV@state.gov; its phone number is 606-526-7500, but they might not answer.

If you will be adjusting your status, you'll need to submit Form I-485, Application to Register Permanent Residence or Adjust Status along with supporting documents and forms to USCIS, and check the box in Part 2 indicating you are a lottery winner.

It's best to also indicate on the envelope and cover letter that you are a DV applicant and are facing a September 30th deadline. Few immigrants who win the lottery have the opportunity to adjust status in the United States. Despite taking such precautions, you could encounter delays over which you have little control. Some people's applications get stalled while their security checks are being completed by the FBI (Federal Bureau of Investigation) and CIA (Central Intelligence Agency). Even if you've never done anything wrong, just having a common name can lead to delays, as the FBI and CIA check and double-check your name and fingerprints against various databases.

Given that you are facing the DV cap and deadline, consider hiring an experienced immigration attorney to help make sure your application is complete the first time around and to respond if and when delays occur. Another problem is that, as with all green card applications, if you win the lottery, you still must prove that you are not "inadmissible" to the United States. For example, if you have been arrested for committing certain crimes, are considered a security risk, have spent too much time in the United States illegally, or are afflicted with certain physical or mental illnesses, you might be prevented from receiving a green card. (For more on inadmissibility, see Chapter 4.)

Proving that you'll be able to support yourself financially in the U.S. can be a challenge for lottery winners. If you can't show this, you'll be considered inadmissible as a potential "public charge"—that is, someone who might need government financial assistance. You will need to show that you are either self-supporting, have sufficient skills and/or education to find employment, or have friends or family who will support you once you're living in the United States. In 2021, for example, the U.S. government said that a family of four who were getting their green cards through the visa lottery would be presumed to need government assistance unless their income was $26,500 per year or more.

You'll face less onerous financial requirements than most other green card applicants. Most people applying for green cards must have a sponsor submit an Affidavit of Support for them on Form I-864, which shows that their sponsor can support them at 125% of the U.S. poverty guidelines. People getting green cards through the visa lottery, however, submit a shorter and simpler Affidavit of Support, on Form I-134. Instead of showing an income that is at least 125% of the poverty guidelines, an I-134 sponsor needs only show an income that reaches 100%. You also have the option of filling out this form yourself if your income is sufficient, avoiding the need for a sponsor.

SEE AN EXPERT
Don't miss your chance—get professional help. A good lawyer will know the latest ways to get your application through the system quickly, and when and who to ask for speeded up handling.

CAUTION
Don't forget to pay the extra fees. Lottery winners must pay a "diversity visa surcharge" in addition to the regular fees for applying for a green card. At the time this book was published, the fee was $330.

D. How to Bring Your Spouse and Children

For the lottery application itself, it's simple to include your spouse and children—in fact, you're required to name them on your application, unless you and your spouse are legally separated (by court order) or divorced, or your children are U.S. citizens or permanent residents. Simply include your spouse and children's names, and remember to attach a digital photograph of each one to your lottery submission. (And remember that your spouse may, if eligible, submit a separate lottery application, which includes your name and photo and those of your children.)

It doesn't matter whether your spouse and children plan to come with you to the U.S. or not—you must still list their names and provide their photos with your lottery application. If you don't list them, not only will they lose their chance to immigrate with you if you win, but your entire application will be disqualified! In fact, even if you and your spouse are no longer living together, you must provide your spouse's photo unless you're either legally separated (by court order) or divorced—a requirement that causes problems for some applicants.

What if you give birth to a child or get married after submitting the lottery application? That's okay—your new child and spouse will be allowed to immigrate with you if you win. However, you could be asked to provide extra proof that this relationship wasn't created fraudulently, to get the newly added person a green card.

If you win the lottery, the rules and paperwork for your family get more complicated. First, you need to figure out which family members are allowed to immigrate with you. Your spouse will be allowed, so long as you're legally married. Your children will also be allowed, so long as they're younger than 21 years of age and remain unmarried up to the date you're approved for green cards. Warn your children that they must remain unmarried until they've entered the U.S., or they'll lose their eligibility!

Next, each family member must submit a separate green card application, as described in either Chapter 17 (discussing consular processing for people coming from overseas) or Chapter 16 (discussing adjustment of status for people already in the United States and lucky enough to have a right to apply for a green card without leaving). No matter where you apply, the application will consist of several forms, fees, medical examination results, and more.

Fortunately, only the lead person—the one who won the lottery—is required to meet the educational and work requirements of the lottery. However, each of your family members must separately prove that they don't have any of the health, criminal, or other problems that make people inadmissible to the United States. And you'll have to show that the family as a whole isn't likely to need government assistance.

You'll also need to pay for your entire family's airfare to the United States, and for housing once you get here. You won't receive any U.S. government assistance with your transition.

CAUTION
Be careful if you have a child about to turn 21. Getting older is, of course, something your children have no control over. But a child who turns 21 before being approved for a green card is, technically, no longer eligible. Fortunately, the law contains some protections for children in this situation. When and if you are approved for green cards, your child will be allowed to subtract from their age the amount of time between the date you could have first applied for the lottery and the date the winners were announced. ●

12

Your Brothers and Sisters as Immigrants

A. Who Counts as Your Brother or Sister..120

    1. Legitimate Brother and Sister..120

    2. Half-Brother and Half-Sister..120

    3. Stepbrother and Stepsister 121

    4. Adopted Brother and Adopted Sister..121

B. Quick View of the Application Process..121

C. Detailed Instructions for the Application Process..122

    1. Preparing the Form I-130 Petition..122

    2. Submitting the Form I-130 Petition 122

D. What Happens After Filing Form I-130...123

I f you are a U.S. citizen, whether by birth, naturalization, or some other means, you can petition for your brothers and sisters to immigrate—but you must be at least 21 years old when you file the petition.

What's more, your brothers and sisters will be put in the family fourth preference visa category, which is so overloaded with applicants that they'll likely face a wait of at least 14 years, and up to around 23 years for applicants from some countries. (See Chapter 5 for more information on waiting periods in visa preference categories.) Nevertheless, the years can pass surprisingly quickly, so it might be worth getting the petition in and reserving your brother or sister a place on the waiting list.

Once a visa number becomes available, your brother or sister will also be able to bring in their spouse and any unmarried children younger than age 21.

CAUTION
Congress might someday eliminate the F4 immigrant preference category for siblings. One of the proposals that Congress regularly brings up when discussing comprehensive immigration reform is to stop allowing U.S. citizens to petition for green cards for their siblings. The good news is that all family petitions before the law changes would likely be allowed to go forward. To be safe, if your sibling wishes to live in the U.S. permanently, it might be worthwhile to apply for a green card as soon as possible.

A. Who Counts as Your Brother or Sister

U.S. immigration laws contain specific definitions of who qualifies as a brother and sister in every family.

When it comes time to submit the paperwork for your brothers or sisters (the Form I-130 petition), you'll need to prove that they fit into one of these relationship categories. The sections below will explain the different possibilities and list the documentation that you'll need to provide as proof.

1. Legitimate Brother and Sister

If your mother and father were married and had other children, all of them are your legitimate brothers and sisters.

Be sure to add the following to your visa petition:
- ☐ your birth certificate, and
- ☐ your brothers' and sisters' birth certificates (to show that you have the same mother and father).

EXAMPLE: Your parents raised your cook's baby as their own child. But to file a petition for that baby, you would have to present proof that your birth certificate and the other child's birth certificate show the same father and mother. Of course, you cannot do this. There is no way you can petition for this person as your brother or sister.

The only way around this strict rule is for someone in the family to legally adopt the child before the child turns 16. If that is not possible, you will have to look for another way for the child to immigrate to the United States, such as an employment visa.

2. Half-Brother and Half-Sister

If you and another person have the same mother or father, but not both parents in common, that other person is your half-brother or half-sister.

It does not matter when the relationship of half-brother or half-sister occurred. As far as the immigration law is concerned, you can petition for them just as if they were your full-blooded brothers or sisters.

Be sure to add the following to your I-130 petition:

- ☐ your birth certificate, and
- ☐ your half-brothers' or -sisters' birth certificates (showing that you have one parent in common).

3. Stepbrother and Stepsister

If your mother or father has married somebody who had children from a previous marriage or relationship, the children of your stepfather or stepmother would be your stepbrothers and stepsisters.

However, for purposes of immigration into the United States, you can file a petition for them only on one condition: Your mother or father must have married your stepparent before your 18th birthday.

Be sure to include the following documents with your visa petition:

- ☐ your birth certificate
- ☐ the birth certificates of your stepbrothers or stepsisters, and
- ☐ the marriage certificate of your mother or father and your stepparent, as well as documents showing that any and all of their prior marriages ended by death, divorce, or annulment.

4. Adopted Brother and Adopted Sister

If your mother and father have adopted a child according to the laws of the state or country they are in, that child is your adopted brother or adopted sister. Or, you might have been adopted by parents who have other legitimate children of their own. Their children became your brothers and sisters when you were adopted into their family.

However, you can petition for your adopted sibling only if the adoption decree occurs before the 16th birthday of your adopted brother or sister if they are the petitioners, or before your own 16th birthday if you were the adopted child.

Be sure to include the following with your visa petition:

- ☐ the adoption decree, and
- ☐ your and your siblings' birth certificates to show you had the same parents.

B. Quick View of the Application Process

To get a green card as a brother or sister, the U.S. citizen must begin the process by submitting USCIS Form I-130, the petition used for family immigrants. We're going to assume that the person reading this is the U.S. citizen.

Form I-130 serves to prove to the immigration authorities that your siblings are truly and legally yours. After that petition is approved, your siblings must complete their half of the process (with your help, of course) by submitting immigrant visa applications and attending interviews, possibly with you accompanying them. Their applications serve to prove that not only do they qualify as the brothers or sisters of a U.S. citizen, but that they're otherwise eligible for U.S. permanent residence.

However, the details of when and how your brothers or sisters complete their half of the process depend on whether they are living overseas or in the United States, as described in Section D, below.

 TIP

Other people can petition for your brother and sister at the same time. There's no limit on the number of petitions that can be filed for a person—and it can be good to have more than one pending, in case one petitioner dies, for example. Let's say your parents are or become permanent U.S. residents—in that case, they could file visa petitions for your siblings (if your siblings are unmarried) in the second preference visa category, which moves much faster than the fourth preference. But you could file for your siblings as well, as a backup.

C. Detailed Instructions for the Application Process

Now we'll break the application process down into individual procedures, some of which will be covered in this chapter, and others in later chapters—we'll tell you exactly where to turn for your situation. We'll start by discussing the I-130 petition, which the U.S. citizen must always prepare to begin the process.

1. Preparing the Form I-130 Petition

To prepare the immigrant petition, the U.S. citizen will need to assemble and prepare the following:

☐ Form I-130, Petition for Alien Relative (available at www.uscis.gov/i-130; and you can download a completed sample at www.nolo.com/back-of-book/GRN.html).

☐ Copy of a document proving your U.S. citizenship, such as a birth certificate, naturalization certificate, or passport.

☐ Copy of your birth certificate.

☐ Copy of your immigrating brother or sister's birth certificate.

☐ Any other required proof of your relationship as detailed in Section A, above.

☐ If you or any of your brothers and sisters have changed your name from the name that appears on the birth certificate, a copy of a marriage certificate or court document that explains the change.

☐ Filing fee (currently $535, but double-check the USCIS website at www.uscis.gov). Don't send cash. Pay by check or money order to the U.S. Department of Homeland Security. Or pay by credit card, by including Form G-1450, Authorization for Credit Card Transaction, with your application. Place this on top of the other papers you send to USCIS.

☐ Form G-1145. This is optional, but filing it is a good idea, so that you'll receive an email and/or text notification from USCIS when your application has been accepted. (Get it at www.uscis.gov/g-1145.) Once USCIS sends you a receipt number, you can use that number to sign up to receive automatic email updates letting you know whenever mail is sent regarding your application.

TIP

Here's how to sign up for automatic email updates: Go to www.uscis.gov and click "Check your case status" on the home page. Then look for the "Click Here" under "Why sign up for an account?" and follow the prompts.

2. Submitting the Form I-130 Petition

After preparing and assembling all the items on the above list, the U.S. citizen should make a complete copy of everything (even the check or money order—this will be helpful if USCIS loses the application, which happens more often than it should). Then create an account and file online at www.uscis.gov, or send it to the USCIS lockbox indicated at www/uscis.gov/i-130 (the exact lockbox choice depends on where the U.S. citizen lives). The lockbox facility will forward it to the appropriate USCIS service center After USCIS receives the I-130 and determines that nothing was left out, it will send the U.S. citizen a receipt notice. In the upper left-hand corner will be a receipt number, which you can use to track the status of the petition at www.uscis.gov. There, you can also sign up to have USCIS send you automatic email updates about the petition.

Immigrant Story:
Reuniting Brother and Sister

Karl, from Sweden, became a U.S. permanent resident after winning the visa lottery. Although most of his family is uninterested in joining him in the United States, his twin sister, Karla, is extremely close to Karl and swears she'll never live more than 20 miles away from him.

Unfortunately, Karl must wait until he is a U.S. citizen to file an I-130 petition for Karla. As soon as his required five years of permanent residence have passed, he files a petition for naturalization. Within a year, Karl is a U.S. citizen. Now he petitions for Karla in the fourth preference category: But unfortunately, the wait in this category is over ten years long. During that time, Karla marries and has two children.

At last, Karla's Priority Date becomes current. After talking to her husband, they agree to give life in the U.S. a try. Based on Karl's original application, Karla and her husband and children all apply for and receive U.S. green cards.

Don't expect a final decision on the petition for many years, however. USCIS often decides to wait until a visa will soon be available to the immigrants before making a decision on the petition—which, in the case of brothers and sisters, could be decades away.

If you move during that wait, be sure to send your change of address to the USCIS office that has the petition. You can change your address online at www.uscis.gov or download Form AR-11.

D. What Happens After Filing Form I-130

And now, your brothers or sisters must sit back and wait. There is no way to hurry up the process—see Chapter 5 for details on the visa preference system, and for information on how to track your brothers'

or sisters' progress on the waiting list (using their Priority Dates).

Having an approved visa petition on file does not give your brothers or sisters any right to stay in the United States. In fact, it could cause problems when they apply for tourist or other temporary visas, because the State Department will know that they also have plans to stay in the U.S. permanently.

If your brothers or sisters are already in the United States, they cannot become permanent residents unless they remain in legal status during all the time they are in the country. They will probably have to return to their home country and proceed with consular processing (see Chapter 17), unless they're lucky enough to qualify for adjustment of status in the U.S. (see Chapter 16).

If your brothers or sisters are in the U.S. illegally, or have spent six or more months here illegally since 1997, they should talk to a lawyer about whether they'll be found inadmissible and barred from returning.

Once the immigrant visa is available to your brothers or sisters, they can extend the immigration privilege to their spouses and all unmarried children younger than 21 years of age at the same time, as "accompanying relatives."

CAUTION

A brother or sister who wants to come to the United States to visit during the waiting period must tell the U.S. consul when applying for a tourist or business visa about the approved I-130 petition. To be silent about this important fact will be looked upon as fraud in an immigrant visa file—and could mean a lost chance for a green card in the future. On the other hand, to be approved for the visa, the sibling will need plenty of evidence of intent to return home after a brief stay in the United States. ●

Refugees and Asylees

A. Who Qualifies..127

  1. What Is Persecution?..127

  2. What Do the Five Grounds Cover?..128

  3. Difference Between Asylees and Refugees..128

  4. Challenges in Proving Your Case...129

B. Who Is Barred From Qualifying..129

  1. Those Who Have Assisted in Persecution...129

  2. Those Who Threaten U.S. Safety or Security..130

  3. Those Who Have Resettled Elsewhere...130

  4. One-Year Deadline for Asylum Application...130

  5. Alternatives to Asylum...130

C. How to Apply for Refugee Status...131

  1. Filing the Application..131

  2. Refugee Interview..131

  3. Action on Your Refugee Application...131

  4. When Refugees Can Apply for a Green Card...132

  5. If Your Green Card Is Denied...132

D. How to Apply for Asylum...132

  1. Where to Request Asylum..132

  2. Asylum Applications at the Border or Port of Entry...132

  3. Preparing and Filing Your Asylum Application...135

  4. USCIS Asylum Offices—Where to File...135

  5. USCIS Interview...136

  6. Comments of the Department of State..137

  7. Decision by the Asylum Officer...137

E. If Your Asylum Application Is Denied...137

F. Asylees Can Bring Overseas Spouses and Children to the United States...........................138

G. Getting a Green Card After Asylum Approval or Refugee Entry...139

H. Revocation of Asylee Status..139

I. Temporary Protected Status (TPS)...140

  1. TPS Benefits..140

  2. Who Designates the TPS Countries...140

  3. Period of Protected Status..140

  4. Who Qualifies for TPS...140

5. Who Is Not Eligible for TPS...141

6. TPS Holders Shouldn't Depart the U.S. Without Advance Parole..................................141

7. How to Apply for TPS...141

8. Termination of TPS..142

J. Deferred Enforced Departure (DED)..142

Since the Refugee Act of 1980 was passed by the U.S. Congress, many people fleeing persecution from their own countries have found a permanent haven in the United States. Those who made it to the U.S. on their own applied for what's called "asylum." (An unlimited number of people can apply for asylum every year.) Others were granted refugee status and a right to come to the U.S. while they were overseas. The U.S. president limits the number of refugees who'll be accepted every year—in recent years, the maximum has usually been set at between 70,000 and 90,000 (though when Trump was in office, it went to a historic low of 18,000 per year). People fleeing natural disasters or war who do not receive this permanent protection may receive what is called "Temporary Protected Status" if they are in the U.S. when their country is designated. (See Section I, below.)

 SEE AN EXPERT

You will need more help than what's in this book. This chapter explains the basic procedures and describes the immigration forms required for people claiming status as refugees and asylees. However, the full legal process requires much more than filling out forms. You must present the facts of your case, in detail, in a convincing and compelling manner and if applying for asylum, you must also document the conditions in your country and make the legal argument that your facts qualify you for asylum. If, after reading this chapter, you think you might qualify as a refugee or an asylee, it is best to consult an experienced immigration lawyer or other immigration professional. Many nonprofit organizations offer free or low-cost services to people fleeing persecution. The current demand for services has overwhelmed many nonprofits and private attorneys, however, so it will be important to contact many agencies and attorneys in order to find someone to represent you. (See Chapter 24.)

A. Who Qualifies

To qualify as either a refugee or an asylee you must be unable or unwilling to return to your country because of actual persecution or a well-founded fear of persecution on account of your:

- race
- religion
- nationality
- membership in a particular social group, or
- political opinion.

1. What Is Persecution?

Persecution can include such things as threats, violence, torture, inappropriate and abusive imprisonment, or a failure by the government to protect you from such things.

You do not have to provide evidence that you would be singled out individually for persecution if you can establish the following:

- There is a pattern or practice in your country of persecuting groups of people similarly situated to you.
- You belong to or identify with the groups of people being persecuted so that your fear is reasonable.

The persecution may have been by your government, or you can claim asylum by showing that you were persecuted by a group that your government is unable or unwilling to control, or that you fear such persecution.

For example, these might include guerrilla groups, warring tribes, or organized vigilantes. Again, however, the persecution must have some political or social basis—for example, a member of a criminal network who comes after you just because you haven't paid him off is not persecuting you according to refugee law unless there is some more specific reason that you in particular are being targeted.

Although U.S. law does not list types of persecution, it does, in one section, specify that refugees and asylees can include people who have undergone or fear a "coercive population control program" (such as forced abortion or sterilization). This provision was directed mainly at mainland China.

2. What Do the Five Grounds Cover?

A large stumbling block for many asylum applicants is that they simply can't show a connection, or "nexus" between the persecution they suffered and one of the five grounds for having been targeted.

Political opinion is a commonly used ground, for example by journalists, activists, dissidents, and the like. Race, religion, and nationality are obvious ones for people in countries with a clear and obvious pattern of persecution of particular groups or tribes.

When other categories don't neatly fit, membership in a particular social group (PSG) can be a useful one to argue for. "PSG" is broadly understood as an identifiable group of people, who perhaps share a similar background, social status, lineage, experience (such as former property ownership or former gang or military conscription), habits, or color, which the government views as a threat. Their shared characteristic must be so fundamental to their individual identities that its members cannot—or should not be expected to—change it.

In recent years, the PSG category has allowed some applicants to gain protection based on having undergone or fearing cultural practices such as female genital cutting or forced marriage. Another social group recognized only in recent decades is one based on sexual orientation.

The definition of "membership in a particular social group" is, however, extremely country-specific, and constantly evolving. During the Trump administration, the Department of Justice attempted to narrow options for people relying on the PSG category. Since the Biden Administration took office, it has taken steps to reverse this. But you should definitely consult an attorney if a PSG category looks like your best bet.

3. Difference Between Asylees and Refugees

The difference between someone who can claim "asylee" status and someone who can claim "refugee" status has nothing to do with basic eligibility (both must meet the same standards). It simply refers to where you are when you file the application. To apply to be a refugee, you must be outside your country of nationality or country of residence but not within the borders of the United States. In addition, the U.S. president is empowered to recognize as a refugee any person who is still residing in their own country.

To apply to be an asylee, you must be either at the border or already inside the United States.

Although the standards are the same, there are major differences in the way refugee and asylee applications are processed. One difference is that each year the U.S. president designates certain countries and areas of the world as places from which the U.S. will fill the annual refugee quota. No such designation exists for asylees. So if a person seeks refugee status from a country that is not designated under that year's quota, a U.S. consular officer can't accept the application, but will instead refer the person to the United Nations High Commissioner for Refugees (the first stop for most would-be refugees in any case).

Also, the U.S. government prioritizes the processing of refugee applications based on several factors, including familial relationships in the U.S. and country of origin. No such prioritizing occurs with asylum applications, which are traditionally handled on a first-come, first-serve basis; although in recent years have been handled on a last-in, first-out basis.

4. Challenges in Proving Your Case

The biggest challenge in applying, especially for asylees, is proving that you were, in fact, persecuted or you reasonably fear that you might be persecuted in the future. You can't just say "I was persecuted" or "I'm afraid" and expect to be approved. But you probably didn't flee your country with a lot of documents to prove what happened, if indeed any such documents exist. Nevertheless, you are required to at least attempt to obtain corroborating evidence of your persecution. (That's a fairly new development in U.S. asylum law, based on the 2005 REAL ID Act.) If you are unable to do so, it is important to explain why and describe your attempts or explain that it is unavailable.

Succeeding with your application will depend a great deal on your ability to tell a detailed, compelling story of what occurred, including names, dates, places, and more. You'll probably need to write down the dates when everything you're talking about happened, and then read them several times to refresh your memory (unless you already have a better memory than most people, who probably couldn't tell you where they were on a particular date last week, much less last year).

Also realize that the official deciding your case is allowed to take into account your demeanor when testifying, as well as any previous statements you made while not under oath. This can create problems for people who, for example, have been culturally trained not to look anyone in the eye.

Looking someone straight in the eye is, in the U.S., considered a sign of honesty, and the judge or U.S. official could interpret looking at your hands or at the floor as a sign that you're lying.

If you underwent torture or suffered other medical or psychological stress, it might help to get a written evaluation by a doctor with expertise in this area who can verify that you suffer from the effects of these things.

You'll also need to show that your own story matches up with accounts by independent sources of what goes on in your country. A good asylum application, in particular, is accompanied by a thick stack of newspaper clippings, human rights reports, and more, all containing information about the kind of human rights violation you're describing. If, for example, you fled because local government officials were threatening to imprison you because you sent a letter to the editor protesting a political matter, you'd need to provide evidence that others who expressed similar political opinions have been imprisoned or threatened with prison. (And you'd definitely want to produce a copy of the newspaper's printing of your letter.)

B. Who Is Barred From Qualifying

A number of people are prohibited from becoming refugees or asylees in the United States.

1. Those Who Have Assisted in Persecution

The opportunity for refugee or asylum status is not open to anyone who has ordered, incited, assisted, or participated in the persecution of any other person owing to that person's race, religion, nationality, membership in a particular social group, or political opinion.

For example, this rule is often used to deny refugee status to military or police officials who assisted in persecuting minority or guerrilla groups (even though they might, indeed, fear for their life because members of those groups are seeking revenge).

2. Those Who Threaten U.S. Safety or Security

No one who has been convicted of a "particularly serious crime" and is therefore a danger to the community of the United States will be granted refugee or asylee status. There is no list of particularly serious crimes—the decision is made case by case, depending on the facts surrounding the crime. However, all "aggravated felonies" are considered particularly serious crimes—and, because of the immigration laws' strict definitions of aggravated felonies, some crimes that might have been called misdemeanors when prosecuted will be looked upon as aggravated felonies.

In addition, no person who has been convicted of a serious nonpolitical crime in a country outside the United States will be granted refugee or asylee status. However, people whose crimes were nonserious or political in nature may still qualify.

Furthermore, no person who has been involved in terrorist activity or who can reasonably be regarded as a threat to U.S. security will be granted refugee or asylee status.

As discussed in Chapter 4, the definition of who is a "terrorist" is broader than you might expect. It could, for example, be interpreted to cover people who have provided food or other "material support" to guerrillas or others trying to overthrow the government, or people who have given money to organizations whose aims the U.S. government believes are, at least in part, terrorist in nature.

Asylum applicants who provided material support under duress (for example, at gunpoint) can in some cases overcome this barrier.

3. Those Who Have Resettled Elsewhere

Would-be refugees or asylees who have become "firmly resettled" in another country will not receive protection in the United States. People are regarded as firmly resettled if they have been granted permanent residency, citizenship, or some other type of permanent resettlement in a nation other than the one from which they're seeking asylum. Other things taken into account are whether they enjoyed the same kind of rights and privileges as citizens of the nation in which they lived, in areas like housing, employment, permission to hold property, and rights to travel.

The Trump administration also made agreements with certain countries in Central America to designate them as "safe third countries." The idea was that if you pass through one of those countries and don't apply for asylum there, you won't be eligible to apply in the United States. However, these actions gave rise to lawsuits and court injunctions, with the result that they were mostly not in effect when this book went to print. However, a related agreement called the "Migrant Protection Protocols" ("MPP") or "Remain in Mexico" policy has so far survived litigation. It means that people who come to the U.S. border seeking asylum must typically wait in Mexico for their U.S. Immigration Court—a process which can take months and sometimes years.

4. One-Year Deadline for Asylum Application

In order to qualify for asylum, you must, by law, apply within one year of entering the United States. There are some exceptions if you have been in some other lawful immigration status (covered by a visa, for example) or if exceptional circumstances prevented you from applying (such as severe mental health issues) or if circumstances in your country recently changed and made it unsafe for you to return.

5. Alternatives to Asylum

Some people who don't qualify for asylum may qualify for Withholding of Removal or protection under the Convention Against Torture (also called "CAT"). These forms of protection require a higher likelihood of persecution and result only in employment authorization and permission to remain in the United States rather than eligibility to apply for a green card in the future. Nevertheless, they can be useful for some people who are otherwise barred from receiving asylum.

C. How to Apply for Refugee Status

If you are outside the U.S. and believe you qualify as a refugee, you cannot apply directly to the United States. You would need to first receive a referral to the U.S. Refugee Admissions Program (USRAP). USRAP accepts refugees based upon its priorities, which usually include cases identified by the United Nations High Commissioner for Refugees (UNHCR), a U.S. embassy, or a reputable nonprofit organization, and cases of people from countries with extreme conflict or who need family reunification.

This means your most likely (although challenging) starting point is to find and register with the UNHCR in the host country where you are living. If you are living in a refugee camp, there might be UNHCR representatives there to assist. If you're an urban refugee, look for the closest UNHCR office. Bring whatever identity documents you have, such as a driver's license, state-issued identification document, birth certificate, student identity card, or military book.

1. Filing the Application

If you get a referral for processing with the United States, you will next meet with officers of an intermediary organization called Refugee Support Center (RSC). It will prepare you to meet with a U.S. refugee officer, who will eventually interview you and decide whether to approve you to travel to the United States as a refugee. With the RSC officer's help, you will prepare and submit various forms and documents, including:

- Form I-590, Registration for Classification as Refugee
- documentation of persecution or a detailed affidavit supporting your request for classification as a refugee

- an assurance from a sponsor, which can be a responsible person or an organization, that employment and housing on entry will be arranged for you, and that you will be provided transportation to your final destination (usually accomplished through an umbrella organization called the American Council for Voluntary Agencies), and
- a medical examination report to ascertain that you are mentally sound and do not have a serious communicable disease.

2. Refugee Interview

After submitting your application, you will be interviewed by an overseas U.S. immigration officer who will decide whether you meet the definition of a refugee.

3. Action on Your Refugee Application

If your refugee application is denied, there is no appeal. You have no further recourse, because you are outside the United States and its legal mechanisms for judicial review.

If your refugee application is granted, you will have four months in which to enter the United States; and again, the RSC will help, in arranging your travel.

After your arrival, a Refugee Resettlement Agency, or RRA, will serve as your sponsor. It will send some-one to meet you at the airport and provide support during your first few months in the United States.

The RRA will provide you with cultural orientation and line you up with low-cost housing, employment options, and English language classes. (Asylees do not receive all these benefits.) You will be granted work authorization for one year as soon as you enter the United States. (After that year, you're expected to apply for U.S. lawful permanent residence, as described next.)

4. When Refugees Can Apply for a Green Card

After one year of physical presence as a refugee in the United States, during which you must not have violated certain laws or regulations, you, your spouse, and your children may apply for permanent residence (a green card).

If you are approved, the date of your permanent residence will be the date that you first arrived in the United States as a refugee. You will be eligible to apply for citizenship five years from that date.

5. If Your Green Card Is Denied

If you are found ineligible for U.S. permanent residence, removal proceedings may be started against you and your family. You will have to present your cases before an Immigration Judge. If this happens, consult with an immigration lawyer who specializes in removal cases. (See Chapter 24.)

D. How to Apply for Asylum

If you are already in the United States and interested in applying for asylum, you must fill out USCIS Form I-589 and explain your case to a USCIS asylum officer or an Immigration Judge.

1. Where to Request Asylum

You can request asylum in the following ways:

- by requesting it upon arrival at the U.S. border, or at a port of entry if you are an alien stowaway, a crewman, or a passenger seeking admission into the United States (remember that at many ports of entry along the southern border, asylum applicants were (as of early 2022) still being forced to wait in Mexico while awaiting a court date, under the MPP (described in Section B3, above))

- by presenting asylum as a defense at a removal hearing before the Immigration Judge, or
- by sending an application to USCIS, after which you'll be interviewed at a USCIS asylum office. You can apply for asylum even if you're in the U.S. without status—but if your application is not approved, it will be forwarded to an Immigration Judge for in-person hearings. If you cannot persuade the judge that you should be granted asylum, you could find yourself with an order of deportation and removal against you.

> **CAUTION**
> **Don't delay in preparing your asylum application (if you're already in the U.S. and not in removal proceedings).** The law says that applications for asylum must be submitted within one year of your U.S. entry. If you entered on a visa, USCIS policy is to allow you to proceed with your application within a period of "a reasonable time" after your visa-permitted stay expires (typically a maximum of six months). But this is up to the discretion of the USCIS officer deciding your case. Similarly, time during which you had Temporary Protected Status (discussed in Section I, below) does not count toward your one year.
>
> If you've already spent more than a year here, talk to an immigration attorney as soon as possible. Exceptions are possible in rare cases, based on changed country conditions, changes in personal circumstances that affect your eligibility for asylum, or other compelling reasons, such as having been younger than the age of 18 when you first arrived in the United States.

2. Asylum Applications at the Border or Port of Entry

If you arrive at a U.S. border or port of entry and the officer says your visa isn't valid or you can't be admitted to the U.S., you are supposed to be able to tell the CBP officer that you fear returning to your home country and plan to request asylum. The officer is supposed to refer you to another officer who is trained to understand, based on very little information, whether you have a believable and valid claim. Unfortunately, these officers do not act consistently, and there are many tragic reports of people being turned around and sent back to places where they were physically harmed.

Immigrant Story: Filing Beyond the One-Year Deadline

Roberto came to the United States alone, without a visa or documents, when he was 14 years old. Three years later, he came out as gay and became publicly and actively involved in gay rights causes. Then, during a demonstration, Roberto was arrested by U.S. immigration agents.

Because Roberto had already been in the U.S. for three years, his lawyer had to make a special request to the judge to extend the one-year deadline for filing for political asylum.

Fortunately, the judge agreed to hear the asylum application because: 1) Roberto had entered the U.S. as an unaccompanied minor, and therefore could not have been expected to know about the one-year asylum filing deadline, and 2) Roberto's circumstances had changed since he publicly came out as gay, which could make him subject to persecution in El Salvador.

Again, note that if you arrive at the southern border to seek asylum, you might have to wait in Mexico for your court hearing. There are nonprofit organizations that can help you. See www.alotrolado.org for help finding an immigration law clinic in Mexico.

If the officer denies your entry despite your request for asylum, you won't be allowed to reapply for U.S. entry for five years without a special waiver. You can, however, potentially avoid this bar by withdrawing your request for entry—in other words, by saying you changed your mind and don't want to enter the U.S. after all. But the border official has the option of deciding whether to allow you to withdraw your request for entry.

If the officer with whom you meet thinks you have a possible asylum case, you'll be placed in removal proceedings, where an Immigration Judge will consider your asylum claim (and any other relevant claims for immigration benefits you want to make). At this point, you'll have to prepare the application described in Section 3, below—and you should, if at all possible, get an attorney's help.

Don't Bow to Pressure From U.S. Officials to Give Up Asylum Case

U.S. Customs and Border Protection (CBP) officials reportedly don't always follow the law when encountering migrants along the U.S.–Mexico border. For example, they've reportedly falsely told migrants that there is "no right to asylum." If you have read this far and think that you meet the qualifications for asylum, you do have the right to request asylum at the U.S. border or another port of entry.

Be aware, however, that even if a U.S. asylum officer finds that your asylum claim has merit, you can be kept in immigration detention—a nicer word for prison—for weeks or months or be forced to wait in Mexico or possibly a third country, such as Guatemala, until you are able to see an Immigration Judge. In case you are detained within the U.S., it is good to carry the name of an immigration lawyer and friends and family members with legal status in the U.S., so that you can contact them for help to request that the Immigration Judge authorize your release upon payment of a bond.

Applying for a U.S. Work Permit

Some years ago, applicants for asylum were eligible for a work permit as soon as they submitted an I-589—but no more. Now, in order to apply for a work permit, you have to either win your case—which can take anywhere between a few months and several years—or be lucky enough to be left waiting for an unusually long time (365 days or more, as of the newest, Trump-era regulations) with no initial decision by the U.S. government on your application.

This obviously creates hardships for asylum applicants, who have to find money to live on and potentially pay their lawyers with, until the case is won. You may want to find help from lawyers at a nonprofit organization who, if you're financially needy, will charge low or no fees.

Also, the Trump-era rule changes lengthening the wait from 180 to 365 days are the subject of ongoing litigation, and could yet change. In fact, they were temporarily put on hold by a federal court in the case of *Casa de Maryland, Inc. v. Wolf*, pending the final outcome of the case. However, this court injunction currently affects only people who are members of CASA de Maryland (CASA) and the Asylum Seeker Advocacy Project (ASAP), although advocates have filed motions with the court to broaden the case to all asylum applicants. Contact those organizations before attempting to apply for a work permit to see whether it's still possible to become a member or otherwise benefit from this litigation.

While USCIS attempts to issue asylum decisions within 365 days, longer wait times are common. If the required number of days pass with no decision,

or if your application for asylum is approved, you'll need to take steps to apply for a work permit (formally known as an "Employment Authorization Document," or "EAD"). You can submit your application once your wait time reaches 150 days, but your work permit can't be granted until your wait time reaches 180 days. Any request for rescheduling or other delay on your part stops the accrual of days toward your ability to apply for a work permit. This is referred to as "stopping the clock." The clock will restart once the delay is resolved.

You can apply for a work permit once you are eligible by filling out Form I-765 (available on the USCIS website). Most of this form is self-explanatory. On Question 27, if you've been waiting for the required number of days or more with no decision, enter "(c)(8)." If your asylum application has already been approved, enter "(a)(5)." Follow the instructions on the form for what to include and where to send it.

Remember that any steps on your part that delay processing of your application can lead USCIS or the Immigration Court to "stop the clock" on your case. That means that if you request a rescheduled asylum interview, ask the Immigration Judge for more time to find an attorney or prepare your application, or do not accept the next available hearing date with the Immigration Judge, you could hurt your chances of getting a work permit before your asylum case is decided, but not doing so might hurt your chances for winning asylum if you aren't really ready to proceed. For more information about this tricky rule, consult an experienced immigration attorney.

3. Preparing and Filing Your Asylum Application

The following documents should be mailed to a USCIS regional service center, if you are not in removal proceedings, or submitted in person to the Immigration Judge (or to the clerk's window or mailed to the court), if you are already in proceedings:

☐ Form I-589, Application for Asylum and for Withholding of Removal—one original and one copy. (Available at www.uscis.gov/i-589; and you can download a completed sample at www.nolo.com/back-of-book/GRN.html.) Also make one copy of all supplementary documents. There is no filing fee for this form. Your spouse and children may be included in the application, as long as you supply an additional copy of your filled-out Form I-589 and attached documents for each. If you include your family members, they will also be granted asylum if you win or be placed in removal proceedings with you if you lose. (Regardless of whether you take the required steps to officially include them, you must provide their names and other requested information on your Form I-589.)

☐ One color passport-style photo of you and each family member applying with you. Write the person's name in pencil on the back.

☐ Copies (two) of your passports (if you have them) and any other travel documents (including from USCIS or the border authorities, such as a Form I-94 Arrival-Departure card)

☐ Copies (two) of documents to prove your identity, such as a birth certificate, driver's license, or national identity document ("cedula")

☐ Copies (two) of documents to prove the relationships between the family members applying, such as birth and marriage certificates

☐ Documentation (two copies) of your experience and the human rights situation in your country, showing why you fear to return, supported by your own detailed written statement

☐ If possible, also include statements (two copies) by any witnesses, doctors, friends, relatives, or respected leaders of your community, relevant news reports, or letters from people in your country.

> ⓘ CAUTION
> **Documents not in English must be translated.** You'll have to provide a word-for-word English translation of any document in another language. Any capable person can do this, but should, on their translation, add the following text at the bottom: "I certify that I am competent in both English and [*your language*], and that the foregoing is a full and accurate translation into English, to the best of my knowledge and ability." The person should add their signature and the date under this statement.

Not long after receiving your application, USCIS will call you in for a "biometrics" appointment to have your fingerprints taken (if you're older than age 14). This is to make sure that you don't have a record of criminal or terrorist acts and that you haven't applied for asylum before.

4. USCIS Asylum Offices—Where to File

There are four regional service centers that handle affirmative U.S. asylum applications. Where you file depends on where you live. To find out which service center to use, go to www.uscis.gov/i-589. If you are submitting your I-589 to USCIS rather than to the Immigration Court, it now requires you to fill in every field on the form even if the answer is just "none" or "not applicable." USCIS can reject the form if even one field is left blank.

5. USCIS Interview

> ⚠ **CAUTION**
> **USCIS currently faces a large backlog of asylum applications.** The wait for an interview at one of the eight U.S. asylum offices and suboffices can be years long. USCIS often states that it suspects people of applying for asylum solely to receive employment authorization (a temporary work permit, during the wait for an interview). USCIS thus rearranged its interview-scheduling priorities, so that they'll interview applicants in this order: 1) those whose interviews have been rescheduled; 2) those with applications pending 21 days or less; and 3) all other pending asylum applicants, in the order their I-589s were received, with the newest cases scheduled first. This means that recent asylum applicants are unlikely to receive work permits. If you have been awaiting an asylum interview, you might expect to wait quite a while longer, while people who are just now applying for asylum might have their cases decided before you. This fast-tracking makes it all the more important for new asylum applicants to get help from an experienced immigration attorney.

The purpose of your interview will be to determine whether you are eligible for asylum. Interviews can last anywhere from one to three hours.

If you aren't comfortable in English, you'll need to bring your own interpreter. This doesn't have to be a hired professional—a family member or friend will do. But if your friends and family aren't truly fluent in both English and your own language, it's worth spending the money on a professional. Many asylum interviews have gone badly because the interpreter wasn't fully competent and the asylum officer, not knowing of the problem, assumed that the applicant couldn't get their story straight. For example, we know of a case in which the interpreter repeatedly translated the Spanish word "padres" (which means "parents") as "father." The applicant was testifying about the death of both his parents in Guatemala, as stated on his Form I-589, and the interviewer became suspicious when the applicant suddenly appeared to be talking about only his father.

The asylum officer will also call a translating service (on contract with the U.S. government), to have a monitor listen in on the interview by telephone. The monitor's job is to interrupt if it appears that your interpreter is not being accurate.

Expect the interviewer to begin by reviewing some basic items in your application, such as your name, address, date and place of birth, and date of entry into the U.S.; then to move quickly into open-ended questions such as "Why are you afraid to return to your country?" The interviewer may interrupt you at any point. They may also ask questions you never expected, sometimes to test whether you are who you claim to be. For example, if you claim to be a member of a persecuted Christian minority in a Middle Eastern country, you might be asked questions about Christian doctrine. These interviewers are highly trained in the human rights situations of countries around the globe, and many have law degrees, so expect intelligent, probing questions.

Protection Under the U.N. Convention Against Torture

Even if you don't qualify for asylum, you may be protected from deportation by the United Nations Convention Against Torture. This prohibits deporting people who can show that they are more likely than not to suffer torture at the hands of their home country's government. The asylum application has a place to mention whether you feel you qualify for this protection. However, it won't get you a green card—it will just stop USCIS from deporting you. Whether USCIS will also allow you a work permit is up to its discretion.

Whether the interviewer will behave courteously is another matter. Many are sympathetic people who took this job because they're interested in human rights issues—others are government bureaucrats whose first concern is to ferret out cases of fraud. You won't be able to choose your interviewer. Women who have been raped or experienced similar trauma can, however, request a female interviewer by contacting the office in advance or including the request in writing when submitting the asylum application.

6. Comments of the Department of State

When USCIS receives your application, the officer may send a copy to the Bureau of Human Rights and Humanitarian Affairs (BHRHA) of the U.S. Department of State for comments on:

- the accuracy of the assertions on the conditions in the foreign country and the experiences described
- how an applicant who returned to the foreign country would be likely to be treated
- whether people who are similarly situated to the applicant are persecuted in the foreign country and the frequency of such persecution, and
- whether one of the grounds for denial might apply to the applicant.

However, the process usually goes faster than the BHRHA's ability to provide comments. Almost no one receives these comments anymore.

7. Decision by the Asylum Officer

After interviewing you, the asylum officer has discretion to approve or deny your application for asylum. However, you won't be told the decision that day. You might have to return to the USCIS Asylum Office at an appointed time weeks later to pick up your decision from the front desk. Or, as is more likely since the COVID pandemic began, the decision might be mailed to you.

If you're approved, you'll be given a document stating this. Take good care of this document, and make copies to keep in safe places. You'll need it to apply for your Social Security card, work permit, and green card (permanent resident status) in a year.

CAUTION
Need to travel after you've been granted asylum? Don't leave the U.S. without first obtaining a refugee travel document allowing you to return. The application is made on Form I-131; see www.uscis. gov/i-131 for the form and instructions. Allow several weeks for your fingerprinting appointment and possibly several additional months for the travel document to be approved. Also check the website to see the projected processing time, and take into account whether you will need any visas for your trip, to give yourself enough time to apply for them in advance. Do not return to the country that persecuted you—this will be taken as a sign that you aren't really in danger there after all. You then might not be allowed to return to the United States. If you feel you have no choice but to return to your home country, talk to an experienced immigration attorney before you leave. Even after receiving your green card, you should not travel to your home country; not even if conditions have changed and it is now safer for you to return. Your safest bet is to not travel to your home country until you have naturalized and become a U.S. citizen.

E. If Your Asylum Application Is Denied

If you are not approved for asylum, your case will be referred to the Immigration Court. There, you will have another chance to have your asylum case considered; this time, by an Immigration Judge. You can also ask the judge for Withholding of Removal or protection under the Convention against Torture. It is very important to get an attorney to help you.

CAUTION

Don't miss the court hearing! If, after you have been notified orally and in writing of the time, place, and date of the Immigration Court hearing, you fail to attend, the judge will order you deported (in your absence) and you won't be able to adjust your status, obtain voluntary departure, or be granted cancellation of removal for a period of ten years. You will be subject to immediate removal if ICE finds you.

Only "exceptional circumstances beyond your control," such as your own serious illness or the death of an immediate relative, are considered to be valid excuses for failing to appear before the Immigration Judge. Your lawyer will need to file a motion to reopen the order of your deportation. Even if your circumstances don't seem to qualify for reopening, consult with an attorney in case there is another argument to be made.

If the Immigration Judge denies your case, you are free to appeal the case to the Board of Immigration Appeals (BIA) and from there to the federal circuit court of appeals. In the meantime, while your case or your appeal is pending, you are able to remain in the United States. If you have already received work authorization, it will continue to be granted for one year at a time. If you haven't, you'll have to continue living without a work permit. Be sure to file your notice of appeal within 30 days of the denial. The BIA must receive your notice within those 30 days, so don't leave it to the last minute.

Some people turn around after they've been denied asylum and try to apply for it again. This won't work. First of all, it's not allowed, and second, USCIS has your fingerprints on file and will check them, so even if you change your name, you'll get caught.

F. Asylees Can Bring Overseas Spouses and Children to the United States

If you're granted asylum and you have a husband, wife, or unmarried children who were younger than 21 when you applied for asylum, and they are still living in the country that persecuted you, you have the right to request asylum for them, too. But you must act within two years of when you're granted asylum, or they'll miss their chance. (When you're a permanent resident or U.S. citizen you can petition for them, but this takes years). No other relatives are eligible—you cannot, for example, bring your parents or grandchildren.

CAUTION

Getting married after you've won asylum won't do it. As an asylee, you can bring in your spouse only if the two of you were already married when you were granted asylum. If, however, your wife gave birth to a child after you won asylum, you can bring the child in so long as it was in the womb when you were granted asylum.

In order to bring your spouse and children to join you, prepare and assemble the following (using separate forms and documents for each person):

- ☐ Form I-730, Refugee/Asylee Relative Petition, available at www.uscis.gov/i-730. (You can download a completed sample at www.nolo.com/back-of-book/GRN.html.)
- ☐ a copy of the document granting you asylum
- ☐ a clear photograph of your family member
- ☐ a copy of proof of the relationship between you and the person you're applying for— a marriage certificate for your spouse, or a birth certificate for your child (or if it's an adoption certificate, the adoption must have occurred before the child was 16); and include a marriage certificate in your child's petition if you're the child's father or stepparent; and
- ☐ if your child is adopted, include evidence that the child has been living in your legal custody for the last two years.

There is no filing fee. For more detailed information, see the USCIS instructions that come with Form I-730. After you've finished preparing the applications, make a complete copy for your records and send it the USCIS service center indicated on the USCIS website. If you were granted asylee status in court and your spouse or children were in the U.S. but not in removal proceedings with you, you can also use this form to apply for asylee status for them.

Despite your status as an asylee, be aware that your family members can be denied entry to the U.S. if they've committed serious nonpolitical crimes, been affiliated with terrorism, or otherwise violated the provisions of the immigration law in I.N.A. § 208(b)(2), 8 U.S.C. § 1158.

> **CAUTION**
> **Your children must remain unmarried until they enter the United States.** Warn them not to get married, or they'll ruin their chance to claim asylum and join you. Of course, turning 21 is something your children have no control over. Fortunately, a law called the "Child Status Protection Act" ("CSPA") protects them. The law says that a child who was younger than age 21 when you filed your Form I-589 with USCIS will still be considered 21 years of age when you file the Form I-730 and the child comes to claim U.S. asylee status.

G. Getting a Green Card After Asylum Approval or Refugee Entry

One year after your asylum application has been approved, or after entering the U.S. as a refugee, you and your family may apply to become U.S. permanent residents. In fact, it's a legal requirement for refugees. (Asylees can wait more than a year, but it's safest to apply as soon as you can.) You are eligible for a green card if you:

- have been physically in the United States for 365 days after being granted asylum or entering as a refugee— although the 365 days do not have to be consecutive
- continue to be a refugee or asylee or the spouse or child of a refugee or asylee (as defined in Section A, above; if conditions in your country have improved a lot, see an attorney), and
- have not violated certain U.S. criminal laws.

If you meet these criteria, it's time to prepare and submit an application for adjustment of status, as described in Chapter 16. You can skip the sections of that chapter that discuss whether or not you're truly eligible to use the adjustment of status procedure—as an asylee or refugee, you are. You also don't need to worry about proving that you entered the U.S. legally, like some applicants do. And unlike most other adjustment of status applicants, you need not submit an Affidavit of Support (Form I-864), because you are not subject to the public charge rules.

Again, there is no deadline for asylees to submit an application for adjustment of status. Asylee status is indefinite. However, the U.S. government has the authority to review your asylee status from time to time to see if you are still eligible and whether conditions in your home country have improved to such an extent that it is no longer dangerous for you to return. Although the government does not often conduct such reviews, your safest course of action is to apply for permanent resident status as soon as you can.

H. Revocation of Asylee Status

If your country's political situation has improved or changed so that you are no longer in danger of being persecuted, USCIS may revoke your asylee status. However, it must first notify you and then convince either an asylum officer or an Immigration Judge that you either:

- no longer have a well-founded fear of persecution upon your return, due to a change of conditions in your country
- were guilty of fraud in your application so that you were not eligible for asylum when it was granted, or
- have committed any of the acts that would have caused your asylum application to be denied—such as a serious felony.

I. Temporary Protected Status (TPS)

Temporary Protected Status (TPS) is a legal category that was fashioned by the U.S. Congress to respond to situations when natural disasters, such as earthquakes, volcanic eruptions, or tidal waves occur, or when war is being waged in a foreign country. It is a form of safe haven for foreign nationals living in the U.S. whose country is in turmoil. Congress responded with this humanitarian gesture to avoid deportations to countries where people's personal safety is threatened or in which normal living conditions are substantially disrupted. It does not, however, lead to permanent residence or a green card.

1. TPS Benefits

Temporary Protected Status offers several short-term benefits:

- **Stay of deportation.** You will not be placed into removal proceedings. If a removal case is already underway, you can claim TPS, and the proceedings will be paused until the end of the TPS period.
- **Work authorization.** You will receive work authorization as long as the TPS is in effect.
- **Temporary Treatment (TT).** When you file for TPS, so long as your application is complete with such documentary proof as a birth certificate showing that you are a national of the designated country, you'll be granted a stay of deportation immediately and work authorization if the approval of TPS is significantly delayed, and they won't be taken away until either the TPS designation is ended or your application is denied.

2. Who Designates the TPS Countries

The U.S. attorney general, working through USCIS, will designate the countries whose nationals deserve

Temporary Protected Status. The following situations may give rise to this designation:

- ongoing armed conflict and civil war that pose a serious threat to the lives and personal safety of deported aliens who are nationals of that country
- earthquakes, floods, droughts, epidemics, or other environmental disasters, resulting in a substantial disruption of living conditions and an inability to handle the return of its nationals, in a foreign country that has requested a TPS designation, or
- extraordinary and temporary conditions in the foreign country preventing its nationals in the United States from returning safely to their country.

3. Period of Protected Status

The U.S. attorney general will designate the initial period of protection as not less than six months or more than 18 months. Sixty days before the end of the period, the attorney general will review the conditions of the foreign country to determine whether to end the TPS, or to extend it for a period of six, 12, or 18 months.

The termination or the extension will be published in the *Federal Register.*

4. Who Qualifies for TPS

Nationals or native-born citizens of the designated foreign countries may apply for Temporary Protected Status if they:

- have been physically present in the United States continuously since the date of the designation
- have continuously resided in the United States since a certain date
- register for TPS during a registration period of not less than 180 days, and
- pay the filing fee.

TPS-Designated Countries

At the time this book went to print, citizens from the countries on the list below were eligible for TPS. However, this list changes rapidly, so keep your eyes on the news and USCIS website at www.uscis.gov:

- Afghanistan, for 18 months beginning approximately April 2022
- Burma (Myanmar), through November 25, 2022
- Cameroon (for 18 months beginning on a date to be announced, in approximately May, 2022)
- El Salvador, Haiti, Honduras, Nepal, and Nicaragua (terminated, but then extended due to a lawsuit until December 31, 2022)
- Somalia (extended through March 17, 2023)
- Sudan (through December 31, 2022 for people who registered under an earlier designation; plus a new 18-month allowance until October 19, 2023 for people who register in 2022 under the latest designation)
- South Sudan (through November 3, 2023)
- Syria (through September 30, 2022)
- Ukraine (through October 9, 2023)
- Venezuela (through September 9, 2022)
- Yemen (extended through March 3, 2023)

Liberians used to have TPS and then something called "DED," extended through June 22, 2022. Congress also said that any Liberian who had lived in the U.S. since November 20, 2014 could apply for permanent residence even if they didn't have TPS or DED in the past. This was called the "Liberian Refugee Immigration Fairness" ("LRIF") Act. However, the application period ended December 20, 2021.

5. Who Is Not Eligible for TPS

TPS is not available to nationals or native-born citizens of a designated foreign country who are outside the United States. In addition, even if you are already in the United States, your application for TPS will be denied if you:

- have been convicted of any felony, or at least two misdemeanors, in the United States
- have ordered, incited, assisted, or participated in persecuting any person
- have committed a serious nonpolitical crime outside the United States, or
- are regarded as a terrorist or danger to the security of the United States.

6. TPS Holders Shouldn't Depart the U.S. Without Advance Parole

If a person who has been granted TPS leaves the United States without getting advance permission from USCIS, the agency may treat the TPS status as having been abandoned.

For humanitarian reasons, USCIS recognizes emergency and extenuating circumstances, and may grant something called "Advance Parole," which is permission to depart for a brief and temporary trip without affecting one's TPS. Use Form I-131 to apply for this. It is a good idea to consult with an immigration attorney or accredited representative before traveling abroad with Advance Parole.

7. How to Apply for TPS

The following forms should be sent to the USCIS address indicated for your specific country on the Form I-821 instructions. The forms include:

- Form I-821, Application for Temporary Protected Status. It's available at www.uscis.gov/i-821. The filing fee is $50 for your initial registration, plus $85 for fingerprinting if you are age 14 or older. There is no filing fee to renew the I-821, but if you are older than 14 years of age and you want to renew your work permit, you must pay the I-765 fee again (currently $410) and the fingerprinting fee ($85). Sometimes, the Department of Homeland Security issues an automatic extension of expiring work permits for TPS beneficiaries from specific countries. For an up-to-date list and more information, go to www.uscis.gov, and search for "Temporary Protected Status."

- Form I-765, Employment Authorization Application (from www.uscis.gov/i-765). Even if you do not want a work permit, you must submit this form for biographic purposes; but you do not need to pay a separate filing fee. If you do want to receive a work permit, submit this form with the fee (currently $410). Work authorization, effective until TPS is ended, is granted for the TPS period. The fee must be paid each time.

- For initial applications, copies of documents showing your physical presence during the period designated: for example, passport used in entering the United States, for example, Form I-94 (Arrival-Departure Record), rent receipts, school records, hospital records, pay stubs, banking records, employment records, and affidavits of responsible members of your community (such as a religious officer, school director, or employer).

- For initial TPS applications, two kinds of documents showing personal identity and nationality: such as a birth certificate, a passport, driver's license, employment ID, or school ID.

- For initials and renewals, two photographs, passport style.

- For renewals, a copy of your expiring work permit and previous approval notices.

8. Termination of TPS

After the U.S. government decides that the situation in the foreign country has improved and there is no longer any reason to retain the Temporary Protective Status for its nationals, the government will announce that the TPS designation will be terminated. Your work authorization will continue until the end date.

If you do not have any other legal right to be in the United States, you are expected to leave at that time. However, if other immigration options are available to you, you might be able to pursue them rather than leave. Consult with an immigration attorney or accredited representative to see if you have any other immigration options available to you.

J. Deferred Enforced Departure (DED)

Another benefit that might be available for people from countries that have political or civil conflicts is known as "Deferred Enforced Departure" ("DED"). This is a temporary form of relief that allows designated individuals to work and stay in the United States for a certain period of time, during which the authorities will not try to deport them.

At the time this book went to print, only Liberia was designated under the DED program, through June 30, 2022.

The law makes certain people ineligible for DED, including those who have committed certain crimes, persecuted others, or have been previously deported, excluded, or removed from the United States.

If you are already in removal proceedings, you may ask the Immigration Judge to defer action on your case based on DED if your country becomes designated. If your case is already up on appeal after a decision by an Immigration Judge at the Board of Immigration Appeals, you should receive notice automatically about the administrative or temporary closure of your proceeding. ●

Military Veterans and Enlistees

A. Which Military Members Qualify to Apply for Citizenship Without
   a Green Card 144

B. Which Military Members Qualify for U.S. Permanent Residence 145

   1. Veterans' Eligibility for U.S. Permanent Residence..................................145

   2. Enlistees on Active Duty and U.S. Permanent Residence 145

   3. Iraqi or Afghan Translators for U.S. Armed Forces 146

   4. How to File for Permanent Residence...146

   5. Applying for Citizenship After Getting a Green Card...............................147

The immigration laws recognize the patriotism and valor of foreign nationals who have defended the U.S. Constitution by serving in the military. Some veterans can jump directly to becoming U.S. citizens. Others have a path to a U.S. green card.

A. Which Military Members Qualify to Apply for Citizenship Without a Green Card

If you have honorably and actively served the U.S. military in a time of war or conflict, you are exempt from all green card requirements and might qualify for immediate citizenship. (See I.N.A. § 329, 8 U.S.C. § 1440.) It's possible your military installation has a designated point of contact to help you through this process, so be sure to check into that. This special benefit depends, however, on the war or conflict in which you fought as a member of the U.S. Armed Forces. It includes:

- World War II, specifically between September 1, 1939 and December 31, 1946
- the Korean War, specifically between June 25, 1950 and July 1, 1955
- the Vietnam War, specifically between February 28, 1961 and October 15, 1978
- the Persian Gulf Conflict, specifically between August 2, 1990 and April 11, 1991, and
- the "War on Terrorism" (also called "Operation Enduring Freedom"), which began on September 11, 2001 and will end on a date to be determined by the U.S. president. (See 8 C.F.R. § 329.2.)

It also depends on where you were when you enlisted. Your enlistment, reenlistment, extension of enlistment, or induction must have been in the United States, the Canal Zone, American Samoa, or Swains Island, or on board a public vessel owned or operated by the U.S. for noncommercial service.

What's more, the government has started requiring that active duty recruits actively serve for at least 180 days and undergo various background and security checks before even beginning basic training, much less being approved for citizenship. (In past years, one could apply right after basic training.) This matter is the subject of lawsuits, so check for updates on the Nolo website or consult an attorney for the latest.

You'll need to submit an application for naturalization in order to become a citizen. This will consist of Form N-400, Application for Naturalization; and Form N-426, Request for Certification of Military or Naval Service (certified by the military; or if you've already left the military, a copy of your DD Form 214, Certificate of Release or Discharge from Active Duty, or NGB Form 22, National Guard Report of Separation and Record of Service). You will need to undergo a security check, including providing fingerprints (biometrics) if USCIS doesn't already have yours on file. Depending on what's available where you are living, you might need to go to your local military police or perhaps a U.S. consulate or USCIS application support center.

As a member of the military, you are exempt from paying the usual application fee.

You'll ultimately need to attend an interview and pass a test of your knowledge of the English language and U.S. civics and government. But you won't have to worry about many of the other U.S. citizenship requirements, including your age and your period of residence within the United States.

If you're eventually separated from the Armed Forces under other-than-honorable conditions before you've served honorably for a total of five years, your citizenship can be revoked (taken away).

B. Which Military Members Qualify for U.S. Permanent Residence

If you were outside the U.S. when you enlisted in the military, or for other reasons don't qualify for immediate U.S. citizenship, you might still be able to apply for a U.S. green card, under the employment-based classification of "special immigrant."

The spouse and minor children younger than 21 years of age who are joining or accompanying the veteran or enlistee are also entitled to immigrant visas.

In order to have enlisted outside the U.S., you must be in a country that has a treaty with the United States allowing this.

Immigrant Story: Major Diaz Becomes a U.S. Citizen

Reynaldo Diaz came to the U.S. from Mexico as a four-year-old, with his family. A cousin helped smuggle them across the border near San Diego. After completing high school in the U.S., Reynaldo decided to join the U.S. Army. He was sent to serve in Iraq, where he received many awards and commendations.

As soon as Reynaldo learns of the law permitting him to apply for citizenship, he talks to a superior officer, who helps him fill out the paperwork. Reynaldo attends his naturalization interview while at home in Kansas on leave, and passes the test easily.

As a U.S. citizen, he can now petition for residency for his parents, brothers, and sisters.

RESOURCE

You can call or email for advice. Members of the U.S. military and their families stationed around the world can call USCIS for help with immigration services and benefits by using a dedicated, toll-free telephone help line, at 877-CIS-4MIL (877-247-4645). Alternatively, you can email militaryinfo@uscis.dhs.gov.

1. Veterans' Eligibility for U.S. Permanent Residence

An alien veteran of the U.S. Armed Forces can apply for permanent residence if they:

- have served honorably
- have served on active duty
- have served after October 15, 1978
- are recommended for a special immigrant visa by the U.S. Armed Forces or Navy officer under whom they serve
- originally enlisted outside the United States
- have served for an aggregate of 12 years, and
- were honorably discharged when separated from the service.

2. Enlistees on Active Duty and U.S. Permanent Residence

An alien enlistee in the U.S. Armed Forces can apply for permanent residence if they:

- originally enlisted outside the United States for six years
- are on active duty when applying for adjustment of status under this law
- have reenlisted for another six years, giving a total of 12 years active duty service, and
- are recommended for a special immigrant visa by the U.S. Armed Forces or Navy officer under whom they serve.

A Break for Illegal Workers

Because of this special law for alien members of the U.S. Armed Forces, the Immigration and Nationality Act allows the applicant—and spouse and children—to get permanent residence even if they might have worked illegally in the United States.

3. Iraqi or Afghan Translators for U.S. Armed Forces

In 2008, Congress created a new program to bring Afghan and Iraqi translators and interpreters who worked with the U.S. military to the United States. (See the National Defense Authorization Act Section 1059.) Under this program, you may apply for a U.S. green card if you are a national of Iraq or Afghanistan and you:

- worked directly with the U.S. Armed Forces as a translator for at least 12 months
- received a letter of recommendation from a general or flag officer in your unit, and
- have passed background checks and screening.

Your application process will be similar to the one described below, except that you'll need to provide documents proving the above three things (instead of the certifications required of other members of the military). Also, you must submit a petition (Form I-360) to the USCIS Nebraska Service Center to start the process; you can't combine it with an adjustment of status application even if you're in the United States. You will not need to pay a filing fee.

(!) **CAUTION**

Afghan and Iraqi interpreters face unique challenges obtaining green cards. What was supposed to be a program to fast-track permanent residence for people who served alongside military personnel in armed conflict at great peril to themselves now has many applicants stuck in "administrative processing" (a bureaucratic term for background checks). This was naturally made worse by the 2021 U.S. withdrawal from Afghanistan. Some visa-eligible persons were paroled into the U.S. and might still be able to obtain a Special Immigrant Visa. But with the U.S. Embassy in Kabul having closed operations, others will have a more difficult time. The Biden Administration is still attempting to deal with this situation.

4. How to File for Permanent Residence

To file for permanent residence as a special immigrant, you must complete and file the following forms. The filing fee is $435 (2021 figure), but Afghan and Iraqi translator applicants need not pay the fee. Others must pay either by money order or certified check made payable to U.S. Department of Homeland Security or by credit card, using Form G-1450, Authorization for Credit Card Transaction (preferably placed on top of the paperwork you send USCIS). Submit the following:

☐ Form I-360, Petition for Amerasian, Widow(er), or Special Immigrant (available at www.uscis.gov/i-360; and you can download a completed sample at www.nolo.com/back-of-book/GRN.html; note that it includes only the pages relevant to veterans and

☐ Form N-426, Request for Certification for Military or Naval Service

☐ certification of past active duty status of 12 years for the veteran, or certified proof of reenlistment after six years of active duty service for the enlistee, issued by an authorized Armed Forces official, and

☐ your birth certificate to show that you are a national of the country that has an agreement with the United States allowing the enlistment of its nationals in the U.S. Armed Forces.

These papers have to be submitted to either:

- the USCIS office having jurisdiction over the veteran or enlistee's current residence or intended place of residence in the United States, or
- the overseas USCIS office having jurisdiction over the residence abroad.

If you are in the U.S., you may (unless you're an Afghan or Iraqi translator, as described in Section B3, above) apply directly for adjustment of status (see Chapter 16), and so may your spouse and your children younger than 21 years of age. Form I-360 and accompanying materials should be included with the rest of the adjustment of status application.

If your spouse and children are outside the United States, you may file Form I-824, Application for Action on an Approved Application or Petition, to be sent to the U.S. consulate where they will apply for immigrant visas as derivative relatives of a special immigrant.

> ⓘ **CAUTION**
> **USCIS will automatically revoke the petition and bar an enlistee from getting a green card who:**
> - fails to complete the period of reenlistment, or
> - receives other than an honorable discharge.
>
> The enlistee's spouse and children will also be barred from getting green cards. If any of them already have green cards, USCIS will begin proceedings to have them taken away.

5. Applying for Citizenship After Getting a Green Card

If you got your green card as a veteran or an enlistee, you're only a few short steps away from being eligible for naturalized U.S. citizenship. Although most people must wait five years after getting their green card, you are immediately able to apply for citizenship.

Servicepeople who got their green cards in other ways than through their military service can apply for citizenship as soon as they've served honorably for one year; it doesn't matter how long they've had the green card for—one day is enough. However, if they've been discharged, the discharge must have been honorable, and they must apply for citizenship within six months of the discharge date.

To file for naturalization, you must file the following forms and documents with USCIS:

- ☐ Form N-400, Application for Naturalization
- ☐ Form N-426, Request for Certification for Military or Naval Service
- ☐ a copy of your green card
- ☐ two photographs, passport style.

There is no fee for filing a naturalization application for servicemembers filing for citizenship on the basis of their military service.

> 📖 **RESOURCE**
> **Want complete information on the application process for U.S. citizenship, including special exceptions applying to members of the military?** See *Becoming a U.S. Citizen: A Guide to the Law, Exam & Interview*, by Ilona Bray (Nolo). ●

Cancellation of Removal:
Do Ten Illegal Years Equal One Green Card?

A. Applying in Court Proceedings 150

B. Who Qualifies for Cancellation of Removal 150

C. Who Is Not Eligible for Cancellation 151

D. Preparing a Convincing Case 151

    1. Proof of Good Moral Character 151

    2. Proof That You Stayed in the U.S. Ten Years 152

    3. Proof of Hardship 152

E. How to File 154

F. Approving Your Application 155

G. Additional Types of Cancellation of Removal 155

    1. Permanent Residents 155

    2. Abused Spouse or Child 155

Immigration law does provide a green card as a form of relief from removal (deportation) to a person who has been in the United States for more than ten years. However, the process can normally be started only if you're already in Immigration Court proceedings, facing removal from the United States. This relief is called "cancellation of removal," formerly known as "suspension of deportation." When granted, a undocumented foreign national immediately becomes a lawful permanent resident —and receives a green card soon after the court hearing.

This area of immigration law has changed drastically over the years. Some people can still qualify under more flexible, pre-1996 rules; others will qualify only if they meet later, more restrictive rules.

A. Applying in Court Proceedings

You cannot file an application to begin cancellation of removal directly with USCIS, as you can with other immigration applications. This process is available only when you are already in Immigration Court (EOIR) proceedings, as a defense against deportation and removal. (The only exception to this rule is for people who qualify for benefits under the Nicaraguan Adjustment and Central American Relief Act.)

Unlike the other kinds of applications discussed in this book, the decision on your case will be made by the Immigration Judge. USCIS will not be part of the decision making. However, a branch of the Department of Homeland Security (DHS) called Immigration and Customs Enforcement (ICE) will serve as "opposing counsel" in your case.

Being in removal proceedings means that DHS has learned of your illegal status and has served you with a summons called a "Notice to Appear" or "NTA" (once called an "Order to Show Cause"). The NTA gives you the time, date, and place to appear for a court hearing on whether or not you should be deported.

If DHS has not started removal proceedings against you, and you want to apply for cancellation of removal, your sole possibility is to turn yourself in to DHS—and it might then start removal proceedings against you. But consult an experienced immigration attorney before taking this risk.

B. Who Qualifies for Cancellation of Removal

If you have been in the United States for ten years or more and you are of good moral character, and your deportation would cause hardship to certain close family members who are either U.S. citizens or permanent residents, there is a chance that your application for cancellation of removal will be granted.

SEE AN EXPERT

It is very risky to ask to be placed in removal proceedings solely to request cancellation. If you are contemplating turning yourself in to DHS, discuss your situation first with an immigration attorney who specializes in cancellation issues or with an immigration law clinic or a group that specializes in counseling on immigration matters. The attorney can help evaluate whether you qualify and the chances of DHS's cooperating with you. Too often, DHS just lets applications sit in its files for years.

CAUTION

Watch out for scammers. Unscrupulous immigration practitioners (also sometimes called "notarios") have spread a myth that after you live in the U.S. for ten years, you automatically qualify for permanent residence. That's wrong: There's no "ten-year green card" you can apply to USCIS for. Rather, ten years' continuous presence in the U.S. provides the possibility of deportation relief, which could result in a green card. But this relief is totally discretionary. Some Immigration Judges won't grant cancellation of removal except in the most dire of circumstances, while others are more generous.

C. Who Is Not Eligible for Cancellation

A number of people are not allowed to apply for cancellation of removal. They include:

- aliens who entered the United States as crewmen after June 30, 1964
- J-1 visa holders who have not fulfilled a two-year home country residency requirement (if they are required to do so), and those who came to the U.S. to receive graduate medical education or training
- certain categories of inadmissible aliens, including those who the U.S. government believes are coming to the U.S. to engage in espionage, unlawful activities to overturn the U.S. government, or terrorist activities, and those who have been members of totalitarian or some communist parties
- people who are deportable for offenses involving national security, espionage, or terrorism
- people who have participated in persecuting others
- certain people previously given relief from removal or deportation
- people who have been convicted of certain crimes involving morally bad conduct or illegal drugs
- people convicted of crimes involving morally bad conduct in the five years after being admitted to the U.S. if the crimes are punishable by a sentence of one year or more (regardless of the sentence actually handed down)
- people who have been convicted of certain offenses involving failure to comply with registration or change of address requirements, or certain offenses involving document fraud, and
- people convicted of aggravated felonies. This includes murder, rape, sexual abuse of a minor, illegal trafficking in drugs or firearms, money laundering, crimes of violence, some theft crimes, burglary, or other offenses, including some misdemeanors. If you have been convicted of a crime, get advice from an experienced attorney.

D. Preparing a Convincing Case

If you decide that your best approach is to file for cancellation of removal, know that you will have some difficult times ahead. Nationwide, Immigration Judges are not allowed to grant more than 4,000 cancellation of removal cases per year, so applicants are to some degree competing against each other to show who is most worthy of this relief— usually by showing whose family will be most devastated by their removal from the United States.

What's more, if you appear in court after the 4,000 annual limit has been reached for that year, the Immigration Judge is likely to continue (postpone) your case until the following year, perhaps without holding a full hearing. Or the judge might allow the hearing to go forward but, if inclined to grant your case, "reserve judgement" (put off issuing a decision) until a green card becomes available. Your first task will be to find a lawyer. (See Chapter 24 for advice on finding a good one.) Together, you will figure out what kinds of evidence you can submit to show that you should be granted cancellation of removal. The following three sections will get you started.

1. Proof of Good Moral Character

You must show that you've been a person of good moral character for at least the last ten years. You might be able to secure a certificate of good conduct from your local police station. This certificate will attest that, according to computer records, you have never been in trouble with the police. Although DHS will also send your fingerprints to the Federal Bureau of Investigation in Washington, D.C., submitting your own record from the local police will help prove to the court that you are a person of good moral character.

You can also submit declarations from relatives, friends, and community members verifying that you have participated in religious institutions, volunteered at schools or other civic places, or in any other way demonstrated that you are a good person.

If you have committed any serious crime during the ten years you were in the United States, the Immigration Judge could find that you lack good moral character. Ten years must pass from the time you committed the crime until the time you can apply for a suspension of deportation. However, committing certain serious crimes will make you ineligible forever.

2. Proof That You Stayed in the U.S. Ten Years

You must show also that you have lived in the United States continuously for at least ten years. Copies of your passport and I-94 (Arrival-Departure Record) from when you first arrived in the United States are excellent proof of this.

In addition, copies of your apartment lease, bank statements, and income tax returns are good evidence that you have been in the United States for ten years. School and medical records, subscriptions and memberships, and statements from friends, landlords, or coworkers are also useful.

3. Proof of Hardship

You must convince the court that if you are deported from the United States, it would cause "exceptional and extremely unusual hardship" to your spouse, child, or parent who is a U.S. citizen or a permanent resident. (The law in effect before 1996 allowed an individual to qualify by showing extreme hardship to himself or herself as well as to one of those family members, but this no longer works.)

Of course, if your spouse, parent, or adult child (21 or over) is a U.S. citizen, you qualify as a candidate for an immigrant visa as an immediate relative or as a family preference beneficiary (see Chapter 4). Cancellation of removal is considered a remedy of last resort, so if you are able to adjust your status based on an I-130 petition filed by any of those family members, you are expected to do so. If for some reason you are not able to adjust your status, however, cancellation of removal might be your only available avenue.

Because cancellation of removal depends almost completely on the discretion of the judge, you can only hope for a judge who is compassionate and humane. You and your lawyer must convince the judge that leaving the United States and returning to your own country would cause exceptional and extremely unusual hardship for your family members due to any combination of personal, economic, sociocultural, and psychological reasons.

What Does "Continuous Physical Presence" Mean?

The court will consider that you have been continuously present in the U.S. even if you departed from the country, as long as your absences did not exceed more than 90 days per trip or 180 days total. There are exceptions for individuals who served honorably in the Armed Forces for at least two years. Also, the time that can be used toward the ten-year presence period will be cut short if you commit an act that makes you deportable or inadmissible, or when DHS issues you a Notice to Appear.

Personal reasons. The Immigration Court will need the birth certificate of your child, your marriage certificate, and your own birth certificate (if your parents are the U.S. citizens or permanent residents who will suffer hardship should you leave the United States).

For starters, your relatives should be prepared to testify in court about how much you mean to them, how much they depend on you, and how disastrous it would be for them if you were not allowed to remain in the United States. Since nearly every family would face some similar pain, the judge wants to see that the hardship your family would face is "exceptional and extremely unusual."

If your American-born children are younger than 14, the judge will normally not ask to hear their testimony. However, the testimony of such young children, detailing their affection for you and the hardships they would endure if they accompanied you to your native country—problems with language, problems being uprooted from friends and schools—could strengthen your case.

Although testimony by your young children that, as Americans, they would rather stay in the United States with their grandparents or with a foster family than leave for a country they don't know could be hurtful for you to hear, such testimony would be further evidence that your deportation would cause them hardship.

Proof that any illness for which you or a family member is being treated in the United States, and evidence that the same treatment or medicine is either lacking or too expensive in your own country should also be given to the judge, supported by letters from doctors and pharmacists in the United States and the foreign country.

Provided they are either U.S. citizens or permanent residents, more distant relatives—including the grandparents or the biological parents of your child, their aunts, uncles, or cousins, or your own brothers and sisters—may all testify that your departure would also be an extreme hardship to them and to the family in general.

Whether or not these people testify, they should all submit letters of support for you. Letters that are sworn under penalty of perjury are usually given more weight than other letters.

If you have are dating someone who is married to somebody else, it is not recommended that they testify either on your behalf, or on behalf of the child they had with you. Although adultery has been repealed from immigration law as proof of the lack of good moral character, many judges will not look with favor upon such situations.

Economic reasons. Although you might be earning much more in the United States than you would in your own country, economic reasons are the least persuasive arguments against deportation. Economic hardship by itself has never been considered by the Immigration Court as sufficient

reason to cancel deportation. If you would be completely unable to support yourself and your family in your home country, however, the judge may consider that as a hardship factor.

If you are receiving welfare, government subsidies, or any form of public assistance, you might have a more difficult time receiving mercy from the judge. A judge is unlikely to grant you permission to stay in the United States permanently if you could be seen as a burden to the government.

Proof of regular and continuous employment is very important. Letters from your employers, past and present, detailing your employment history and your value as an employee, your most current pay stubs, and evidence of your work product, in the form of photos or newspaper articles, are all useful in demonstrating your contribution to the economic life of the nation. Try to contrast this to how different your employment opportunities would be in your home country.

You should have filed income tax returns for the past ten years, so submit copies as proof. These will show that, except for your illegal immigration status, you have been law-abiding. If you have not filed any tax returns because you do not have a Social Security number or because you have always been paid in cash, consult a tax expert at once. You might have to pay back taxes.

If you are in business for yourself, submit copies of documents demonstrating this. These could include your business license, your business checking account showing activity, a financial statement from an accountant to the court, and incorporation papers showing you as the major or sole stockholder. Also consider providing photos of your business in operation, payroll records for any employees, and a letter from your bank giving your account history and the average balance of your business account. Letters from your business partners and testimony in court explaining how the business would be affected if you were forced to leave it should also be presented during the hearing.

If you have invested in real estate, present proof of ownership, mortgage papers, and a letter from a real estate broker concerning how much your property would be worth if sold in the present market and especially how much financial loss this would cause you.

Sociocultural reasons. Convince the court that you are in good standing in your community in the United States. Present letters from your church, temple, or mosque about your active membership, from your block or village association, from the Parent-Teacher Association, from volunteer organizations, and from people you have cared for or helped. All are important to show that your life has been intimately entwined with U.S. society and that you have been a useful member of your community.

Letters from the union supervisor or from your coworkers explaining the kind of person you are and how valuable you are to them, personally and in terms of work, are also persuasive documents to present to the judge.

The judge will want to know whether you have any other possible forms of relief from deportation available to you, whether you have any pending petitions submitted on your behalf by a relative or an employer, and why it is advantageous for the U.S. government to grant you permanent residence through an immediate cancellation of removal instead of waiting for the Priority Date of any other immigration petition that might be pending.

Psychological reasons. You will have to acquaint the judge with the social, cultural, and political situation in your country and how your family could be subjected to prejudice, bigotry, or ostracism.

If you have a child born outside of marriage, or who is of a different race or is physically handicapped, provide evidence of how such children are treated in your country. Explain how going back to your country would affect your emotional and psychological health, thereby affecting your U.S. citizen and permanent resident family members. Also explain how going back would directly affect the emotional or psychological health of any relative

who is a U.S. citizen or permanent resident. Testimony from an expert witness, such as a psychiatrist or a psychologist, would bolster your case.

If you have a child who is a U.S. citizen, explain how the child's inability to fluently speak the language of your native country would be harmful to the child's education, and how removal from relatives, friends, and classmates could cause the child great psychological trauma.

E. How to File

You and your lawyer must submit the following documents to the Immigration Judge, along with a filing fee of $100:

- Form EOIR-42B, Application for Cancellation of Removal and Adjustment of Status for Certain Nonpermanent Residents
- Form G-325A, Biographical Information
- Documentary evidence as described in Section D, above
- A color photograph taken within 30 days of submitting the application, and
- Proof that you paid the $85 biometrics (fingerprinting) fee; DHS will provide instructions on how to do this.

Notice that we don't provide sample, filled-in forms at www.nolo.com/back-of-book/GRN.html. That's because you'd be foolish to go into Immigration Court without the help of an attorney; and the attorney will help you fill out the forms. You must also submit a copy to the Assistant Chief Counsel for DHS.

You can apply for a work permit once you have filed Form EOIR-42B, by filing Form I-765 at the address indicated on the form's instructions, along with the filing fee (currently $410).

Your answer to Question 27 (eligibility category) is "(c)(10)."

The Immigration Judge will set a hearing date for your case—giving enough time for you and your lawyer to prepare and for USCIS to investigate your case. In the meantime, USCIS should issue you a work permit.

The hearing might not finish the first day. In fact, it could be postponed one or more times because the Immigration Court devotes only a few hours at a time to each case on its calendar. Unless you are being detained at the immigration jail, your case could easily take one or two years before it is fully heard and a decision is reached.

F. Approving Your Application

If the Immigration Judge approves your application for cancellation of removal, you will be granted permanent residence that day (if there are still visa numbers available for the current year).

Winning Is Not Enough

Remember, even if an Immigration Judge decides to cancel your removal order, you could face a delay. Only 4,000 people each year are granted formal cancellation of removal. Immigration Judges have the power to grant conditional or temporary cancellation of removal orders until the person becomes eligible. The removal proceedings will not be formally ended, and permanent residence will not be formally granted, until your waiting number is reached.

G. Additional Types of Cancellation of Removal

There are two additional varieties of cancellation of removal. One is for permanent residents (green card holders) who have become deportable or removable. The other is for people who have been subjected to extreme cruelty or battery by a spouse or parent who is a U.S. citizen or permanent resident while in the United States.

1. Permanent Residents

An Immigration Judge may cancel the removal of, and regrant a green card to, a permanent resident if the person:

- has five years as a permanent resident
- has lived continuously in the U.S. for at least seven years after having been admitted in any status, and
- has not been convicted of an aggravated felony.

This relief will serve as a waiver of removal for many permanent residents who commit acts that make them deportable. See a lawyer for help with this (and Chapter 24).

2. Abused Spouse or Child

An abused spouse or child of a U.S. citizen or permanent resident may apply for cancellation of removal under different rules provided by the Violence Against Women Act, or VAWA. In this case, the applicant must show that they:

- suffered physical abuse or extreme mental cruelty in the U.S. at the hands of a permanent resident or U.S. citizen who is or was the applicant's parent or spouse—or the applicant is the parent of such an abused child
- has been physically present in the U.S. for a continuous period of at least three years at the time of the application
- has had good moral character for at least the three-year period, and
- is not inadmissible due to a conviction for a crime involving moral turpitude or drugs, or on national security or terrorism grounds or other specified grounds, and has not been convicted of an aggravated felony.

The applicant must also show that the removal would result in extreme hardship to the applicant, or their child or parent (if the applicant is a child).

Congress added this provision so that spouses and children who are victims of abuse by their petitioning relative would have a way to obtain status if they left the household of the abuser.

Again, seek a lawyer's help with this type of application. Many nonprofits offer free or low-cost help.

Adjustment of Status

A. Who Is Allowed to Use the Adjustment of Status Procedure 158

  1. Immediate Relatives Who Entered Legally 159

  2. People Who Entered Legally and Remain Legal 161

  3. People Who Qualify Under Old Laws 162

B. People Who Can't Adjust Status at All 162

C. How to File 163

  1. Whether You Need to Wait for USCIS Approval of Form I-130 163

  2. Adjustment of Status Forms and Documents 163

  3. Submission Procedures 167

D. After You Apply 167

E. Interview and Approval 168

Are you ready for the final step toward getting a green card while you're living in the United States? By now, you should have already completed some preliminary steps, such as winning the visa lottery, receiving approval of a petition on Form I-130 filed by a member of your family, or having spent one year in the U.S. as an asylee or a refugee. Or you should have figured out that, because of special circumstances (most likely that you're the immediate relative of a U.S. citizen and entered the U.S. legally), you don't need to get advance approval of a Form I-130 before continuing with your application. In any case, it's now your turn, as the immigrant, to file your application for a green card.

The procedure for obtaining a green card while you're in the United States is called "adjustment of status." It involves submitting forms to USCIS and attending an interview at a local USCIS office. It literally means you're changing your status from that of an undocumented person or a nonimmigrant visa holder to that of permanent resident. The alternate way to obtain a green card is through what's called "consular processing" (discussed in Chapter 17), in which you correspond with and attend interviews at an overseas U.S. embassy or consulate.

If you're living or staying in the United States right now, you might prefer the convenience of applying for your green card without leaving, using the adjustment of status process. Unfortunately, it's not always that easy. Many people who are eligible for green cards—because they're family members of U.S. citizens or permanent residents, or fall into other immigration categories—are nevertheless not allowed to stay in the United States to get their green card. Read on to find out the possibilities and potential problems that surround adjustment of status.

This chapter will discuss:

- who is allowed to use the adjustment of status procedure (Section A)
- who doesn't qualify, and what effect this has on the person's efforts to immigrate (Section B), and
- if you qualify, what forms and application procedures you'll need to use (Section C).

How Do You Decide?

If you are eligible for both adjustment of status in the United States and consular processing abroad, it is often best to choose adjustment of status because:

- You will save the expense of traveling back to your home country.
- If your application to adjust your status is denied, you can remain and work in the U.S. while you appeal that decision.
- If you go for consular processing and your application is denied, there is no right to appeal.
- When adjusting status, there is no risk of being kept out for three or ten years due to past illegal stays in the United States.

Nevertheless, adjustment of status is not the best choice for everyone. For example, if you don't face any problems with the time bars, and are planning to visit your home country anyway—you might want to choose consular processing for a less expensive green card.

A. Who Is Allowed to Use the Adjustment of Status Procedure

You are allowed to choose adjustment of status as your green card application method only if you fall into one of the following three categories:

- You are the immediate relative of a U.S. citizen and your last entry into the U.S. was done legally (see Section 1, below).
- Your last entry into the U.S. was done legally and you have remained in legal status ever since (see Section 2, below).
- You are "grandfathered in" under certain old laws because you had a visa petition on file before the laws changed (unlikely; see Section 3, below).

In addition, you must not be inadmissible based on the "permanent bar." This bar applies to people who lived in the United States illegally for more than a year and then left or were deported, but who returned to the United States illegally (or were caught trying to). Such people might never be allowed to get a green card. See a lawyer if you believe this bar might apply to you.

1. Immediate Relatives Who Entered Legally

If you meet the following two criteria, you are one of the lucky few allowed to use the adjustment of status procedure:

- You are the immediate relative (spouse, parent, or minor, unmarried child) of a U.S. citizen.
- Your most recent entry to the United States was done legally, most likely using a visa (such as a tourist or a student visa), a visa waiver (in which you simply showed your passport and were admitted for a 90-day tourist stay), or some other entry document like a border crossing card. There are exceptions, however: You cannot adjust under this category if you entered as a crewman on a boat or plane, regardless of what visa you had, or you were in transit to another country without a visa (for example, changing planes in a U.S. airport).

CAUTION

Remember, this chapter discusses only procedures, not your underlying eligibility for a green card. Unless you've already completed the steps explained in another chapter—most likely one describing family- or lottery-based visas—you shouldn't be in this chapter. It's only for people with approved immigrant petitions—or immediate relatives who are filing an I-130 petition with their application for adjustment of status—or for people with winning lottery letters who are now completing their green card application process.

EXAMPLE: Katerina is a foreign student from Germany who has used her student visa to enter the United States many times, most recently on her return trip after summer vacation. She is engaged to marry a fellow student named Mark, a U.S. citizen. Once they're married, Katerina will be an immediate relative, whose last entry to the U.S. was done legally. (In fact, it wouldn't matter if she let her student visa expire before applying to adjust status, though we don't recommend this method, since it means spending time in the U.S. illegally.) Katerina will be able to apply for her green card without leaving the U.S., using the adjustment of status procedure.

However, there's one major, and common, difficulty for some immediate relatives: Your use of the visa or visa waiver to enter the U.S. has to have been an innocent one, merely to study, travel, or whatever it was your visa was meant for. If instead you used the visa specifically for the purpose of getting yourself to the U.S. so you could adjust status, that's visa fraud, and will make you ineligible for a green card. Visas are meant to be used only for the limited purpose of coming to the U.S. for a temporary stay—any secret plans to stay permanently can be seen as a big problem.

EXAMPLE: While Sally was a foreign student in the Netherlands, she met Joost, and they became engaged. After Sally's studies ended, she returned to the United States. Joost stayed behind for a few months, to finish an architecture project. Because citizens of the Netherlands are not required to obtain visas to visit the U.S., Joost simply picked up his passport when he was ready, and flew to New York. He told the border official he was there to visit friends for a few months, and was let in. They got married at city hall the next week, and Joost immediately began preparing his green card application. Joost's actions could easily be considered visa fraud. Although, technically, Joost would be able to use the adjustment of status procedure—in fact, he would probably have no problem submitting his full green card application—when the time comes for Joost's interview, the USCIS officer will likely question him closely about whether he purposely lied when he entered the U.S. and told the border official that he would stay here for only a few months. If Joost can't come up with a good answer, his application will be denied. (There is a waiver Joost can apply for, with the help of an attorney, but it's hard to get.)

DOS Makes It Easier to Accuse Applicants of Visa Fraud (Changes 30/60-Day Rule)

In late 2017, the DOS made changes to its *Foreign Affairs Manual*, specifically to what was commonly called the "30/60 rule." This concerns a ground of inadmissibility under I.N.A. 212(a)(6)(C) applying to any alien "who, by fraud or willfully misrepresenting a material fact, seeks to procure (or has sought to procure or has procured) a visa, other documentation, or admission into the United States." (For more information on inadmissibility, see Chapter 4.)

Under the former 30/60 rule, consular and USCIS officials presumed that the immigrant lied if they did something inconsistent with the terms of the visa (such as take a job while on a student visa or come to the U.S. to get married and stay permanently while on a tourist visa) within 30 days of U.S. entry. Any such actions after 30 days but before 60 days were typically not considered fraud unless separate evidence showed otherwise. If the relevant conduct took place after 60 days of U.S. entry, there was no presumption of misrepresentation.

However, this has been replaced with the "90-day rule," under which a consular officer may presume misrepresentation for actions within 90 days of entry and may also make a determination that fraud existed long after 90 days have passed if enough evidence supports it. This policy is much broader and gives immigration officials far more discretion in determining whether immigrants lied in obtaining a visa or immigration benefit.

Although USCIS (which operates separately from DOS) has not yet updated its own policy manual to include the new 90-day rule, it will likely follow suit. This is a huge issue for adjustment of status based upon marriage after entering the U.S. on a tourist visa, the Visa Waiver Program, or another short-term visa. Note the example below.

An unbelievable number of married couples make the same mistake that Sally and Joost did. A few get lucky and the immigration official who interviews them simply overlooks the problem. If you wait long enough after your entry to either get married or submit the green card application—hopefully three months, at least—you'll face fewer questions, because USCIS might presume you were thinking your plans over in between. And some people are able to convincingly explain that their intentions when entering the U.S. were truly just to visit (or do whatever their visa was intended for), but while here, they talked it over with their relative (or soon-to-be spouse) and decided that the immigrant should stay and apply for a green card.

> **EXAMPLE:** John, a U.S. citizen living near Washington D.C., and Fernando, a citizen of Spain, are engaged. They know about the K-1 visa that would allow Fernando to travel to the U.S. to be married and stay permanently; and that they have the option of getting married and later applying for an immigrant visa at a consulate abroad. However, they decide it will be less expensive and inconvenient for Fernando to simply travel to the U.S. on the Visa Waiver Program (VWP), which allows nationals of certain countries to enter without a visa and stay for a maximum of 90 days; then to marry and file for adjustment of status afterwards. Fernando travels to the U.S. and tells the border official at the airport that he is staying with a friend and plans to sightsee but does not mention any wedding plans. Two weeks later, the couple is married at a reception with 100 of their friends and family attending.

While it's not against the law to get married in U.S. while on a tourist visa or using the VWP, it is a violation of law to misrepresent your intentions to a border official in order to gain U.S. admission. If Fernando decides to stay in the U.S. and adjust status rather than returning to Spain, he might have difficulty convincing USCIS he did not commit visa fraud by failing to mention that he was going to get married and planned to live in the U.S. permanently. This is especially true since the couple will need to submit marriage evidence with their adjustment application, which will show that they planned a big wedding reception months before Fernando came to the U.S.—and got married two weeks later! Best-case scenario is that the USCIS officer overlooks the indiscretion and approves Fernando's green card, but there is the possibility that his green card will be denied, a fraud finding made, and he will be returned to Spain with diminished hopes for ever again living in the United States.

The safest thing for Fernando to do is return to Spain within 90 days and obtain his green card through consular processing rather than applying using adjustment of status procedures. While he might face questions about why he told the border official that he was coming to the U.S. to sightsee when he actually got married, he will be able to sidestep any questions about lying about his intentions to live in the U.S. permanently after his travel on the VWP.

Additional difficulties can occur if you entered the U.S. on the Visa Waiver Program. In this situation, you should submit a complete adjustment application to USCIS and, ideally, submit it before the expiration of the 90-day period of your visa-waiver–authorized stay. USCIS may approve your I-485 application even if you overstayed, but in most jurisdictions, if your application is denied, you won't get a "second bite at the apple" by asking an Immigration Judge to consider your application.

2. People Who Entered Legally and Remain Legal

Even if you're not the immediate relative of a U.S. citizen, you're allowed to get a green card using the adjustment of status procedure if you meet all the following criteria:

- You entered the U.S. legally, most likely using a visa (such as a tourist or a student visa) or some other entry document like a border crossing card. There are exceptions, however: You cannot adjust under this rule if you entered using a visa waiver, you entered as a crewman on a boat or plane (regardless of what visa you had), or you were in transit to another country without a visa (for example, changing planes in a U.S. airport).
- You have never been out of legal status (your right to stay, as most likely shown on your I-94, hasn't expired).

- You have never worked without INS or USCIS authorization.

Whether or not your permitted stay has expired is an important issue. If you were granted a tourist visa (B-2), for example, the visa itself might be valid for many years and allow multiple entries. However, the important issue is how long the border officials said you could stay on this particular trip. You'll find this information on your I-94, which you must obtain online, and will show the expiration date of your authorized stay. You might also find this date stamped on your passport. If you've overstayed that date, and didn't get any extension or change of status, your status is now illegal, no matter how long your visa is good for.

Note to students: Your I-94 might not have an expiration date, but instead simply say "D/S," which means "duration of status." In other words, you're allowed to stay in the U.S. as long as you continue your studies (and don't violate the other terms of your student visa).

Working without authorization is also a troublesome issue for many would-be immigrants. Tourist and student visa holders, for example, are frequent violators of the work permit rules (tourists aren't allowed to work at all, and students can work only under limited circumstances).

> **EXAMPLE:** Ahmed and Ali, two brothers age 24 and 26, come to visit their mother in the United States, where she lives as a permanent resident. A month into their six-month stay, their mother's U.S. citizenship finally comes through. Because the mother petitioned for the brothers some years ago, they can use their old Priority Date, and they find that they're immediately eligible for green cards in the family first preference category (see Chapter 9). But can they apply for adjustment of status? They entered legally, and their stay is still legal. However, Ali has picked up a part-time job in a local restaurant. Only Ahmed will be able to adjust status. Ali will have to return home and try to get his green card through consular processing (where he might face questions about his illegal work).

Another problem that comes up for some applicants is the use of visa fraud to enter the United States. After waiting outside the United States for many years for their Priority Date to become current, many applicants figure they can simply get a visa to the U.S. and submit an adjustment of status application once they're here. Many of them are disappointed to find out they've just committed visa fraud. Again, visas are meant to be used only for the limited purpose of coming to the U.S. for a temporary stay, and your activities on that visa must remain within its purposes—visitor visa holders must act like tourists, student visa holders must act like students, and so on. Although immigration officials will sometimes look the other way, it's best to avoid the problem, stay in your home country, and finish your application through the local consulate.

EXAMPLE: Meijin is a U.S. permanent resident who filed visa petitions for her two children, aged 26 and 28, in the second preference category, many years ago. Their Priority Date finally becomes current, and they receive forms and information from the U.S. consulate in Beijing, China, near where they live. The older child, Guofeng, can't wait—he uses a tourist visa he already happens to have to enter the United States. He tells the border officials in San Francisco he's just coming to sightsee (otherwise they would have turned Guofeng around and sent him home). Guofeng submits a green card application. The application is denied, because Guofeng inappropriately used a tourist visa when his real intention was to stay permanently. His sister, Jinqing, stays home and files her paperwork with the U.S. consulate, and she succeeds in getting an immigrant visa and a green card.

SEE AN EXPERT

Not sure whether you can adjust status under these rules? If you have any doubts at all about whether you qualify to adjust status, consult a qualified immigration attorney. See Chapter 24 for advice on finding a good one.

3. People Who Qualify Under Old Laws

As you've seen, a number of people are barred from adjusting status, including those who entered the U.S. illegally; overstayed their visa or other permitted time; worked without authorization; entered while in transit without a visa; or entered as crew on planes or boats. However, there are two exceptions, based on changes in the laws over the years.

At one time, a law called "245(i)" allowed all people who were otherwise unable to adjust status to do so by paying a penalty fee. That law is now gone, but a few people who were around when the law was still in effect are allowed to make use of it. You can apply to adjust status under § 245(i) if you:

- had an approvable immigrant petition or labor certification filed on your behalf before January 14, 1998 (it doesn't matter whether it was filed by the same person or employer as the one through whom you're now immigrating)
- had an approvable immigrant petition or labor certification filed on your behalf before April 30, 2001, as long as you were physically in the U.S. on December 21, 2000 (again, it doesn't matter whether it was filed by the same person or employer as the one through whom you're now immigrating), or
- in certain circumstances, are the spouse or child of someone described above.

There is a financial catch to using these old laws to adjust status, however: You'll have to pay a penalty fee, currently $1,000.

B. People Who Can't Adjust Status at All

If you don't fall into any of the categories described above, you do not qualify to use adjustment of status as your green card application method. This means that many people who only recently became eligible to immigrate—for example, by marrying a U.S. citizen—but who entered the U.S. without being inspected and admitted by a border official, and had no immigrant petitions filed for them by any of the important 1998 or 2001 dates, will be ineligible to adjust status.

Unfortunately, this can create a difficult trap, because if a person has spent more than 180 days in the U.S. illegally, leaving the U.S. to try to apply through an overseas U.S. consulate could result in being barred from returning for three or ten years. Some, but not all people facing this trap might be able to get around it by applying for a provisional waiver of unlawful presence, allowing them to receive an answer before leaving the United States. (Review Chapter 4 for details.) See a lawyer if you're in this or a similar situation.

C. How to File

If you are one of the lucky people who can adjust status in the U.S., a number of picky rules control how and when you can submit your various application forms. Follow them exactly, to be sure that your paperwork can be processed quickly and properly.

1. Whether You Need to Wait for USCIS Approval of Form I-130

Most people who are eligible to adjust status can do so only after receiving some official government statement about their basic eligibility for a green card—for example, USCIS receipt or approval of their Form I-130 petition, a State Department letter indicating they won the lottery, or a grant of asylum (which can be used as the basis for a green card after one year). However, one exception allows certain applicants applying through family to turn this two-step application process into one step.

If you are the spouse, parent, or minor child of a U.S. citizen (an immediate relative), then you can file the I-130 and adjustment of status paperwork at the same time. If you've already filed the I-130, file your adjustment application with either the approval or with a request for USCIS to request that the pending file be transferred.

If you are applying through a family member but do not match the description in the paragraph above, then your family member must file Form I-130 and accompanying documents at a USCIS service center first. (The procedures for I-130 submissions are explained in the various chapters of this book that apply to different types of eligibility for family members.) Only after the I-130 is approved and your Priority Date is current can you continue with your application.

2. Adjustment of Status Forms and Documents

To apply for adjustment of status, you must submit the following forms to USCIS:

☐ **Copy of government document proving your basic green card eligibility.** This might be a USCIS approval or receipt notice for an I-130 petition (unless you're a family member who can submit this petition together with the adjustment of status application as described in Section 1, above), a State Department letter notifying you that you've won the lottery, a grant of political asylum or refugee status, or, if you entered on a K-1 or K-2 fiancé visa, copies of the I-129F fiancé petition approval notice, your marriage certificate, and your Form I-94 (which is either a card tucked into your passport or a page you've printed from the U.S. Customs and Border Protection (CBP) website).

 TIP
Getting a copy of your I-94. Until 2013, all nonimmigrants (such as students and tourists) entering the U.S. needed to complete Form I-94, Arrival/Departure Record, a small white piece of paper. The border agent would then indicate the date by which the entrant would need to depart the U.S., and staple the form to the person's passport. Now, paper I-94s have been mostly phased out. You will, however, still need your I-94 number for your adjustment of status application. To find and print it, go to https://i94.cbp.dhs.gov/I94/#/home. If you can't locate your information on the first try, try different variations of your name. For example, include your middle name along with your first name, or both last names, if applicable. Still out of luck? Call a

Customs and Border Patrol Deferred Inspection Site for more information. Some adjustment applicants have had luck by simply submitting a statement that they were unable to locate their I-94 number on the CBP website. Otherwise, USCIS will likely instruct you to file Form I-102, Application for Replacement/Initial Nonimmigrant Arrival-Departure Document, along with the $445 filing fee. Another possibility for locating your I-94 (especially if it was a paper document) is to submit a Freedom of Information Act (FOIA) request online with CBP at www.cbp.gov/site-policy-notices/foia.

☐ **Proof that you're eligible to use the adjustment of status procedure.** What you use as proof depends on the reason you're able to adjust status. For example, if you're an immediate relative who entered the U.S. legally, a copy of your Form I-94 would be sufficient. If you're an asylee or a refugee and have been present in the U.S. for one year or more, submit proof of the day your status started. This could be your I-94, the Asylum Office approval letter, or the order of the Immigration Judge. If you entered the U.S. on a fiancé visa (K-1, K-2, K-3, or K-4) and got married or met your other visa requirements, submit a copy of your visa and I-94. If you're claiming eligibility because you fall under the Section 245(i) law from 1998, you'll need to submit a copy of your I-130 petition or labor certification approval notice, with proof that your application was received by the January 14, 1998 deadline. If you are claiming eligibility under the Section 245(i) law from 2001, you'll need to submit the Approval Notice with proof that the application was received by April 30, 2001, as well as proof that you were in the U.S. on December 21, 2000. Such proof might include medical or dental records from that date, a pay stub, or even a traffic ticket. If you don't have a document issued exactly on December 21, 2000—and most people don't—submit documents that are close in time to that date.

☐ **Form I-485, Application to Register Permanent Resident or Adjust Status.** This is the primary form used to adjust status, which collects information on who you are, where you live, how you're eligible for a green card, and whether any of the grounds of inadmissibility (disqualification) apply to you. (It's available from www.uscis.gov/i-485; and you can download a completed sample at www.nolo.com/back-of-book/GRN.html.)

☐ **Form I-485 Supplement A.** Use this form only if you're applying to adjust status based on old laws (245(i)). Also remember to pay the penalty fee.

☐ **If you want permission to work, Form I-765.** (Obtain from uscis.gov/i-765; and you can download a completed sample at www.nolo.com/back-of-book/GRN.html.) Several months could pass before you're approved for a green card, during which time you can't work without getting permission. Use this form to ask permission (the current filing fee is $410). If for some reason you submit your work permit application later, you'll have to submit a copy of your Form I-797C Notice of Action receipt showing you filed the I-485, in order to show you're eligible for the work permit. You'll be given an Employment Authorization Document (EAD), which is an identification card with your photo. Even if you don't plan to work, this card is a handy way to prove who you are. Question 27 on the form can be confusing (and the instructions list many ways that different types of applicants must answer it). As an adjustment applicant, you simply answer it "(c)(9)," regardless of how you became eligible for your green card.

☐ **Form I-131, Application for Travel Document.** This is optional, but very handy. (Obtain it from www.uscis.gov/i-131; and you can download a completed sample at www.nolo.com/back-of-book/GRN.html.) Submitting this will result in your obtaining an "Advance Parole" (AP) document, which you'll need if you leave the U.S. before your green card application has been approved. Even if you don't have plans to leave the U.S. anytime soon, having this AP document will save a lot of time and worry if circumstances arise requiring you to leave before you receive your green card (such as an emergency in your home country or a required trip abroad for work). Ignore the part of the form that says you have to supply a separate explanation as to why you deserve Advance Parole. Approval is fairly automatic for adjustment of status applicants who haven't already left the U.S., so you really don't need to explain anything. Leaving the U.S. without Advance Parole will lead to your adjustment of status application being canceled. The current filing fee is $575. As with the EAD application, if you apply after submitting your I-485 application, be sure to submit a copy of your I-797 Receipt Notice to show you have a pending I-485. If you also apply for an EAD and are approved, you will receive an "EAD-AP" combo card, which both serves as your work permission and enables you to leave the U.S. while you await a decision on Form I-485.

TIP

Advance Parole does NOT guarantee readmission into the U.S. You can still be denied reentry at the discretion of Customs and Border Protection (CBP) or if you're inadmissible. This was, in the past, a particular problem for people who'd been unlawfully present in the U.S. for 180 days or more. Fortunately, the Board of Immigration Appeals (BIA) ruled in *Matter of Arrabally Yerrabelly*, 25 I&N Dec. 771 (BIA 2012) that people with a pending permanent residency application who leave the U.S. with Advance Parole do not trigger the three- and ten-year unlawful presence bars. However, to be cautious, you might want to consult an immigration attorney before leaving.

☐ **Form I-864, Affidavit of Support.** (See the discussion in Chapter 17.) If you're applying through a family member (not through an employer or as an asylee or a refugee, nor if you're a self- petitioning widow(er) or a battered spouse or child), you must submit this sworn statement from the petitioner (the U.S. citizen or lawful permanent resident who submitted the visa petition for you, who has sufficient income and who promises to support you and to reimburse the U.S. government if you must receive public assistance after receiving your permanent residence).

☐ **Form I-864W (if you fall within an exception to Form I-864 requirement).** Certain exceptions apply: The petitioner need not submit a Form I-864 if either the immigrant or the immigrant's spouse or parent has already worked in the U.S. for 40 quarters as defined by the Social Security system—about ten years. Nor do you need the Form I-864 if the beneficiary is a child (adopted or natural born) who will become a U.S. citizen automatically upon entering the U.S. If you're exempt from the affidavit of support requirement due to one of these exceptions, fill out Form I-864W instead of the regular Form I-864.

☐ **Documents to support Form I-864.** The latest year's tax returns (or IRS transcripts) of the citizen or permanent resident should be attached to the affidavit as proof of financial capacity (or up to three years' worth if it will strengthen your case). Proof of the sponsor's employment should also be attached.

☐ **Additional Form I-864 or I-864A (Contract Between Sponsor and Household Member) if getting help with sponsorship.** If your petitioner doesn't earn enough to meet the government requirements, you'll have to find an additional financial sponsor or another member of the sponsor's household who can add income and assets to the mix.

Sample Sponsor's Job Letter

ABC Company
123 Main Street
Anytown, Anystate 12345

April 24, 20xx

U.S. Citizenship and Immigration Services
26 Federal Plaza
New York, NY 10278

Dear Sir or Madam:

This letter is to certify that Jon Fratellanza has been employed by this company since March 2005 as a widget inspector.

His salary is $850 per week and he is employed on a full-time, permanent basis. His prospects for continued employment with this company are excellent.

Our personnel records indicate that this employee is married. In case of emergency, his spouse, Danielle Fratellanza, must be notified at their home telephone: 111-222-3456.

Sincerely,

Milton Mutter

Milton Mutter
Personnel Director, ABC Company

☐ **Form I-864EZ (for simple cases).** If you are the only person that your petitioner is sponsoring, and your petitioner can meet the sponsorship requirements based upon income alone, it's okay to instead use a shorter version of the form called "I-864EZ."

☐ **Job letter for immigrant.** If you are working (with USCIS authorization), you can submit a job letter from your employer in the United States stating your work history, when you started to work, whether your employment is permanent, and how much you earn, along with a payroll statement confirming your earnings.

If you are applying for a green card based on marriage, ask your employer whether it's willing to add to this job letter basic information about your marital status, such as name of spouse and confirmation that they are listed as the person to be notified in case of an emergency

☐ **Form I-693, Medical Examination of Aliens Seeking Adjustment of Status.** This must be filled out by a USCIS-approved doctor and submitted in an unopened envelope. To find a USCIS-approved doctor, go to https://my.uscis.gov/findadoctor and enter your zip code or call the USCIS Contact Center (800-375-5283). You can submit the Form I-693 with your I-485 Application or later, either in response to a USCIS Request for Evidence or when appearing at the local office for your interview.

☐ **Refugees, take note:** If you had your medical exam overseas, a USCIS-approved doctor will need to complete only the Part 9. Vaccination Record and Parts 1–4 and 6 of Form I-693, as long as your earlier exam didn't turn up any medical grounds of inadmissibility. Your state or local refugee health coordinator might be able to complete Part 9 of the form for you.

☐ **Derivative asylum applicants, take note:** If you had your medical exam overseas, a USCIS-approved doctor will need to complete only the Part 9. Vaccination Record and Parts 1–4 and 6 of Form I-693, as long as no medical grounds of inadmissibility were noted during your exam and you are applying for adjustment of status within one year of becoming eligible to file.

☐ **K nonimmigrant visa holders, take note:** You are not required to have another medical exam, so long as no medical grounds of inadmissibility were noted during your overseas exam (or you received a waiver) and if the Form DS-3025 vaccination record was properly completed and included. Carefully check your overseas medical exam and vaccination record. If you did not have the vaccinations before traveling to the U.S., you will need to have a USCIS- approved doctor complete the Part 9 Vaccination Record and Parts 1–4 and 6 of Form I-693.

☐ **If applying as an asylee or a refugee, proof that you've been physically present in the U.S. for at least a year.** This could be a letter verifying your employment, an apartment lease, or school records. You'll also need to include evidence of any trips you've made outside the U.S. since gaining asylum. (Remember, if you've made any trips to the country you fled from, you might have canceled your eligibility and should see a lawyer.)

☐ **A copy of your birth certificate.** Include a word-for-word translation, if it is not in English. Be sure the translator is not related to you and signs an attached statement confirming that the translation is complete and accurate and that the translator is competent to translate from the foreign language into English.

☐ **Passport-style color photographs.** If requesting Advance Parole and an EAD, submit a total of six passport-style, color photographs. USCIS requires two for each of Forms I-485, I-765, and I-131. It's a good idea to put your name and A number (if any) on the back of the photos. If filing Form I-130 along with your adjustment package based on marriage to a U.S. citizen, also include two photos of the U.S. citizen petitioner.

☐ **Filing fee.** USCIS charges fees for handling applications, based on which forms you submit and the applicant's age. Check www.uscis.gov/i-485 for a current list of fees. As of when this book went to print, the fee to file Form I-485 is $1,140 (with the exception of refugees, who pay no fee, and applicants younger than age 14 who are filing with at least one parent, who owe a fee total of $750). There is an additional fingerprinting ("biometrics") fee of $85 for people between ages 14 and 78, which can be paid with the filing fee. Make checks or money orders payable to the U.S. Department of Homeland Security. You can also pay by credit card, using Form G-1450, Authorization for Credit Card Transactions and placing this on top of the other paperwork you send. Keep in mind that the few applicants who will file Form I-485, Supplement A with their applications will also need to pay a penalty fee of $1,000.

☐ **Form G-1145.** While not required, it is a good idea to also file Form G-1145, so as to receive an email and/or text notification from USCIS letting you know that your application has been accepted.

3. Submission Procedures

Years ago, people could walk the application right into a local USCIS office. Now, however, you'll have to mail your application to a service center or an out-of-state processing office. See the USCIS website for the appropriate address.

D. After You Apply

After you've submitted your adjustment of status application, USCIS should send you a receipt notice (on Form I-797C). This will confirm that your application contained everything it should have, and that you're now in line for an adjustment of status interview.

> ### Travel Outside the U.S. While Awaiting Your Interview
>
> As discussed earlier, you or your minor children should not leave the United States while waiting for your adjustment of status interview without first applying for and receiving Advance Parole. If you didn't apply for Advance Parole when you filed your adjustment of status application, you can do so later, by submitting Form I-131 to the designated lockbox for the office handling your file, plus a copy of your filing receipt. Check the USCIS website for the current address.
>
> If you leave without this permission, USCIS will cancel your adjustment of status application. It will assume that your departure shows your lack of interest in receiving your green card in the United States and that you have abandoned your application.

You can use the number on your receipt notice to sign up for automatic email and/or text updates letting you know when mail is sent regarding your application. Go to the USCIS website, www.uscis. gov, and click "Check your case status." Enter your receipt number, then click "Check Status." On this page, you can also create an account to get case status updates about your application.

If your application was incomplete, you will receive a letter called a "Request for Evidence" or RFE indicating what's missing, and should reply as soon as possible.

Some weeks after you submit your application, you'll be called in to have your fingerprints taken for your security checks.

How long you'll have to wait for your adjustment of status interview depends on how backed up your local USCIS office is. (These interviews are held locally, at a different office than the one you submitted your application to.) Several months is typical, but it's not unheard of for it to take a year or longer.

During this wait, it's best not to take any long trips or move to a different address. USCIS won't give you much advance notice of your interview date, usually about a month or so.

E. Interview and Approval

Although USCIS makes exceptions, it requires most applicants to attend an interview at a local USCIS office before approving them for permanent residence and a green card. You'll get a form letter (see the sample below) advising you of the interview date and location, and telling you what to bring along.

The required documents normally include a photo identification; recent financial records from whoever signed the affidavit of support to show continuing employment and ownership of assets; documents updating other information in your application, for example if you've changed your name; and originals of your birth certificate, passport, visas, and other documents you've submitted copies of in connection with your application (these are for the USCIS officer to view, not keep); and documents showing any changes in the information on your application, such as a new employer.

If you're applying based on marriage, you'll also need to bring documents proving that your marriage is the real thing, such as copies of your home mortgage or lease, joint credit card statements, children's birth certificates, and more.

Then there's the question of whom to bring along.

Everyone who submitted a green card application and is mentioned in the interview notice should go, including children. And if the green cards are based on marriage, the U.S. petitioner needs to be there as well. For other family relationships, however— for example if you're getting a green card as the brother, sister, parent, or child of a U.S. citizen—the rules are less strict. USCIS would prefer to see the petitioner there, first off to make sure that they are still alive, and in case questions arise about the affidavit of support. But if that's inconvenient, for example if the petitioner lives in another part of the U.S., you can go to your appointment without the petitioner. However, it's best to bring a recent, signed, sworn statement by the petitioner explaining the situation and providing a phone number in case USCIS wants to follow up.

When bringing new documents, be sure to make copies of any that you don't want to leave with USCIS—they're usually happy with copies, particularly if they can view the original when you bring it. They're often unable or unwilling, however, to make photocopies for you, so you must either bring a copy or lose your original to the USCIS file.

If you don't speak English, you'll need to bring your own interpreter. You don't need to spend money on a professional—a friend or family member older than 18 who is a legal U.S. resident will do. But it's worth spending the money if you don't know anyone who's truly fluent in both English and your native language—your future is at stake here, and a little confusion could delay or destroy your hopes of getting a green card.

> ⓘ **CAUTION**
>
> **Arrive on time—and follow the rules.** Leave extra time for parking and passing through the security guard post at the USCIS office. Remember, this is a federal government building, so they'll X-ray your possessions and confiscate pocket knives or other illegal materials. They may also prohibit other items, such as cell phones and food. And you'll need to follow the latest COVID guidelines, for example wearing a mask that complies with government specifications. If you arrive late, you will probably lose your chance to be interviewed that day, and go through major hassles getting USCIS to reschedule you.

At your interview, a USCIS officer will review your application, ask some questions, and hopefully approve you for a green card. Most of the questions will relate to what's already on your application, such as your current address, how you last entered the United States, and whether you have a criminal record or are otherwise ineligible for a green card.

If you're applying based on marriage, be prepared to answer additional questions to prove that your marriage is the real thing, such as how you met, details of your wedding, and details about your house and your life together.

Interview Tips for Spouses

If you are requesting an adjustment of status as the spouse of a U.S. citizen or permanent resident, USCIS will require a personal interview with you both before granting your application.

Bring copies of all the forms relevant to your application, along with evidence of a bona fide marriage—such as wedding pictures, joint bank statements, rental agreements, children's birth certificates, health insurance contracts, and more. (See Chapter 7.)

If you've got solid documentary evidence of your real marriage, the officer is likely to ask only a few questions. If, on the other hand, the documents are weak, or you and your spouse don't seem able to answer the questions about your marriage, you may be sent for what's called a "fraud interview." This means that you and your spouse will each separately meet with the USCIS officer, who will ask each of you the same set of questions, and then check whether your answers match up. If you don't already have an attorney, this is a good time to ask that the interview be postponed, so that you can return with legal help.

Sample Interview Appointment Notice

Department of Homeland Security U.S. Citizenship and Immigration Services	**Form I-797C, Notice of Action**

THIS NOTICE DOES NOT GRANT ANY IMMIGRATION STATUS OR BENEFIT.

REQUEST FOR APPLICANT TO APPEAR FOR INITIAL INTERVIEW	Notice Date November 07, 2021
Case Type FORM I485, APPLICATION TO REGISTER PERMANENT RESIDENCE OR ADJUST STATUS	A# 099 909 909

Receipt Number **MSC2112345678**	Received Date September 09, 2021	Priority Date September 09, 2021	Page 1 of 2

HAI-ZI ZHANG c/o ILONA BRAY 950 PARKER ST. BERKELEY, CA 94710	A Number A 099 909 909 Receipt Number MSC 211 234 5678

You are hereby notified to appear for the interview appointment, as scheduled below, for the completion of your Application to Register Permanent Residence or Adjust Status (Form I-485) and any supporting applications or petitions. *Failure to appear for this interview and/or failure to bring the below listed items will result in the denial of your application.* (8 CFR 103.2(b)(13))

Who should come with you?
- **If your eligibility is based on your marriage, your husband or wife must come with you to the interview.**
- If you do not speak English fluently, you should bring an interpreter.
- Your attorney or authorized representative may come with you to the interview.
- If your eligibility is based on a parent/child relationship and the child is a minor, the petitioning parent and the child must appear for the interview.

NOTE: Every adult (over 18 years of age) who comes to the interview must bring Government-issued photo identification, such as a driver's license or ID card, in order to enter the building and to verify his/her identity at the time of the interview. You do not need to bring your children unless otherwise instructed. Please be on time, but do not arrive more than 30 minutes early. We may record or videotape your interview.

YOU MUST BRING THE FOLLOWING ITEMS WITH YOU: (Please use as a checklist to prepare for your interview)
- This Interview Notice and your Government issued photo identification.
- A completed medical examination (Form I-693) and vaccination supplement in a sealed envelope (unless already submitted).
- A completed Affidavit(s) of Support (Form I-864) with all required evidence, including the following, for each of your sponsors (unless already submitted):
  - Federal Income Tax returns and W-2's, or certified IRS printouts, for the most recent tax year;
  - Letters from each current employer, verifying current rate of pay and average weekly hours, and pay stubs for the past 2 months;
  - Evidence of your sponsor's and/or co-sponsor's United States Citizenship or Lawful Permanent Resident status.
- All documentation establishing your eligibility for Lawful Permanent Resident status.
- Any immigration-related documentation ever issued to you, including any Employment Authorization Document (EAD) and any Authorization for Advance Parole (Form I-512).
- All travel documents used to enter the United States, including Passports, Advance Parole documents (I-512) and I-94s (Arrival/Departure Document).
- Your Birth Certificate.
- Your petitioner's Birth Certificate and your petitioner's evidence of United States Citizenship or Lawful Permanent Resident Status.
- If you have children, bring a Birth Certificate for each of your children.
- If your eligibility is based on your marriage, in addition to your spouse coming to the interview with you, bring:
  - A certified copy of your Marriage Document issued by the appropriate civil authority;
  - Your spouse's Birth Certificate and your spouse's evidence of United States Citizenship or Lawful Permanent Resident status;
  - If either you or your spouse were ever married before, all divorce decrees/death certificates for each prior marriage/former spouse;
  - Birth Certificates for all children of this marriage, and custody papers for your children and for your spouse's children not living with you;
- Supporting evidence of your relationship, such as copies of any documentation regarding joint assets or liabilities you and your spouse may have together. This may include: tax returns, bank statements, insurance documents (car, life, health), property documents (car, house, etc.), rental agreements, utility bills, credit cards, contracts, leases, photos, correspondence and/or any other documents you feel may substantiate your relationship.
- Original and copy of each supporting document that you submitted with your application. Otherwise, we may keep your originals for our records.
- If you have ever been arrested, bring the related Police Report and the original or certified Final Court Disposition for each arrest, even if the charges have been dismissed or expunged. If no court record is available, bring a letter from the court with jurisdiction indicating this.

If you have questions, please call the USCIS Contact Center at 1-800-375-5283 (hearing impaired TDD service is 1-800-767-1833)

PLEASE COME TO: U.S. Citizenship and Immigration Services 550 MAIN STREET JW PECK FEDERAL BLDG, ROOM 4-001 CINCINNATI, OH 45202	ON: Friday, December 20, 2021 AT: 10:30AM

1

If this is an interview or biometrics appointment notice, please see the back of this notice for important information.	Form I-797C 04/01/19

Most interviews last 20 to 30 minutes. Answer the questions courteously and honestly—but don't volunteer extra information. Saying too much wastes the officer's time and might bring to light information that would have been better left unsaid.

If everything is in order, your application for adjustment of status should be approved. If you are not approved at your interview, you will later be notified of the approval by mail.

Your green card—which resembles a driver's license in size and format—will be sent by mail to your address within several weeks after approval. Be sure to inform USCIS of any change of address, because your green card might not be forwarded to you by the post office. Even after you get your green card, you are obligated to send USCIS written word every time your address changes—see Chapter 23 for this and other important rules on keeping your right to a green card.

You are now a lawful permanent resident who is authorized to work and stay in the United States legally.

SEE AN EXPERT

If your application is denied, consult an experienced immigration attorney. Unless you have some other visa or legal status in the United States, your file will be transferred to the Immigration Court for removal proceedings. See Chapter 24 for advice on finding a good attorney.

Immigrant Story: Proving a Real Marriage

Brian, a U.S. citizen, and Toshi, from Japan, met and fell in love while they were in college in Champaign, Illinois. Brian graduated two years ahead of Toshi, and got a great job in Atlanta. They corresponded long distance, and the next year got married and applied for Toshi's green card.

However, by the time Toshi got called for her adjustment of status interview, the couple was still not living together. They were worried that the immigration officer would not believe that their marriage was the real thing. After much thought, here are the documents they came up with to prove their relationship:

- college receipts showing that Brian was helping pay for Toshi's education
- sworn statements from Toshi's dormmates attesting to Brian's frequent visits
- documents showing that Toshi is the beneficiary of Brian's life insurance policy and 401(k)
- letter from a fertility specialist that Brian and Toshi had consulted about her difficulty in getting pregnant, and
- copies of emails, texts, and phone bills showing their frequent communication.

Brian and Toshi easily answered all the officer's questions at the interview, and Toshi was granted U.S. permanent residence.

Consular Processing

A. How Your Case Gets to the U.S. Consulate...175

B. Forms and Documents You'll Need to Provide...177

C. Attending Your Visa Interview..179

D. Approval of Your Immigrant Visa..180

E. Arriving in the United States...180

The second type of U.S. government procedure for getting a green card (other than adjustment of status) is "consular processing." It means that the immigrant goes to a U.S. embassy or consulate to complete the green card application. Only after the consulate interviews and approves someone for an immigrant visa can they enter the United States and claim permanent resident status.

Most immigrants will have no choice but to use consular processing as their application method. Immigrants who are overseas are almost all required to use consular processing, though many would love to enter the U.S. and finish their application there. However, with the exception of fiancés and people immigrating based on marriage (who can use a K-3 fiancé visa to enter the U.S. and then adjust status) most immigrants will only get themselves in trouble (for example, accused of visa fraud) if they try to enter the U.S. to finish their green card application.

Immigrants who are already in the United States might be required to use consular processing if they are not eligible to use the adjustment of status procedure described in Chapter 16. Unfortunately, this lack of choice creates a potential trap for immigrants who have lived unlawfully in the U.S. for 180 days or more. By leaving the U.S., they become inadmissible; basically, subject to legal penalties for their illegal stay. Even if they otherwise qualify for a green card, the consulate must, under the law, bar them from reentering the U.S. for three years (if their illegal stay was between 180 days and one year) or ten years (for illegal stays over one year). See an attorney if you're in this situation—there are waivers you can apply for, including a "provisional waiver" that allows some applicants to receive an answer before they actually leave the U.S., but it's hard to get one approved.

This chapter will discuss the paperwork and other requirements involved in consular processing.

CAUTION

Remember, this chapter discusses only procedures, not your underlying eligibility for a green card. Unless you've already completed the steps explained in another chapter—most likely one describing family- or lottery-based visas—you shouldn't be in this chapter. It's only for people with approved immigrant petitions or winning lottery registrations who are now completing their green card application process.

If You Have a Choice of Procedure

While the requirements for adjustment of status (getting a green card at a USCIS office) are rather restrictive, if you qualify, there are a number of advantages to that procedure over consular processing. If you are currently in the U.S., read Chapter 16 carefully to see whether you qualify to get a green card through adjustment of status.

TIP

Are you a K-3 spouse applying for a green card by applying for a fiancé visa and later using adjustment of status procedure? The consular processing procedures and fee amounts outlined in this chapter apply only to spouses applying for immigrant visas who will not have to adjust status after arriving in the United States. If USCIS approves your Form I-130 prior to or at the same as your Form I-129F, your application will be converted to consular processing and will be subject to the procedures (and fees) in this chapter. This is because your main reason for applying for a K-3 visa—the shorter processing times—is now no longer a concern for you. See Chapters 6, 7, and 16 for more information about using the K-3 visa and adjusting status in the United States.

A. How Your Case Gets to the U.S. Consulate

When your U.S. relative filled out your I-130 immigrant petition, or when you filled out your lottery application, your address or other information will have indicated to the U.S. government which consulate would be most convenient for you. After your immigrant petition has been approved or you've won the lottery, a central office known as the National Visa Center (NVC) will transfer your file to the appropriate consulate. (Remember that if you're not an immediate relative but a "preference relative," you might have to wait years before your Priority Date becomes current and your case is transferred to a consulate—see Chapter 5 for details.)

A lot has to happen, however, before the NVC transfers your case. You will have to visit the Consular Electronic Application Center (CEAC) at http://ceac.state.gov/ceac and complete DS-261, Online Choice of Address and Agent. Log in using the case number that the NVC sent you. It's a fairly simple form, but keep in mind that by choosing an "agent," you are essentially deciding where and how all the important notices from the U.S. government will be sent—to your overseas address by mail or to the U.S. petitioner or via email. If mail service from the U.S. has been unreliable where you live, or if you might be moving before your visa interview, it's safest to choose the petitioner (in the U.S.) as your agent or to choose to be contacted by email. Since the majority of the steps you need to take on your I-130 petition are online, it makes sense to enroll in email notifications.

After you submit the DS-261, you will receive information about filing fees. If you are immigrating through a family member, the NVC will send the U.S. family member petitioner a bill for the Affidavit of Support review and send either you or your agent a bill for the immigrant visa processing fee (currently $325). If any family members who are included on your petition are immigrating with you, a separate filing fee for each will be required. However, all family members can be included on the one $120 filing fee for the Affidavit of Support.

The NVC prefers that you pay these fees online, by entering your checking account number and bank routing number. That's also the best way to ensure that your fees get credited to your account, all your documents are kept together, and that the NVC doesn't lose your paper check. The affidavit of support and the immigrant visa processing fees may be paid online at https://ceac.state.gov/IV/Login.aspx.

If you don't have a checking account, you will need to pay by mail using a bank check or money order. Make sure to have your visa bill handy, because it contains a bar code that the NVC will need in order to credit your fee to your application.

After paying your fees, you will need to submit DS-260, the online immigrant visa application. This form will ask you a number of biographical questions, such as all names used, all addresses where you have lived, work and educational history, and family member information. You will also be asked questions to determine your admissibility to the United States.

The DS-260 application can be submitted only online. You will again need your NVC invoice number and receipt number in order to complete it. You can save your DS-260 and come back to it later if you need to. Keep in mind that you need to complete this form in English using English characters only, so have someone ready to help if necessary.

This online form requires a lot of detail. You'll be asked for all your addresses since the age of 16 and the exact dates that you lived there. Make sure that all your answers correspond with those given on the petitioner's Form I-130. If an answer does not apply to you (such as U.S. Social Security number), you will be given the option to choose "Does Not Apply."

After submitting the DS-260, print the confirmation page and bring it to your interview. It doesn't hurt to print out a copy of the entire form as well, so that you can refer to it when needed.

 TIP

Got questions about the process? The Department of State website has an outline of the entire process. At https://travel.state.gov, click "U.S. Visas," then "Immigrate," then choose the basis upon which you're immigrating to see a step-by-step chart. Or, click "When and how to Contact NVC" on the right side of the page, to access its Public Inquiry Form. You will receive further instructions and a checklist on what else the NVC needs from you before your interview. See the next section for our own checklist of the forms and documents you'll most likely need.

Fees for Visa Services

The following chart shows the fees required for immigrant visa processing (as of the date this book went to print in mid-2022) after your Form I-130 is approved by USCIS. For an updated list of fee amounts, go to https://usvisas.state.gov and click "Fees/Reciprocity" then "Fees-Visa Services." These fees are required only for immigrant visas, not nonimmigrant visas.

Fee Type	Fee Amount	Payment Details
Affidavit of Support Review Fee	$120	Only one fee is required for the applicant and all family members included in the visa application
Immediate Family and Family Preference Applications Immigrant Visa Fee	$325	Separate filing fee is required for each family member included in the visa application
Diversity Lottery Visa Fee	$330	Only required for diversity lottery visa applicants
USCIS Immigrant Fee	$220	Separate filing fee is required for each family member after the consulate interview and visa approval. You may pay this fee after you receive your visa to enter the U.S., but you will not receive a green card until the fee is paid. It's best to pay this fee after receiving your visa packet from the U.S. consulate.

Also, any consulate-specific websites offer details and information in the country's native language. There's a list of U.S. embassies and consulates at www.usembassy.gov.

All foreign-language documents must be translated into English. For more information on the requirements, see Chapter 21.

After the NVC is satisfied that you have submitted the necessary documentation and have paid all fees, it will schedule an interview date and transfer your visa file to the appropriate U.S. consulate or embassy.

Before your visa interview, you will need to attend a medical examination with an authorized physician. To find one in your country and learn more about the what the medical exam involves, go to the DOS chart described under "Got questions about the process?" above.

Medical exam fees vary among doctors, so it's worth calling around to inquire. Bringing your vaccination records and any recent chest X-rays will help you to avoid additional costs for shots and X-rays (if necessary).

This exam is not like the ordinary one you'd have with your own doctor. Its sole purpose is to spot any grounds of inadmissibility that might prevent you from getting a green card. See Chapter 4 for a discussion of the grounds of inadmissibility. If you do have a medical ground of inadmissibility, you could be eligible for a waiver (also discussed in Chapter 4), and should consult an immigration lawyer. See Chapter 24 for tips on finding a good lawyer.

B. Forms and Documents You'll Need to Provide

Here's a summary of the forms and documents that you'll need to give to either the NVC or the consulate between now and the end of the process:

- ☐ Confirmation page for Form DS-260, which you'll fill out online (as described above)
- ☐ Copies of current passports. You'll be asked to send in a copy of the key pages of your family members' passports—but not the originals. You'll bring the original passports to your interview at the U.S. consulate.
- ☐ Birth certificates or adoption records for you and your spouse or children, with English translations if they are not in the language of the country in which you are interviewed
- ☐ A police clearance certificate for each person older than 16 years of age from the country of nationality or current residence if they lived there for more than six months, and from any other country where the applicant lived for more than one year
- ☐ Marriage certificate, death certificate, divorce or annulment decree—whichever shows your current marital status and history
- ☐ Military record of any service in your country, or any country, including certified proof of military service and of honorable or dishonorable discharge
- ☐ Certified copy of court and prison records if you have been convicted of a crime
- ☐ Form I-864 or I-864EZ, Affidavit of Support. (Obtain the one you need from www.uscis.gov/i-864; and download a completed sample at www.nolo.com/back-of-book/GRN.html. Notice that in our sample, the sponsor didn't have enough income, and therefore had to add a Form I-864A in which his daughter, who lives with him, also promised to add her income to help the immigrant.) Which form you must submit depends on your situation. You must file Form I-864 if your petition is family based (except K-1 fiancé visas). But if you

are the only person that your petitioner is sponsoring, and your petitioner can meet the sponsorship requirements based upon his or her income alone, the petitioner can use a shorter version of the form, called "I-864EZ." On both Form I-134 and I-864, a U.S. citizen or permanent resident promises to repay the U.S. government if you become impoverished and go on public assistance after you arrive in the United States.

☐ Documents to support form I-864. Your sponsor who fills out the form must also include financial documents, including an employment verification letter or other proof of income such as a "year-to-date" pay stub, the sponsor's latest U.S. income tax transcript and W-2s (or the last three years', if it will strengthen the case). If the sponsor is relying on assets to meet the poverty guidelines, then proof of those assets—such as bank statements—must be submitted.

☐ Form I-864W (in cases where an I-864 is not required). In certain exceptional cases, a Form I-864 need not be filed. One of these is where the beneficiary is a child (adopted or natural born) who will become a U.S. citizen automatically upon entering the United States (see Chapter 20 for details). The other is where the beneficiary, or the beneficiary's spouse or parent, has worked 40 "quarters" (about ten years, as defined by the Social Security Administration) in the United States. If you're exempt from the affidavit of support requirement due to one of these exceptions, you should fill out and sign Form I-864W.

You will also be required to submit to fingerprinting, for a background check by the FBI and

CIA. (See Chapter 21, Section F, for more about these security checks.)

The final set of documents you'll normally need to prepare for your interview include:

☐ Two color photographs, passport style

☐ Current passports for you and for everyone in your family who is getting an immigrant visa (they must not expire earlier than six months after your interview date)

☐ Medical examination report. During the exam, your blood will be tested and you will be X-rayed. You could be barred from immigrating if these tests show that you have a contagious disease of public health concern such as tuberculosis, or if you have a severe mental disorder. If any of these bars apply to you, you could be eligible for a waiver (see Chapter 4), and should consult an immigration lawyer.

☐ U.S. income tax transcripts. If you have worked in the U.S., you must present proof that you filed income tax returns for every year you worked.

☐ Visa fees, if not already paid or a receipt showing you paid the fees online.

For a printable checklist of this information, go to https://travel.state.gov and click "U.S. Visas," then "Immigrate," then "The Immigrant Visa Process," then "Prepare for the Interview," then "Items You Must Bring to Your Visa Interview."

CAUTION

Unmarried children beware. If you are an unmarried son or daughter of a U.S. permanent resident or a U.S. citizen, and you marry before you have your your immigrant visa interview, be prepared for a shock: Your visa will be denied because you are no longer in the immediate relative or second preference category under which you were petitioned.

If you married after your visa interview but before you entered the U.S. with your immigrant visa, you could also be in serious trouble. Although you might be admitted into the United States (because the border officer has no way of knowing that you are no longer eligible), USCIS could later discover this fact if you apply to bring your spouse or to become a U.S. citizen.

It will not matter that you have been admitted as a permanent resident. Removal proceedings will be started against you, you and your spouse will not be reunited in the United States, and you will eventually have to go back to your country and start all over in the preference category for married sons and daughters of U.S. citizens. You could completely lose your immigrant eligibility if your parent is only a green card holder.

If you fall into this situation, see an experienced attorney. (Chapter 24 offers tips on finding one.)

C. Attending Your Visa Interview

The final step in obtaining your immigrant visa is to attend an interview with a U.S. consular official. Until the day of your interview, it's quite possible that neither you nor your petitioning spouse or family members (if any) will have had any personal contact with any U.S. immigration official. At last, you can deal with a real human being—for better and for worse.

With all the paperwork you've submitted by now, you might wonder why the interview is even necessary. However, the government regards it as its opportunity to confirm the contents of your application after you've sworn to tell the truth. If you're applying based on marriage, it also allows them to ask personal questions designed to reveal whether your marriage is the real thing or a sham.

Tips for the Visa Interview

The most important thing to do is relax. Wear conservative but comfortable clothes. The interviewer will ask you mostly about information you have already written on your immigration forms and using other documents.

Answer all questions truthfully. If you cannot understand one, be brave and ask for an interpreter. It is better to be embarrassed about not understanding English well than to be denied your immigrant visa because you misunderstood the question.

If you're being petitioned by a spouse or another family member, they're not expected to attend the interview—although it can help to have them there. If yours is a marriage case, your spouse's willingness to travel and be with you at the interview is a good sign that your marriage is not a sham. Some, but not all, consulates also allow you to bring a lawyer, if you feel you need one.

To prepare for your interview, the most important thing is to review all your paperwork. Look at all the questions and answers on all the forms, including any that were submitted for you by your U.S. family member. Though boring, this information is all important to the consular officials. Be alert for any inconsistencies and mistakes, and bring along any documents that will help correct them.

If you're applying through a spouse or fiancé, spend some time together reviewing the details of how you met, how you've corresponded and visited each other or each other's families, and when and why you decided to get married. If already married, review the details of the wedding—number of guests, where it was held, what food and drink was served, and the like.

If you don't live in the same city as the consulate, try to get there a few days in advance, particularly for purposes of getting your medical exam and photos done. Some consulates require a longer waiting period, to ensure that the medical exam results are complete before the interview. (In Indonesia, for example immigrant visa interviews are done at the consulate in Jakarta, which requires that the medical exam be completed ten days before the interview. Applicants who do not live nearby have the choice of either visiting Jakarta for longer than ten days or going there a month before the interview just to do the medical exam.) This is why it's important to review the consulate-specific instructions carefully.

Arrive at the consulate early, in case there's a line. Consulates often schedule applicants in large groups, telling them all to arrive at the same time. The interview itself will probably last 30 minutes. And be careful regarding personal security outside the consulate—it's a common place for pickpockets and con artists to hang around.

D. Approval of Your Immigrant Visa

If the U.S. consulate or embassy needs more information, it will tell you that further administrative processing is necessary and what types of documents it needs. If it denies your case, it will give you a letter detailing the reasons. In any case, you are unlikely to receive the visa at the end of the interview.

The consulate will let you know the how to check on your case status, submit any required documents, and after you're approved, receive your visa (either by mail or in-person pick- up). It will give you back your passport with your immigrant visa, a sealed packet (DO NOT open this), and an envelope with your X-rays, all of which you will need to carry with you when you arrive at the U.S. border and are inspected by Customs and Border Protection (CBP).

Check the visa for any spelling or other factual errors. You will also have to the USCIS immigrant fee, in order to receive the actual green card after entering the United States. Do so at https://my.uscis.gov/uscis-immigrant-fee.

Your immigrant visa is valid for six months, and you must arrive in the United States within that time. Your permanent resident status does not start until you actually enter the United States.

If you are unable to leave for the United States and your visa is about to expire, you may apply for an extension of your immigrant visa by submitting an affidavit, or written statement signed before a notary public, explaining to the consulate why you are unable to leave on time. But unless you have a very good reason, the U.S. consulate will be reluctant to approve an extension.

E. Arriving in the United States

When you arrive at your U.S. port of entry, the U.S. citizens who were on the plane with you will be admitted in one line, while all the noncitizens will be queuing in another line.

When it is your turn, the immigration officer will take your immigrant documents and keep them—all but your X-rays—and make them part of your permanent record in the USCIS office. Your passport will be stamped to show that you have entered as a lawful permanent resident.

Your green card will be mailed to you within some weeks to months. You must inform USCIS if you change addresses within ten days of your move (or you can be deported). Besides, if you don't tell them, you might not receive your green card until you have made several trips to the USCIS office and filled out countless forms. See Chapter 23 for more information on changing addresses and keeping your right to a green card.

At last! You are a bona fide immigrant—able to live and work legally in the United States.

Deferred Action for Childhood Arrivals

A. Who Are the DREAMers?... 182

B. How to Renew DACA 182

   1. Timing Your DACA Renewal Application... 182

   2. Making Sure You Are Still DACA Eligible 183

   3. DACA Renewal Forms... 183

   4. Documentation and Fees for DACA Renewal.. 183

   5. After Submitting Your DACA Renewal Application.. 184

   6. Leaving the U.S. With Advance Parole 184

In June 2012, the Obama administration created a new remedy for young immigrants in the U.S. who had no legal status. Called "Deferred Action for Childhood Arrivals" or "DACA," it allowed noncitizens who were brought to the U.S. as children and who meet various other requirements to apply for two years' protection from deportation (removal), as well a work permit.

In 2017, President Trump announced he would be ending DACA, after a wind-down phase. Immigration advocates filed lawsuits alleging, among other things, that the U.S. government failed to follow the necessary procedural requirements under federal law when it abruptly announced the termination. At the time this book went to print in mid-2022, DACA renewals were still being accepted, due to decisions by federal courts and the Supreme Court. But no new applications were being accepted, owing to a July 2021 decision by a Texas federal court. Members of Congress have discussed enacting legislation giving permanent residency to young, DACA-holding or eligible immigrants. This would open a path to U.S. citizenship after a certain number of years.

So far, however, these proposals have failed, to get enough votes to pass. Still, hope remains that DACA recipients ("DREAMers") could receive green cards in the future. DACA is a turbulent and contentious topic in immigration law, and it's worth paying attention to the news in order to stay up to date

A. Who Are the DREAMers?

Despite being called "DACA kids" by some, many DACA recipients are by now in their mid-30s and have children of their own.

Noncitizens were considered DACA eligible if they:

- had not yet turned age 31 as of June 15, 2012

- had not yet turned age 16 upon entering the United States
- continuously lived in the U.S. after at least June 15, 2007 (excluding brief casual, and innocent departures)
- were physically present in the U.S. on June 12, 2012 and at the time of submitting a DACA application
- were in school, had graduated from high school or received a general education development (GED) certificate; or were honorably discharged from the Coast Guard or U.S. Armed Forces
- had not been convicted of a felony, significant misdemeanor, or three or more other misdemeanors, and
- did not otherwise present a threat to U.S. national security or public safety (such as by being a member of a gang).

B. How to Renew DACA

If you currently hold DACA, you will likely want to renew your deportation protection and extend your work permit if you are so eligible. Although no one can predict whether or when Congress will pass a law giving green cards to DREAMers or how long the DACA program will last, the best hope for benefitting from any upcoming legislation is to maintain your DACA approval. It's true that DACA is temporary, but you will be able to renew it in additional two-year increments for as long as court actions requiring the government to continue accepting DACA renewals remain in effect.

1. Timing Your DACA Renewal Application

When this book went to print, USCIS was accepting DACA renewals only from people whose DACA expired one year ago or less.

You can submit a DACA renewal application 150 days before your work permit (employment authorization document or EAD) is due to expire. For example, if your work permit expires on September 15, 2022, you should submit your DACA renewal on or after April 18, 2022. But if you were to submit your application before April 18, 2022, USCIS could reject it.

2. Making Sure You Are Still DACA Eligible

The basic criteria for DACA eligibility are detailed in the previous section of this chapter. In order to renew your DACA and work permit, you must continue to meet the criteria stated there. There are also additional criteria you'll need to meet for DACA renewal, including that you:

- haven't left the U.S. since August 15, 2012 (at least, not without first obtaining permission from USCIS, in the form of what's called "Advance Parole")
- have continuously lived ("resided") in the U.S. since submitting your initial DACA application
- haven't been convicted of a felony, significant misdemeanor, or three or more other misdemeanors, and
- haven't done anything suggesting that you present a threat to U.S. national security or public safety (such as being a known member of a gang).

Age requirements are irrelevant when renewing; it does not matter how old you have become. Even if you are now in your mid-30s, if you were initially granted DACA, you have met the age requirements, and don't have to worry about them again.

If you think you might no longer qualify for DACA because of any of the factors listed above, see a qualified immigration attorney to evaluate whether you should apply for a renewal. Absolutely see an attorney if you have been convicted of

any crime or you no longer meet the educational requirements; for example, you failed to continue on your path to a GED. In such a case, you might no longer be DACA eligible. Although USCIS doesn't actually require you to show that you're still in school or have otherwise met the educational criteria when renewing, the agency does want to be told if you've failed to do so.

3. DACA Renewal Forms

The forms to submit to USCIS to renew your DACA include:

- ☐ Form I-821D, Consideration of Deferred Action for Childhood Arrivals (from www.uscis.gov/i-821d), and
- ☐ Form I-765, Application for Employment Authorization (from www.uscis.gov/i-765), accompanied by a worksheet called "Form I-765WS" (which you'll also find on USCIS's I-821D page). The eligibility category for purposes of Question 27 is "(c)(33)."

DACA renewal applicants do not need to complete Part 3 of the application.

4. Documentation and Fees for DACA Renewal

You need not submit all the sorts of documentation that you did in support of your initial I-821D DACA application. That's because USCIS has a copy of your original file.

You may submit a copy of your passport biographic page or another photo ID to establish your identity. Other than that, you will need to provide only documentation of anything that has changed since your last DACA application.

If you have received new documentation from an Immigration Court or evidence concerning any criminal issues, include copies in the renewal application. But be sure to discuss such developments with an attorney before filing to renew.

For the Form I-765 employment authorization, submit a copy of the front and back of your current EAD (work permit) card and two passport-style photographs of yourself, with your name and alien registration number ("A number") written on the back. Your A number is on your EAD; it starts with A and has 9 numbers.

The fee for the DACA renewal application is $495, which includes the standard $85 biometrics (fingerprinting) fee for a background check and the fee for a work permit. You may pay the fee with a money order, personal check, or cashier's check made payable to "U.S. Department of Homeland Security." Or, you can pay by credit card, using USCIS Form G-1450, Authorization for Credit Card Transactions (available on the USCIS website).

5. After Submitting Your DACA Renewal Application

After you have mailed your DACA renewal application to USCIS, you will be able to keep your DACA only until its original expiration date, unless you receive an approval notice before it expires.

Unlike with some other types of immigration applications, submitting Form I-821D will not extend your work authorization while USCIS reviews your case. If, therefore, you do not receive your approval notice and an EAD before that time, you will unfortunately not have DACA protection, and your work permit will expire (even if the delay is the fault of USCIS).

While immigration authorities such as Immigration and Customs Enforcement (ICE) don't typically arrest people with lapsed DACA, you are always vulnerable if do not have proof that you are legally authorized to remain in the United States.

You might want to carry your receipt notice with you as proof of your pending DACA renewal, just in case.

6. Leaving the U.S. With Advance Parole

DACA holders may travel outside the U.S. and return legally, but only if they first obtain an "Advance Parole" document. Leaving without this would cause you to lose your DACA status and be denied permission to enter.

Even with Advance Parole, however, traveling is nor risk-free. First off, if you push things until the last minute and plan to return just before your Advance Parole document expired, then encounter travel delays, perhaps due to transportation or COVID issues, you will be blocked from U.S. entry entirely.

Also, the Customs and Border Protection (CBP) officer whom you will meet upon return can deny your entry if you are "inadmissible," most likely for health or security reasons. You'll be in a weaker arguing position than someone who has, say, held a U.S. green card (lawful permanent residence) for a number of years. At least you probably won't be found inadmissible based on your past unlawful presence in the U.S., since this bar requires a "departure" from the U.S. and leaving with Advance Parole doesn't count as one. Nevertheless, if you've entered the U.S. illegally more than once, you'll need to make sure the permanent bar doesn't block you. Or if you have an outstanding order of removal or deportation on record, or neglected to show up for a court hearing, leaving the U.S. could be viewed as your having followed through with the deportation. You would not be allowed to return to the U.S. for many years. Definitely talk to an attorney regarding any such situation.

a. Who Is Eligible to Apply for Advance Parole as a DACA Recipient

Simply wanting to take a vacation or say hello to family is not enough to qualify DACA recipients for Advance Parole. You will need to show that you are traveling for either:

- humanitarian purposes, which include medical assistance, to attend a family member's funeral, visiting a sick relative, or some other urgent family-related matter
- educational purposes, including taking part in a study abroad program or doing academic research, or
- employment purposes, including overseas assignments or client meetings, interviews, conferences, training, and travel needed to pursue a job with a foreign employer in the United States.

Along with your application (described next), you will need to supply authoritative documentary evidence to back up whichever of these purposes you claim.

b. How to Apply for Advance Parole as a DACA Recipient

To apply for Advance Parole, you will need to submit the following to U.S. Citizenship and Immigration Services (USCIS):

- ☐ Form I-131, issued by USCIS (see below).
- ☐ Copy of a photo identity document, such as a driver's license or passport identity page.
- ☐ Proof that you have been approved for DACA (Form I-797).
- ☐ Documents in support of your claimed basis for travel (with a full, certified English-language translation if they're in another language). Send copies, not originals.
- ☐ Proof of family relationships if they're relevant to your request. For example, people claiming a need to travel to a grandparents' funeral should supply birth certificates for their parents and themselves, showing the lineage.
- ☐ Two passport-style photos of you, taken within 30 days of filing your Advance Parole application.
- ☐ Information about your intended dates of travel and the duration of your trip or trips (which you should provide in Part 4 of Form I-131), and
- ☐ Application fee (currently $575, plus $85 for biometrics if you're between the age of 14 and 79; see the USCIS website for the latest).

The more official the documents you provide, the better. For example, if you wish to travel for educational reasons, you'd want a letter from an official at your school explaining why the travel is required or beneficial or a document showing that you've enrolled in a program or class requiring travel. Or, if a family member is seriously ill, you'd want to submit a doctor's letter and other medical or hospital reports, as well as proof of the family relationship.

Assuming you include all the correct materials, you can expect a wait of three to 30 months, depending on which Service Center handles applications from your region.

c. If USCIS Grants Advance Parole

If USCIS approves you, it will send you a Form I-512L, Authorization for Parole of an Alien into the United States. Take this (the original, not a copy) with you when leaving the United States. You'll need to show it before getting on the plane, ship, bus, or train headed back to the U.S. and to the CBP officer when you return.

Look closely at the form, because it contains the last date you can use it to return. Make sure you don't stay outside the U.S. past that date. ●

U Visas for Crime Victims
Assisting Law Enforcement

A. Who Is Eligible for a U Visa 188

   1. What Crimes Qualify Their Victims for a U Visa 189

   2. When Indirect and Bystander Victims May Be Eligible for U Status.............189

   3. Satisfying the Requirement That You Suffered Substantial Physical
      or Mental Abuse..190

   4. Satisfying the Requirement That You Are Helping U.S. Law Enforcement.....190

   5. Available Waiver If You Are Inadmissible...191

   6. Qualifying Family Members May Receive Derivative U Visas.........................191

B. How to Apply for a U Visa 192

   1. Preparing the Petition...193

   2. Obtaining a Certification of Helpfulness...193

   3. Preparing Documents to Support Your U Visa Petition..................................194

   4. Filling Out Form I-765..194

   5. Submitting Your U Visa Petition to USCIS..194

   6. Attending a U Visa Interview..195

C. Your Legal Status While U Visa Is Pending..195

D. Green Card Possibilities After U Visa Approval...196

   1. Which U Nonimmigrants Are Eligible for a Green Card..................................196

   2. You Have Continuous U.S. Physical Presence of at Least Three Years...........196

   3. You Must Continue to Cooperate With Law Enforcement.............................196

   4. Your Residence Is Justified on Humanitarian, Family Unity, or Public
      Interest Grounds...197

   5. Your Immediate Relatives May Also Apply for Green Cards...........................197

   6. How to File for a U.S. Green Card 198

   7. What Happens After Submitting Adjustment of Status Application...............199

The Victims of Trafficking and Violence Protection Act of 2000 authorized a new visa for immigrant victims of serious crimes, called the "U" visa. The legislation was enacted in response to rising public safety concerns, with the idea that foreign victims of crimes in the U.S. should be allowed to remain here so as to provide law enforcement officials with information helpful in apprehending and prosecuting criminal offenders.

Although the U visa is temporary in nature, it can eventually lead to a U.S. green card, albeit after a long wait. It has, in fact, become an important option for many noncitizens in the United States. (The same legislation also created a "T" visa for victims of severe human trafficking, but because this is used less commonly, we will not cover it within this book.) However, the U visa program is not without potential risk to the applicant.

If you are approved for a U visa, you will be granted legal status in the U.S. for up to four years (which may be extended in "exceptional circumstances"). After you have held your U status for three years, you might be eligible to apply for a green card.

As with all U.S. visas, you will need to take several steps to prove that you qualify for it. In other words, it is not enough to simply claim that you have been a victim of a serious crime. You will need to provide a "certificate of helpfulness" from a qualifying law enforcement agency and also prove that you suffered mental or physical abuse by the U.S. criminal perpetrator.

Additionally, if you are "inadmissible" to the U.S. due to past immigration violations or for other reasons, you will need to apply for a waiver of these grounds.

This chapter will discuss the eligibility criteria for a U visa and how to apply. A final note: Although we use the term "U visa" throughout this chapter, only the applicants who come from outside the U.S. will, in literal terms, receive a visa in their passport. (A visa is an entry document.) Applicants from within the U.S. will receive "U status," and will, if they leave the U.S., need to go to a U.S. consulate to get an actual visa stamp in their passport before returning.

A. Who Is Eligible for a U Visa

In order to qualify for a U visa or U status in the U.S., you must meet the following criteria:

- ☐ You must have been a victim of a "qualifying criminal activity," and this crime must have occurred in the U.S. or violated U.S. law. Indirect and bystander victims are also eligible to apply in certain circumstances, though approvals are increasingly rare.
- ☐ In the course of—or as a result of—this criminal activity, you must have suffered substantial physical or mental abuse.
- ☐ You can provide useful information about the criminal activity (or if younger than age 16, your parent, guardian, or "next friend" such as a counselor or social worker can provide this information for you).
- ☐ You (or your parent, guardian, or next friend) are cooperating with U.S. law enforcement in order to bring the perpetrator of the crime to justice.
- ☐ You are admissible to the U.S. or you are applying for a waiver using Form I-192, Application for Advance Permission to Enter as a Non-Immigrant.

You can apply for a U visa either from within the U.S. or abroad (at a U.S. consulate).

1. What Crimes Qualify Their Victims for a U Visa

In a typical U visa case, you will have been the victim of a serious crime that took place in the United States. In some cases, however, the crime might have violated U.S. laws overseas (such as a human trafficking or kidnapping crime). Examples of qualifying crimes are:

- **Violent crimes.** murder, manslaughter, vehicular homicide, robbery, felonious assault (which usually involves the use of a deadly weapon, and can include statutory rape and other offenses), domestic violence, or stalking
- **Enslavement crimes.** criminal restraint, kidnapping, abduction, being held hostage, forced labor, slavery, human trafficking, indentured or debt servitude, or false imprisonment
- **Sex crimes.** rape, incest, sexual trafficking, sexual assault and abusive sexual contact, prostitution, sexual exploitation, or female genital mutilation, and
- **Obstruction of justice crimes.** perjury, witness tampering, blackmail, extortion, or with-holding evidence.

The crime need not have been "completed" in order for it to qualify. An attempt, solicitation, or conspiracy to commit one of the above-mentioned crimes is enough. For example, obviously a murder victim wouldn't be applying for a U visa. But if you are the victim of attempted murder, you may qualify for a U visa.

2. When Indirect and Bystander Victims May Be Eligible for U Status

In limited circumstances, USCIS may grant U status to people who are not the direct victims of crime. The two examples of this are close family members of the direct victim who suffer indirectly, or bystander victims. In either instance, however, the applicant must meet all the other requirements for a U visa, meaning that they: have been helpful, are being helpful, or will be helpful in the investigation, suffered substantial harm as a result of the crime, and are either admissible to the U.S. or qualify for a waiver of inadmissibility.

Certain family members can apply for U visas as indirect victims if the primary victim died due to murder or manslaughter or was rendered incompetent or incapacitated and therefore cannot help authorities with the criminal investigation. For crime victims who are age 21 or older, their spouse, as well as their children younger than 21 years of age, may be considered indirect victims. For victims younger than age 21, their parents and unmarried siblings younger than 18 can be considered indirect victims.

> **EXAMPLE:** Leticia's son Rodrigo was murdered when he was 20 years old. Leticia, from Mexico, had a nervous breakdown soon after hearing the news. She helped the police investigation by providing information about her son and the events that happened on the day of the murder. Leticia would qualify as an indirect victim because she is the parent of a deceased victim younger than 21, she suffered harm as a result of the crime, and she helped in the investigation. She may still qualify even if several years have passed since the murder, because USCIS looks at the age of the victim when the murder took place to determine whether parents were indirect victims, and Rodrigo was 20.

USCIS ordinarily considers minors to be "incapacitated," and therefore their family members often qualify as indirect victims.

EXAMPLE: Minjun, who overstayed a visa from Korea, has a four-year-old daughter, born in the United States. The daughter became the victim of child molestation by a nanny. As soon as Minjun realized his daughter was being abused, he reported the incident to the police, and assisted with the investigation. He suffered serious emotional harm because of what the daughter went through, especially because he was also the victim of abuse as a child. Because the daughter was born in the U.S., she does not need to apply for immigration relief. Minjun therefore could not be a derivative on her U status application. However, he may qualify for U status as an indirect victim, because his daughter was incapacitated (by definition, due to her young age), he helped the investigation, and he suffered harm as a result of the crime.

In both the above examples of indirect victims, the noncitizen would also have to meet the other requirements for eligibility for U status or a U visa, by showing admissibility to the U.S. or qualifying for a waiver of inadmissibility.

USCIS can also grant U visa status to noncitizen bystanders to crimes who suffered unusually severe harm as a result of having witnessed the criminal activity. The example most often used is that of a pregnant woman who suffers a miscarriage as a result of witnessing a criminal activity.

3. Satisfying the Requirement That You Suffered Substantial Physical or Mental Abuse

It is not enough to merely be the victim of a qualifying crime. You must have also suffered "substantial" physical injury or mental anguish as a result of this criminal activity and must provide USCIS with supporting evidence of this, such as medical records and affidavits. The burden of proof is on you to prove that your suffering is "substantial."

In determining whether the injury was "substantial," USCIS reviews applications on a case-by-case basis. USCIS will consider the nature of the injury inflicted; the severity of the perpetrator's conduct; the severity of the harm suffered; the duration of the infliction of the harm; and the extent to which there is permanent or serious harm to the appearance, health, or physical or mental soundness of the victim.

You will need to provide a personal statement detailing the physical or mental harm you suffered, as well as medical records or statements from treating physicians and psychologists, photographs of physical injuries, and affidavits from social workers. Question 7 of Part 3 on the law enforcement certification, Form I-918B, asks the law enforcement officer to detail injuries to the victim, as well. Ensuring that law enforcement is aware of the extent of your injuries can therefore strengthen your case.

4. Satisfying the Requirement That You Are Helping U.S. Law Enforcement

One of the reasons that Congress authorized U visas was out of concern that many U.S. immigrants refuse to provide information to U.S. police and other law enforcement authorities, due to cultural differences, language barriers, and fear of deportation. The unfortunate result is that many perpetrators of serious crimes view immigrants as easy targets; and go on to commit more crimes.

In order to further the public safety objectives of the U visa, your visa petition must be certified by a law enforcement official or judge. Obtaining a strong certification is absolutely necessary for a successful U visa application. The official must attest that you were a victim of a qualifying crime and that you have been, are being, or are likely to be helpful to an investigation or prosecution of the crime.

The chances of your getting a law enforcement official to cooperate with your U visa application are greatly improved if you are forthcoming with information that could lead to the identification, arrest, and conviction of a serious criminal. (Nevertheless, the achievement of such results isn't required.) Relevant information could include (but is not limited to):

☐ an identification of the criminals involved, such as their names and addresses, or by your choosing the correct person in a lineup identification

☐ information that helps apprehend the perpetrators, such as your tips as to where they might be "hiding out," names of their friends and family who might give information about their whereabouts, or identifying details about their vehicle (make, color, license plate number)

☐ descriptive details that help the prosecution convince a jury that the accused is guilty of the crime, rebut the criminal's alibi, support a motive for committing the crime, or determine what penalty (or sentencing) it should request

☐ evidence that could help law enforcement classify the crime as more serious or charge the criminals with additional crimes. (This might be the situation if, for example, the officer is investigating a felony assault but you have evidence that could lead to an attempted murder charge, or you have information that might lead to an additional charge of sexual assault.)

☐ agreement to testify as a witness if the case goes to trial.

Law enforcement agencies can choose not to issue certifications, at their own discretion. On the other hand, they are encouraged to help, for the sake of victim assistance and fostering community trust.

5. Available Waiver If You Are Inadmissible

To be eligible for a U visa, you must not be "inadmissible" to the United States. This means that you are not barred from U.S. entry due to factors such as multiple criminal convictions, immigration violations (including entering without inspection), certain medical conditions, or any of several other reasons.

Most potential U visa applicants are inadmissible, especially if they entered the U.S. without a visa or other official permission. Luckily, a waiver of inadmissibility is available. In order to apply for the waiver, you must submit to USCIS Form I-192, Application for Advance Permission to Enter as a Nonimmigrant. Unlike many other immigration waivers, this one does not require a showing of "extreme hardship." Almost all grounds of inadmissibility may be waived in conjunction with a U visa application (the only exceptions being for national-security or terrorism-related grounds). However, just because a ground of inadmissibility can be waived doesn't mean that USCIS will do so. U visa waiver applications are reviewed on a case-by-case basis. You'll definitely want to get a lawyer's help, in order to identify and prove the reasons you deserve the waiver.

If USCIS approves your waiver, the same grounds of inadmissibility will also be waived for your future application for adjustment of status (if any) and a green card.

6. Qualifying Family Members May Receive Derivative U Visas

Certain family members may be eligible to become derivative U visa recipients if the principal petitioner's application is approved. These include your:

• unmarried children younger than age 21

• spouse

• parents (if principal petitioner is younger than age 21), and

• unmarried siblings younger than 18 years old (if principal petitioner is younger than age 21).

To obtain derivative status for family members, you (as the primary petitioner) would submit Form I-918, Supplement A, Petition for Qualifying Family Member of U Visa Recipient, along with your own petition or after your U visa is approved. Any derivative relatives that you include must also be "admissible" to the U.S. (or apply for a waiver) and have good moral character.

B. How to Apply for a U Visa

Applying for a U visa involves the following steps:

1. Prepare USCIS Form I-918, Petition for U Nonimmigrant Status (you can download a completed sample at www.nolo.com/back-of-book/GRN.html).
2. Have a qualifying agency provide certification of your helpfulness, to accompany this I-918 petition (on Form I-918B).
3. Gather evidence to substantiate your eligibility and claim of substantial injury.
4. If you have derivative family members who wish to work in the U.S., prepare Form I-765 for a work permit.
5. Submit your petition and supporting documents to USCIS.
6. Attend an interview at a USCIS office or your local U.S. consulate, if required.

CAUTION

Don't follow these instructions if you're in removal proceedings. This chapter discusses only how to apply for a U visa if you are not in removal proceedings in Immigration Court. If you are, or if you have a final order of removal, the process is considerably more complex. Filing for a U visa might not prevent your removal at all, due to the long wait times for your case to be decided. Consult an immigration attorney for help with a U visa application if your case is being handled by the Immigration Courts.

We'll explain each of the normal application steps below. Here is a summary of the items you will need to assemble:

☐ Form I-918 (No fee is required with this form.)
☐ Form I-918, Supplement A (if you want derivative status for a qualifying family member)
☐ Form I-918, Supplement B (completed and certified by a qualifying law enforcement agency)
☐ supporting documents, as described in Section 2
☐ evidence that you have helpful information about the crime. Form I-918, Supplement B should be sufficient, but if you have any further information about how you are being helpful to authorities in providing information about the crime, you should submit it.
☐ evidence that the crime violated U.S. laws. Again, Form I-918, Supplement B should cover this, but if you have any additional information about the crime, especially if it occurred outside of the U.S. (but violated federal law), you should provide this.
☐ Waiver of Grounds of Inadmissibility, if applicable. Submit Form I-192, Application for Advance Permission to Enter as a Nonimmigrant, with check or money order ($930 as of this book's print date), made payable to "U.S. Department of Homeland Security." If you cannot afford this amount, you may apply for a fee waiver.
☐ information to prove relationship of derivative family members. Provide documentation to prove that your family member qualifies for derivative U status (for example, birth or marriage certificates). Make sure that any foreign language documents are accompanied by a full English translation

that is certified as complete and accurate by a translator competent to translate from the foreign language into English.

☐ Form I-765, Application for Employment Authorization Document (EAD), with appropriate filing fees (or fee waivers), for any derivative family members who wish to work and are currently in the United States. Principal U visa holders will automatically be sent a work permit when approved.

1. Preparing the Petition

Form I-918 can be obtained from www.uscis. gov/i-918; and you can download a completed sample at www.nolo.com/back-of-book/GRN.html. As a general caution when preparing Form I-918 or the Form I-918 Supplement A for a derivative, realize that you must fill out all fields, unless they are optional. For example, a petitioner who does not have children should not leave the question about children blank, but instead enter "N/A" (not applicable) in the appropriate space. Out of an abundance of caution, since the forms do not always clearly indicate which fields are "optional," applicants should complete all fields.

2. Obtaining a Certification of Helpfulness

As part of your application for a U visa, you will need to show USCIS that a law enforcement official has "vouched" for your petition. A judge, police officer, prosecutor, or other law enforcement official must complete a "certification of helpfulness" (I-918 Supplement B, U Nonimmigrant Status Certification) on your behalf. This document shows that you have been a victim of qualifying criminal activity, have information that will be useful to law enforcement, and are cooperating in order to bring the perpetrator to justice.

The agencies that will most commonly certify a U visa petition are local, state, federal, tribal, and territorial police departments, law enforcement agencies, and prosecutors. Even a judge may sign a U visa certification, although many will refuse to do so in order to avoid a showing of bias for the prosecution. However, any state or federal agency that has "responsibility for the investigation or prosecution of a qualifying crime or criminal activity" may complete the certification of helpfulness. For example, if you are the victim of a crime that requires the involvement of Child Protective Services (CPS), you could bypass the police and justice departments and instead have CPS help you with your application. Or, a department of labor or the Equal Employment Opportunity Commission (EEOC) could provide a certification.

Government guidelines state that people who are in a supervisory role and have responsibility for issuing certificates of helpfulness must be the ones to actually sign the petition, but it allows the agency to designate another certifying official if it chooses to do so.

Ultimately, it's up to the law enforcement authorities acting in your case to decide whether or not you are "helpful" to them and whether they should fill out the certification of helpfulness for you.

If the agency signs the certification for you, it will place the Form I-918B and any supporting documentation into an envelope and seal it, then write on the front, in capital letters: "DO NOT OPEN. FOR USCIS USE ONLY," and on the back, write the signer's initials across the seal, then cover that with clear tape. You will be given the sealed envelope for submission with your Form I-918; and obviously should follow the instructions and not open it.

You must file the Supplement B with USCIS within six months of the date the certifying official signed this, or it will no longer be valid.

TIP

Get to work on obtaining the certification of helpfulness as soon as possible. Not only is it a vital part of your application, but by showing interest and providing helpful evidence to authorities, you will help show that you are eager to participate in the investigation. Also, if the criminals involved are arrested and plead guilty to the criminal charges before you contact police or answer a request for cooperation from law enforcement, your evidence and testimony might not be as useful, since the case will not go to trial.

3. Preparing Documents to Support Your U Visa Petition

Filling out the required forms will not be enough, by itself, to qualify you for a U visa. You will also need to prepare or gather various documents to support your claim, such as:

- a personal narrative statement, describing how you are a victim of criminal activity and the circumstances surrounding the crime. You can use this statement to show that you were not at fault in the criminal activity and that you were helpful (if you called the authorities to report the crime, for example). Also describe the extent of your injuries.
- evidence that you are the victim of a qualifying criminal activity. This could include trial transcripts, newspaper articles, police reports, affidavits, or orders of protection (restraining orders).
- evidence that you suffered substantial physical or mental abuse. This could include affidavits from case or social workers, medical personnel, and police; photographs of injuries; and affidavits from people who have personal knowledge of the criminal activity.

An attorney can help you gather these documents, but you will still need to play a role in considering what the best sources might be, and in talking to friends, doctors, and others who might help.

4. Filling Out Form I-765

You will not be eligible to work while your U visa application is pending, unless you receive deferred action (discussed more in "How Long Does It Take to Get a U Visa?"). The principal petitioner does not need to worry about applying for a work permit (EAD). If the I-918 is approved, the petitioner will be sent an EAD automatically. Any derivative family member who wants to work must, however, separately submit Form I-765 (available at www.uscis.gov/i-765) to request an EAD. They can do so either by including their form with the I-918 petition or by sending in a separate Form I-765 after USCIS has approved the I-918 petition. Derivatives likewise cannot work while the U visa is pending, unless they receive deferred action.

Form I-765 is fairly short and self-explanatory. For Question 27, the applicant's eligibility category, you would fill in "(a)(19)" for the principal applicant and "(a)(20)" for any derivative family members.

Your family members will also need to pay the Form I-765 fee ($410 as of this book's print date) or request a fee waiver.

5. Submitting Your U Visa Petition to USCIS

After completing the application, make a copy for your files. Then send the packet of forms and documents to the USCIS address indicated on its website.

6. Attending a U Visa Interview

If you are applying from within the U.S., chances are you will not be required to attend an interview at a local USCIS office, which is why it is important to provide a strong statement with your I-918 applications. However, it's always possible that you might be required to attend an in-person interview. If you're in the United States, this would be at a local USCIS office. If you (or your family members) are applying from overseas, this interview would be held at the U.S. embassy or consulate in your home country.

The purpose of the interview will be for U.S. officials to review your file and talk with you personally about your eligibility for a U visa or your relationship with the principal applicant (if you are a family member applying for derivative status) and to make sure you are not inadmissible to the United States.

How Long Does It Take to Get a U Visa?

There is an annual limit of 10,000 U visas per year, and demand normally far outpaces supply. The backlog has become so bad that all available visas each year are typically allocated to people on the waiting list, which can last five years or more. Fortunately, USCIS has taken steps to ensure that prospectively eligible U visa applicants receive a work permit and "deferred action" (protecting them against deportation) while they wait.

Unfortunately, your wait time does not count towards the three years of continuous presence required for adjustment of status and to receive a green card.

C. Your Legal Status While U Visa Is Pending

Until you have received a U visa or deferred action, you do not have legal immigration status in the United States. In theory, that means that during your long wait, you could be picked up by Immigrations and Customs Enforcement (ICE) and placed into detention or removal proceedings.

To deal with this issue, the government created a new process in 2021 known as the "Bona Fide Determination" ("BFD"). It allows U visa applicants in the United States to receive four-year work authorization and a quasi-status known as "deferred action" while they wait for USCIS's decision.

You don't have to apply separately for this. USCIS will review applications (in the order received). If an application is complete and appears on its face to meet the basic criteria for approvability, and if the applicant has attended the biometrics (fingerprinting) appointment and isn't blocked from eligibility due to crimes and such, will issue the work permit and deferred action status. For further detail, see the USCIS *Policy Manual* at Volume 3, Part C, Chapter 5.

If your U visa is ultimately denied, however, USCIS may refer your case to ICE for enforcement. This makes applying for a U visa a calculated risk, particularly for people who have significant grounds of inadmissibility. If your U visa is denied, you might be able to appeal that denial, but will need to consult with an immigration attorney. If deported, you have the option of appealing or filing again from overseas.

D. Green Card Possibilities After U Visa Approval

If you have received a U visa or U status as a victim of a serious crime assisting law enforcement, you might be able to adjust your status (receive a green card) after three years of continuous presence in the United States. This does not include time spent in deferred action status. If interested, you should apply for a green card as soon you can, because you must continue to be eligible as a U visa crime victim at the time you apply.

1. Which U Nonimmigrants Are Eligible for a Green Card

Here's a breakdown of the requirements you must meet in order to apply for a U.S. green card:

- You must continue to be eligible for U nonimmigrant status. This means that you must continue to assist law enforcement by providing helpful information used to investigate and prosecute the criminals who victimized you.
- You must not have abandoned this status (for example, by refusing to cooperate with government agencies or by living outside the U.S. for an extended period of time).
- You have been physically present in the U.S. continuously for at least three years.
- You have not unreasonably refused to cooperate with the law enforcement officials investigating and prosecuting the crime against you.
- Your continued presence in the U.S. is justified either on humanitarian grounds, to ensure family unity, or because it is in the public interest.

You will have a difficult time showing USCIS that you are eligible for a green card if your help is no longer necessary to investigate and prosecute the crime against you (for example, the criminal case is now closed and a government official will not vouch for your "helpfulness"). For this reason, you might want to maintain contact with your certifying law enforcement agency while in U status.

2. You Have Continuous U.S. Physical Presence of at Least Three Years

In order to successfully apply for permanent residence, you must show that you have lived in the U.S. continuously for three years. "Continuous" presence for immigration purposes means that you have not taken a trip outside the U.S. for 90 days or more or spent more than 180 days abroad during your time in U status.

You can demonstrate your continuous presence by documenting each trip outside the U.S. (to show that you were abroad only briefly) and providing proof that you now make your life in the United States. This can include pay stubs, tax transcripts, school records, and affidavits from people who know you and can attest to your U.S. presence.

If you can't show continuous presence, you will need to provide a written explanation by a government official who is working on your case, stating that your presence outside the U.S. was necessary in order to assist the investigation or prosecution of the crime or that it was otherwise justified.

3. You Must Continue to Cooperate With Law Enforcement

In order to be eligible for a green card, you must continue to provide helpful information to law enforcement officials, and you cannot have "unreasonably refused" to provide requested assistance.

Ideally, you will submit another certification of helpfulness (Form I-918 Supplement B, U Nonimmigrant Status Certification) with your green card application. This will prove that you are a willing participant in the investigation and prosecution of the crime (or crimes) against you.

If you are unable to obtain another certification of helpfulness, contact an experienced immigration attorney to help, because you will need to instead submit an affidavit and other supporting evidence showing all of your contacts and meetings with law enforcement officials. You will also need to explain that you attempted to obtain a certification from a qualifying agency, but were unable to for good reason.

Additionally, if you ever refused a request for cooperation, you must explain your reasons. USCIS will determine whether the request was "unreasonable" given a variety of factors. Its decision will depend on the nature of the crime, your circumstances, and the extent of the assistance required.

For example, if you are a rape victim and a police investigator asked you to meet with your attacker, USCIS would likely consider this to be an unreasonable request, and would excuse you for refusing it. However, if a police officer asked you to identify your attacker in a lineup where he would not see you and you refused, your denial could cost you a green card.

4. Your Residence Is Justified on Humanitarian, Family Unity, or Public Interest Grounds

Unlike many other green card applicants, U visa holders do not have to apply for a waiver of any applicable inadmissibility grounds. The only ground of inadmissibility that applies to U adjustment applicants concerns participants in Nazi persecution, genocide, or extrajudicial killings. There is no waiver available for these grounds.

However, adjustment of status to permanent residence from a U visa is a discretionary benefit,

which means it is completely up to the USCIS officer handling your case whether or not to grant it. Therefore, you should submit evidence with your application to show USCIS that you "deserve" a green card. For example, your family ties in the U.S., achievements and accomplishments, and any reasons why you would be subjected to hardship if you were to return to your home country will be relevant. This is especially true if there are any negative factors in your record (such as arrests or criminal convictions).

5. Your Immediate Relatives May Also Apply for Green Cards

If you have qualifying family members in the U.S. in derivative U status, the procedures to apply for adjustment of status are the same as for the principal U applicant.

However, if you have an immediate family member—spouse, child, or parents (if you are younger than age 21)—who has never received U derivative status, that person can also apply for adjustment of status or an immigrant visa at the same time you apply or after your approval. To bring this about, file Form I-929, Petition for Qualifying Family Member of U-1 Nonimmigrant, with USCIS. The filing fee as of 2022 is $230.

You must show that you or your family member would be subjected to "extreme hardship" if not permitted to reside with you in the United States. This is not an easy task; you'd do best to consult an immigration attorney.

Keep in mind that these relatives (unlike you) WILL be subject to the inadmissibility grounds that prevent many noncitizens from entering the United States.

6. How to File for a U.S. Green Card

If you meet all the requirements, the next step is to file for adjustment of status. You (and each of your derivative family members) will need to assemble:

- ☐ Form I-485, Application to Register Permanent Residence or to Adjust Status
- ☐ the filing fee or, or if you cannot afford it, a waiver request filed on Form I-912, Request for Fee Waiver
- ☐ Form I-693, Report of Medical Examination and Vaccination Record
- ☐ Form I-765, Application for Employment Authorization and supporting documentation (optional; your I-797 Receipt notice can also be used as verification of your employment authorization)
- ☐ Form I-131, Application for Travel Document and supporting documentation (optional)
- ☐ a copy of Form I-797, Notice of Action, showing that USCIS approved you for U nonimmigrant status
- ☐ a copy of your I-94, Arrival/Departure Record. All arriving foreign visitors had this white card stapled into their passports until this form was automated in April 2013; subsequent visitors can obtain a copy of their I-94 from the U.S. Customs and Border Protection (CBP) website at https://i94.cbp.dhs.gov.
- ☐ if any of your family members has not yet obtained derivative status, Form I-929, Petition for Qualifying Family Member of U-1 Nonimmigrant, as described in Section C5, above
- ☐ a copy of all pages of your passport, including the U nonimmigrant visa page. If you do not have a U visa, because you have not departed the U.S. since you were granted U status, make copies of all of your passport pages regardless. If you don't have a passport, provide an explanation as to why you do not have one, such as loss or theft.
- ☐ a copy of your birth certificate (along with an English translation)
- ☐ two passport-style photos for each of Forms I-485, I-765, and I-131
- ☐ evidence that you have three years of continuous physical presence in the U.S. This can include tax transcripts, pay stubs, leases, receipts, and utility bills for a U.S. residence, a letter from your school or employer, and affidavits from people who can vouch for your U.S. presence.
- ☐ evidence that you complied with requests for assistance from law enforcement officials. The best evidence of this is a new Form I-918 Supplement B. Second-best would be your affidavit, describing your attempts to contact law enforcement officials during your time in U status and reasons for any failure to comply with a request for cooperation.
- ☐ evidence that you "deserve" permanent residence. U visa holders are not subject to a majority of the inadmissibility grounds that others face when applying for a green card. However, because adjustment of status for U visa holders depends on whether USCIS believes it is justified, be prepared to submit evidence that you should be granted a green card on humanitarian, public interest, or family unity grounds.

! CAUTION

What if your U status will expire before you can apply for a green card? Your U status, as the principal applicant, will likely last four years. To be eligible to adjust status, you must be in valid U visa status. If your U visa expires before you file to adjust status, immigration law allows for an extension of status based on law enforcement need or upon a determination that the extension is warranted due to exceptional circumstances.

Derivative U visa holders can also find themselves at risk of having their status expire before they can file to adjust status. Due to consular processing delays, many derivative U visa holders are authorized to stay in the U.S. for only three years or less. If your U status will expire before you are able to accrue the continuous presence needed, you might able to extend the time to a period not exceeding four years.

Whether you are a principal applicant or a derivative U visa holder, you can apply to extend your U status by filling out and submitting USCIS Form I-539. Provide the documents described on the USCIS instructions to the form (available at www.uscis.gov/i-539). You should consult with an attorney before preparing an I-539, because the process is complex and the stakes are high. If your U visa expires before you file for adjustment of status, you risk being deported.

7. What Happens After Submitting Adjustment of Status Application

After you file Form I-485, you should first receive a receipt notice. Later, you will be sent a biometrics appointment notice, requiring you to appear to have your photograph, fingerprints, and signature taken. You are allowed to work while your adjustment of status application is pending. Following that, USCIS will normally schedule you for an interview at a local USCIS field office. Bring a copy of everything you sent to USCIS and an interpreter if you are not fluent in English. ●

Acquiring Citizenship Through U.S. Citizen Parents

A. Who Qualifies for Acquisition of U.S. Citizenship 202

   1. Birth Prior to May 24, 1934 202

   2. Birth Between May 25, 1934 and January 12, 1941 203

   3. Birth Between January 13, 1941 and December 23, 1952 204

   4. Birth Between December 24, 1952 and November 13, 1986 204

   5. Birth Between November 14, 1986 and the Present 204

   6. Exception to Requirements for Retaining U.S. Citizenship 205

B. Obtaining Proof of U.S. Citizenship 205

   1. U.S. Passport 205

   2. Certificate of Citizenship 206

   3. Certificate of Consular Report of Birth 206

C. Dual Citizenship 206

Okay, we know it's unlikely, but every so often someone struggling to qualify for a U.S. green card discovers that they were a U.S. citizen all along. How? Because their parents or even grandparents held U.S. citizenship at the time of their birth in another country. This is called "acquisition" of citizenship. This chapter will describe who qualifies for acquisition of citizenship, how to prove you're a U.S. citizen, and how to figure out whether you qualify for dual citizenship (simultaneous citizenship in the United States and your home country).

RESOURCE

This book does not describe how people who have already gotten a green card can apply to become naturalized citizens. For complete information on eligibility and the application process, see *Becoming a U.S. Citizen: A Guide to the Law, Exam & Interview,* by Ilona Bray (Nolo).

A. Who Qualifies for Acquisition of U.S. Citizenship

In many circumstances, even though a child is born outside the U.S., if at least one parent was a U.S. citizen at the time of the child's birth, the child automatically "acquires" U.S. citizenship. When this child marries and has children, those children may also acquire U.S. citizenship at birth.

The laws governing whether or not a child born outside U.S. boundaries acquires U.S. citizenship from parents have changed several times. The law that was in effect on the date of the child's birth determines whether the child acquired U.S. citizenship from a parent—and, if relevant, whether the parent was a citizen because of acquisition from the child's grandparent. If there is anyone in your direct line of ancestry whom you believe might be a U.S. citizen, it is worth your time to read what the U.S. laws were on the date of your birth and that of your ancestor.

Most laws controlling the passing of U.S. citizenship from parent to child require that the parent, the child, or both have had a period of living in the United States ("residence"). Sometimes the residence is required to be for a specified length of time (for example, five years) and sometimes it is not. When the law doesn't say exactly how long the residence period must be, you can assume that even a brief time, such as a month, might be enough. The key element is often not the amount of time but whether or not USCIS or the State Department believes it was a residence and not a visit. If the period of stay has the character of a residence, the length of time doesn't matter.

1. Birth Prior to May 24, 1934

If you were born before May 24, 1934, the law originally provided that only your U.S. citizen father (not mother) could pass citizenship on to you. The rules were very simple. In order to pass on U.S. citizenship, the father must have resided in the U.S. at some time before the child's birth. The law didn't require any particular length of time or dates when the residence took place. Technically, a day or a week would be enough if it could be regarded as a residence and not just a visit. Once a child obtained U.S. citizenship at birth through a U.S. citizen father, there were no conditions to retaining it. These rules also applied to so-called "illegitimate" children (children born to unmarried parents), provided the U.S. citizen father had at some time legally legitimated the child (acknowledged his paternal responsibility). U.S. citizenship was then acquired at the time of legitimation, without regard to the child's age.

This law has been challenged several times as discriminatory, with some courts holding that citizenship could also be passed by the mother to the children. Congress finally addressed this issue in 1994 and amended the law, retroactively, to provide that either parent could pass his or her U.S. citizenship to children.

Consider that if you were born before May 24, 1934, and either of your parents was a U.S. citizen, that citizenship might have been passed on to you. Consider also that if either of your parents was born before May 24, 1934, they might have acquired U.S. citizenship from either of their parents, which they then passed on to you under laws in existence at a later date. A check of the family tree could well be worth your while.

2. Birth Between May 25, 1934 and January 12, 1941

If you were born between May 25, 1934 and January 12, 1941, you acquired U.S. citizenship at birth on the conditions that both your parents were U.S. citizens and at least one had resided in the U.S. prior to your birth. The law at this time placed no additional conditions on retaining U.S. citizenship acquired in this way.

You could also get U.S. citizenship if only one of your parents was a U.S. citizen, as long as that parent had a prior U.S. residence. If your U.S. citizenship came from only one parent, you too would have been required to reside in the U.S. for at least two years between the ages of 14 and 28 in order to retain the citizenship you got at birth. Alternatively, you could retain citizenship if your noncitizen parent naturalized before you turned 18 and you began living in the U.S. permanently before age 18. Otherwise, your citizenship would be lost.

What If You Were Born "Out of Wedlock" to a U.S. Citizen Father?

Your right to U.S. citizenship might depend on your relationship to a U.S. citizen father. However, if your parents weren't married at the time you were born, the laws of the time might refer to you as "illegitimate," meaning in legal terms that you have no recognized father. As you'll see in the sections below, your right to claim citizenship could depend on your providing evidence that your father took the actions necessary to satisfy the legitimation law of your birth country. Legitimation laws require fathers to legally acknowledge their children.

Change might be on the horizon, however. In June 2017, the U.S. Supreme Court declared in a case called *Sessions v. Morales-Santana* that such gender-based distinctions, specifically in § 309(c) of the I.N.A., violate the U.S. Constitution. The case concerned the laws in effect in 1962, the year Mr. Morales-Santana was born in the Dominican Republic. To acquire citizenship through his unmarried father, he needed to show that the father had lived in the U.S. for at least ten years, with five of those years occurring after he turned 14, and the father must have either been listed on the birth certificate or taken other steps to acknowledge paternity, such as "legitimating" him prior to his 21st birthday and before he married.

Meanwhile, to acquire U.S. citizenship through an unmarried mother in and around 1962, the law required only that the mother had U.S. nationality when the child was born, and have previously been physically present in the U.S. or one of its outlying possessions for a continuous period of only one year. Justice Ruth Bader Ginsburg, who wrote the opinion, called this law's variation in treatment of mothers versus fathers "stunningly anachronistic," and found that it fails to achieve its supposed purpose of ensuring that children born overseas have a strong connection to the United States in order to be allowed U.S. citizenship.

Unfortunately for Mr. Morales-Santana (facing deportation from the U.S. for a criminal conviction), the Supreme Court did not feel it had the power to extend the shorter period of required physical presence to children of unwed citizen fathers. Such a move, it said, was up to the U.S. Congress. Perhaps Congress will, someday, act to create a uniform prescription for acquisition of citizenship that's not based on gender. Until then, however, the Court said that the longer residency requirement should continue to apply to everyone seeking to acquire U.S. citizenship under this (and of course, any other) section of U.S. law.

If the one U.S. citizen parent was your father and your birth was illegitimate (took place while your parents weren't married), the same rules applied provided your father legally legitimated you (acknowledged paternal responsibility). Citizenship was passed at the time of legitimation without regard to your age, as long as you had met the retention requirements.

3. Birth Between January 13, 1941 and December 23, 1952

If you were born between January 13, 1941 and December 23, 1952, both your parents were U.S. citizens, and at least one had a prior residence in the U.S., you automatically acquired U.S. citizenship at birth, with no conditions to retaining it.

If only one parent was a U.S. citizen, that parent must have resided in the U.S. for at least ten years prior to your birth, and at least five of those years must have been after your parent reached the age of 16. With a parent thus qualified, you then acquired U.S. citizenship at birth, but with conditions for retaining it. To keep your citizenship, you must have resided in the U.S. for at least two years between the ages of 14 and 28. Alternately, you could retain citizenship if your noncitizen parent naturalized before you turned 18 and you began living in the U.S. permanently before age 18. As a result of a U.S. Supreme Court decision, if you were born after October 9, 1952, your parent still had to fulfill the residence requirement in order to confer citizenship on you, but your own residence requirements for retaining U.S. citizenship were abolished—you need not have lived in the U.S. at all.

The law during this time period also contained easier U.S. presence requirements for parents who served honorably in the U.S. armed forces. From December 7, 1941 to December 31, 1946, the parent still needed ten years' U.S. residence, but could count five years of that beginning at age 12. And between January 1, 1947 and December 24, 1952, the parent needed ten years' physical presence in the U.S., at least five years of which were after the age of 14.

If your one U.S. citizen parent was your father and your birth was illegitimate (took place while your parents weren't married), the same rules apply provided you were legally legitimated (your father acknowledged paternal responsibility) prior to your 21st birthday and you were unmarried at the time of legitimation.

4. Birth Between December 24, 1952 and November 13, 1986

If at the time of your birth both your parents were U.S. citizens and at least one had a prior residence in the U.S., you automatically acquired U.S. citizenship, with no other conditions for retaining it.

If only one parent was a U.S. citizen at the time of your birth, that parent must have resided in the U.S. for at least ten years, and at least five of those years must have been after your parent reached the age of 14. If your one U.S. citizen parent is your father and your birth was illegitimate (took place while your parents weren't married), the same rules apply provided you were legally legitimated (your father acknowledged paternal responsibility) prior to your 21st (or 18th if you were born between November 15, 1971 and November 13, 1986) birthday and you were unmarried at the time of legitimation.

5. Birth Between November 14, 1986 and the Present

If at the time of your birth both your parents were U.S. citizens and at least one had a prior residence in the U.S., you automatically acquired U.S. citizenship, with no conditions for retaining it.

If only one parent was a U.S. citizen at the time of your birth, that parent must have resided in the U.S. for at least five years and at least two of those years must have been after your parent reached the age of 14. Even with only one U.S. citizen parent, there are still no conditions to retaining your citizenship. If your one U.S. citizen parent is your father and your birth was illegitimate (took place while your parents weren't married), the same rules apply provided you were legally legitimated (your father acknowledged paternal responsibility) prior to your 18th birthday. Additionally, your father must have established paternity prior to your 18th birthday either by acknowledgment or by court order, and must have stated, in writing, that he would support you financially until your 18th birthday.

⚠ **CAUTION**

The situation is more complicated for children born through assisted reproductive technology or ART (intrauterine insemination and in vitro fertilization). Some tragic situations have arisen in which the U.S. government denied citizenship where there wasn't a genetic link with the U.S. citizen parent. In 2014, however, the U.S. State Department changed its policy so as to acknowledge a biological connection based on gestation, as well. USCIS eventually followed suit. Thus if the child's legal parents are married to one another at the time of birth and at least one of them has a genetic or gestational relationship to the child, citizenship should be recognized.

---

6. Exception to Requirements for Retaining U.S. Citizenship

It is not unusual for a child born and raised outside the U.S. to have acquired U.S. citizenship at birth from parents without knowing it. The child, ignorant of the laws and circumstances affecting their birthright, then proceeds to lose U.S. citizenship by failing to fulfill U.S. residency requirements.

Congress sought to address this by adding a law for people who once held U.S. citizenship but lost it by failing to fulfill the residency requirements that were in effect before 1978. Such persons can regain U.S. citizenship by simply taking the oath of allegiance to the United States. It is not necessary that they apply for naturalization. Contact a U.S. consulate or USCIS office for more information. The relevant statute is 8 U.S.C. § 1435(d)(1), I.N.A. § 324(d)(1).

B. Obtaining Proof of U.S. Citizenship

If you have a legitimate claim to U.S. citizenship, in order to establish that claim you must apply for some kind of citizenship document, either a:

- U.S. passport
- certificate of citizenship, or
- certificate of consular registration of birth.

1. U.S. Passport

If you were born abroad to U.S. citizen parents, you can apply for a U.S. passport in the same way as someone born in the United States. However, you will have the added requirement of establishing your citizenship claim. Passports are available from passport offices in the U.S. (run by the U.S. Department of State) and at U.S. consulates outside the U.S., but experience shows that you have a better chance at a U.S. consulate. Wherever you apply, you will be required to present proof of your parents' U.S. citizenship and evidence that they—and you—complied with any applicable U.S. residency requirements. Review the sections on birth to a U.S. citizen for what you must prove under these circumstances. You will need to present documents such as birth or citizenship records of your parent or grandparent and work or tax records establishing U.S. residency for your parent or grandparent.

2. Certificate of Citizenship

Certificates of citizenship are issued only inside the U.S. by USCIS. Anyone with a claim to U.S. citizenship can apply for a certificate of citizenship. In most cases, it is more difficult and takes much longer to get a certificate of citizenship than a U.S. passport.

Certificates of citizenship must be applied for on Form N-600. The current fee is $1,170. Copies of the form and detailed instructions are available on the USCIS website, www.uscis.gov.

We recommend that you also prepare a cover letter explaining the basis of your claim to U.S. citizenship and describing the documents you are offering as proof. These should include your parents' birth certificates, marriage certificate, and citizenship or naturalization certificates.

You should also present your own birth certificate, as well as marriage certificates and any divorce decrees to show legal changes in your name since birth. Your letter should also list whatever evidence you will be presenting to show that you have met any residency requirements as described in this chapter.

Form N-600, the documents, and the cover letter can be submitted online by creating an account at www.uscis.gov or by mail by sending your application package to the USCIS Service Center address noted under Form N-600 on the website. You will most likely be called in for an interview on your application. In the busier USCIS offices, it can take a year or longer to get a decision on an application for certificate of citizenship.

3. Certificate of Consular Report of Birth

Your parents might have registered your birth with a U.S. consulate to establish your right to U.S. citizenship and create an official birth record. If so, the consulate would have issued proof that you are a U.S. citizen, most likely either as as:

- FS-545, Certification of Birth (issued by the Department of State prior to November 1, 1990)
- DS-1350, Certification of Report of Birth (issued by the Department of State prior to December 31, 2010), or
- FS-240, Consular Report of Birth Abroad (currently issued by all U.S. embassies and consulates).

Such documents can be prepared only at U.S. consular offices overseas, and only while the child is younger than the age of 18. Replacement copies can be obtained at any time, either overseas or in the United States. If an application for a replacement is made in the U.S., a Certification of Report of Birth (DS-1350) is issued, rather than a replacement consular report.

C. Dual Citizenship

Whenever a child is born to U.S. citizen parents but the birth takes place outside U.S. territory, the child may acquire dual citizenship. In this situation, the child will, depending on the laws of the country where the birth took place, usually have the nationality of the country in which he or she was actually born, in addition to U.S. citizenship through the nationality of the parents. U.S. law recognizes dual citizenship under these circumstances, and if you have acquired dual citizenship in this manner, under U.S. law, you will be entitled to maintain dual status for your lifetime.

Filling Out and Submitting Immigration Applications

A. Don't Give False Answers 208
  1. Criminal Penalties for Providing False Information to Immigration Authorities 208
  2. Civil Penalties for Providing False Information 208
B. Get the Latest Forms and Fee Amounts 208
C. Tips for Filling Out Forms 209
  1. Your Family Name 209
  2. Your Address 209
  3. Social Security and Alien Registration Numbers 210
  4. Technical Difficulties Filling Out USCIS Forms Online 210
D. When Additional Proof Is Required 210
  1. Proving a Family Relationship 210
  2. Proving an INS or USCIS Approval 212
  3. Proving U.S. Citizenship 213
  4. Proving U.S. Lawful Permanent Residence 214
E. Submitting Photographs for Identification 214
  1. The Photographs 214
  2. Your Image Within the Photo 214
F. Fingerprinting Requirements 215
G. Keep Your Own File 215
H. Tips for Filing Applications 215
  1. Submitting Applications by Mail or Courier 216
  2. Some Applications Can Be Filed Online ("e-Filing") 217
  3. Always Use Your Alien Registration Number 217
  4. Use One Check for Each Filing Fee 218
  5. Looking at Your USCIS File 218

The most important part of obtaining a green card is the paperwork. The key is to pay close attention to the immigration forms and other documents you submit as evidence to the U.S. government.

A. Don't Give False Answers

While answering the questions on the immigration forms, honesty is truly the best policy, and not only for reasons of morality.

For example, if you have been previously married, admitting this and providing the documents to prove that your previous marriage ended by divorce, annulment, or the death of your spouse will lead to a far better result than lying—and possibly getting caught.

If you have children by a previous marriage, or you have had any children while you were unmarried, list all of them on the immigration form, together with their correct names and dates of birth as shown on their birth certificates.

Once you submit the immigration forms, it is very difficult to change your answers. If you attempt later changes, you run the risk of having your petition denied.

> **EXAMPLE:** Suppose you never told your American husband that you had an illegitimate child. For this reason, you do not mention this child in your immigration papers. Later on, you decide to reveal the truth to your husband. If you want to petition for an immigrant visa for the child you left behind in your country, you will have a hard time convincing USCIS that you had a child prior to your marriage.

1. Criminal Penalties for Providing False Information to Immigration Authorities

Lying or failing to mention things on your immigration paperwork can have consequences beyond your immigration case. You also run the risk of being prosecuted criminally for obtaining U.S. entry by a "willfully false or misleading

representation or willful concealment of a material fact." This can also affect U.S. citizens or permanent residents who file petitions for an immigrant.

If found guilty of committing these offenses, you may be imprisoned for as long as five years or fined as much as $10,000, or receive both forms of punishment. If you received your green card by a fraudulent marriage, the punishment is more severe.

2. Civil Penalties for Providing False Information

There are also civil (noncriminal) penalties for people who "forge, counterfeit, alter, or falsely make any document" to satisfy a requirement of immigration law.

If found guilty, you can be fined $250 to $5,000 for each fraudulent document that you have in your possession or have already submitted to USCIS. In addition, a foreign national may be excluded from entering the United States or, if already here, may be removed or deported.

B. Get the Latest Forms and Fee Amounts

The law and the rules on immigration procedures change frequently. Using old, outdated forms can cause your immigration petition to be delayed or, worse, denied. And if your immigration papers are filed with the wrong fee, they will be returned; this will further delay your legal entry as an immigrant. Therefore, before submitting any immigration application, take the time to obtain the most recent forms and to double-check the filing fees on the USCIS website at www.uscis.gov/fees, or on the State Department website at https://travel.state.gov or with an American consulate in your country of residence, whichever is most convenient.

When mailing USCIS applications, you must pay the fees by personal check or money order made payable to "U.S. Department of Homeland Security," or you can pay by credit card by using

Form G-1450, Authorization for Credit Card Transactions. Do not mail cash! Some USCIS and State Department fees (such as the immigrant visa fee) can or must be paid online.

C. Tips for Filling Out Forms

A number of immigration forms ask for basic identifying information—name, address, and identification numbers. While the answers often seem obvious, USCIS requires that they be phrased in specific ways.

1. Your Family Name

When an immigration form asks you to fill in your name, write the complete name that you were given on your birth certificate or the name written in your passport, to match whichever document is required.

If the name on your birth certificate is not your name at present, explain the difference in a letter and submit the corresponding court papers or other documents that show the change.

> **EXAMPLE:** If you are a woman named Jane and you're using the surname of your husband, John Smith, as your family name, write your husband's surname—that is, Jane Smith.
>
> On the space that says "other names used," write your maiden name and any other names you have used—that is, Jane Doe.
>
> If you were married previously, write your previous married name on that space. Attach your marriage certificate or divorce decree.

2. Your Address

Your address, as far as USCIS is concerned, is the place where you receive mail. The post office is very important in your immigration relationship because most everything from USCIS will come by mail—notice of approval of petition, notice of incomplete submission, notice of interview, notice of proceedings, and your green card.

Do I Need to Answer Every Question?

Try to obtain all the information necessary to fully and completely answer every question on any USCIS or Department of State form. This might, at times, require extra research—or be entirely impossible.

For example, you will be asked for your parents' biographical information, including the city/town and country where your father was born. What if you don't know the answer? Try asking relatives, or obtaining a birth certificate or other relevant records. If your search is fruitless, type "Unknown" in the space provided. However, if you know that your father was born in Ecuador, but are unsure of the city where he was born, write "Unknown City, Ecuador."

If, continuing with the above example, your father is no longer alive and you are asked "Country of Residence," type "Deceased" in the space provided. Or if you do not know your father's identity and it is impossible to obtain his name, write "Unknown" if asked. You might also want to attach a sworn statement informing the immigration officials about how you tried to obtain this information and why it is not available.

It was previously advisable to write "None" or "Not applicable" (or "N/A") when asked a question on a USCIS form that doesn't apply to you, in order to avoid leaving any lines blank. However, with the introduction of new automated USCIS barcoded online forms, this is no longer necessary in most cases.

For example, many forms ask for a USCIS online account number or an Alien Registration Number, and you might not have these. It's okay to leave them blank. Or, if applying for a green card based upon marriage to a U.S. citizen, it could ask for the U.S. citizen's date of naturalization. If your U.S. citizen spouse was born in the U.S., this question will not apply; so leave it blank. Some questions in the online forms will become inaccessible if you click "yes" or "no," or you might be asked to skip to a different section of the form. As a result, many sample forms at www.nolo.com/back-of-book/GRN.html have blank spaces. When in doubt, double-check the USCIS form instructions, which usually provide line-by-line guidance about which questions need to be answered.

If the mail carrier does not deliver mail in your locality, rent a post office box. However, some USCIS forms ask not only for your mailing address but also for your actual address. In that case, write the exact address or location of your home or indicate c/o—meaning "in care of"—if another person at that address will be receiving your mail.

3. Social Security and Alien Registration Numbers

The Social Security number requested on immigration forms is issued by the U.S. government, not by your country's own Social Security administration. You should have one only if you've lived in the U.S. and had a legal right to work there.

An alien registration number, also called your "A#," is issued by USCIS (or, formerly, the INS), usually to people who have applied for an immigration benefit or been in deportation proceedings.

4. Technical Difficulties Filling Out USCIS Forms Online

The latest version of many USCIS forms allows you to save them as PDF documents and fill them out on your computer before printing and mailing them. However, you might run into glitches. Applicants have even reported that some of their answers were changed or erased after they had saved and printed the form.

You might also find that some answer boxes are impossible to place a check mark in, or that checking one box will erase the answer in another.

What's more, some of the blanks are too short to include accurate information in (such as long names and foreign addresses). And because the forms cannot tell the difference between numbers and letters, writing "N/A" or "none" in the blanks for things like Social Security number (which was once the best practice) is often not allowed.

Our advice? Do your best, but double- (and triple-) check everything before you send it to USCIS, to make sure it is accurate and unchanged from what you entered.

Many forms now have an addendum to provide information that does not fit in other sections of the form. Use the addendum, which normally is the last page of the form, or attach your own page and reference the page, section, and item number for which you're providing extra details.

You also might need to manually write an "X" in your boxes using black ink after printing the form. Although it could be USCIS's fault that its online system changed or deleted your entry, that excuse won't do you much good if USCIS rejects or delays your application as a result.

D. When Additional Proof Is Required

USCIS requires specific proof to be submitted along with the answers on many of its forms. This is because you are entitled to a green card only when you can prove by convincing documentation that you meet specific qualifications. You can go a long way toward eliminating delays and confusion if you take the time to make sure your additional proof is accurate and complete.

1. Proving a Family Relationship

As requested on the immigration forms, you must provide copies of documents to prove that a relationship permits you to apply as a family-based immigrant. If you do not submit the right documents, your materials will be returned and the whole process will be delayed. In some cases, harsh new guidance concerning "required initial evidence" allows USCIS simply to cash your check and deny your application or petition. Check the USCIS website for "required initial evidence" under the form you're submitting.

Do Not Send Your Originals to USCIS

Whenever possible, make a copy of your original document—and send the copy to USCIS. Things often get lost in the mail. Added to that, USCIS offices are busy places crowded with people and documents, so things get lost there. USCIS often makes no effort to return originals to their owners, and takes no responsibility if they are lost. Keep the originals of your documents in a safe place—fireproof, if possible. Then show them to the USCIS officer at your interview.

If you are consular processing, however, you might be required to send your original documents to the National Visa Center. When sending original documents, use a form of delivery that comes with a receipt, so you have proof of delivery and can track them through the system.

You must have the official documents. To prove a family relationship, you must have the original birth certificate, marriage certificate, or death certificate issued by the civil registry of your country with the official government seal, stamp, or ribbon attached, depending on how official documents are marked in your country. Nongovernmental documents, such as church or hospital certificates, are usually not sufficient. Although you won't mail the originals in—unless you are processing through the National Visa Center and are instructed to send it the originals—you'll probably be asked to show them to USCIS or a consular officer at your interview.

Use your fingers to verify the indentation of the government seal that is embossed or pressed into the paper. USCIS will often assume that a document without such a seal is fraudulent.

If you have lost the documents, you can request certified copies from your government for an additional charge. Be sure these copies also have the official government seal. Because some unscrupulous people create counterfeit documents, USCIS has to carefully examine the documents presented.

You should write or type the following statement on the back of each photocopy:

> Copies of documents submitted are exact photocopies of unaltered original documents, and I understand that I may be required to submit original documents to an immigration or consular official at a later date.

Include your signature and the date. There is no need to have your signature verified by a notary public.

Using the Department of State Documents Finder

Ever wonder how to get a birth certificate in Belarus or a divorce certificate in Djibouti? Go to https://travel.state.gov to find out. (Click "U.S. Visas" then "U.S. Visa: Reciprocity and Civil Documents by Country.")

This helpful Web page tells you how to get documents for immigration cases (like proof of military service or lack of a police record) or replace documents you thought you had but can't lay your hands on. If you really can't get a certain document (such as a birth certificate), the website will suggest acceptable alternatives.

If you don't have the official document. Sometimes, you cannot get your original documents because of war, destruction of the civil registry, your government's prohibition on emigration, or simple oversight or ignorance. Even if you cannot get the particular document, you still likely will need a "nonavailability certificate" or another statement from the office that should have the record saying that a search was conducted but no record found.

In such cases, family relationships, such as parent-child, brother-sister, or husband-wife, can be proved by what is called "secondary evidence"—a combination of documents that do not come from the civil registry, but which nevertheless prove a relationship. These may include:

- Church records, for example, can sometimes be submitted. A baptismal certificate will show the parents' names and the date and place of birth of the child.
- Annotations in a family Bible, old letters, school records, or data from a relevant government census are other types of secondary evidence.
- USCIS might also accept the sworn statements, or affidavits, of two people who have witnessed your birth, your marriage, the death of a spouse, or whatever event you need to prove. The statement should include the witnesses' names and addresses, their relationship to you or your family, and why and how they know about the alleged event. The strongest evidence is from witnesses who were present at the event you need to prove.

For example, if you've never had a birth certificate or you could not obtain a copy, a sworn statement written by your sister could read as the sample below.

The witnesses have to swear to the truth of their statements before a notary public—a person who is authorized by the state to verify signatures.

You can search for a notary online, or check with your bank—many have one on staff.

Most notaries will charge around $15 for their services. If required by the U.S. embassy in your country, the affidavits might have to be sworn to before the U.S. consular official, who will also charge a fee for the service.

You might need to submit your own affidavit stating why you cannot obtain the original documents and what efforts you have made to try to do so.

Sample Sworn Statement

My name is Jane Doe, and I am the older sister of John Doe.

I live at 123 Middle Abbey Street, Dublin, Ireland.

I was seven years old when my brother, John Doe, was born to our mother, Carolyn Doe, on July 4, 1954, at our home in Cork, Ireland. I remember the midwife coming to our house and I was sent outside to play. After it got dark, my brother was born and they called me inside to see him.

This affidavit is submitted because the civil registry in Cork was burned in 1956 and my brother's birth certificate was lost when the family moved to Dublin in the same year.

Signature: _____

Signed and sworn to before me on March 1, 20xx

[Notary Stamp]

USCIS might further investigate your family relationship, or request that you and your relative undergo DNA tests or give additional testimony. An investigation could even be conducted in the neighborhood in which you lived in your native country.

Before it confers an immigration benefit, the U.S. government must be certain that the person immigrating is truly the child, brother, sister, husband, or wife—and not the niece, nephew, aunt, uncle, cousin, or friend—of the U.S. citizen or permanent resident petitioner.

2. Proving an INS or USCIS Approval

In some situations, you might have an application or petition that has been approved by USCIS (or the formerly named INS) but need further action because:

- You lost the approval notice or you need a duplicate.

- The U.S. embassy or consulate that originally received the approval notice closed down or you simply could not go to your home country, and another U.S. consulate is willing to process your immigration visa and needs to be officially notified.
- You need USCIS to notify the U.S. consulate in your country that you became a green card holder in the United States so that your spouse and children can receive visas to join you.

Documents in Languages Other Than English

If the documents you are submitting are not in English, have them fully (and accurately) translated. The only exception to this is if you are consular processing, and the document is in the language of the country where the consulate is located. In that situation, the document does not need to be translated. Any translations should be word for word. An English summary of the main points in the document is usually not enough. However, you do not have to hire a professional to do the job. Somebody who is competent in both English and the language in which the documents are written should be able to do the translation.

The translator must attach the following statement to the translated document and sign and date it:

I hereby certify that I am competent to translate this document from [the foreign language] to English and that this translation is accurate and complete to the best of my knowledge and ability.

The translator should also include an address and contact number.

In any of these circumstances, you must file Form I-824, Application for Action on an Approved Application or Petition, with the USCIS office that approved the original application or petition. The filing fee was $465 at the time this book went to print.

If you have a copy of the approval, make a copy of that and attach it to your Form I-824.

3. Proving U.S. Citizenship

U.S. citizens have the right to petition for their spouse, parent, child, brother, sister, fiancée or fiancé, so that their relative can apply for permanent resident status. The widow or widower of a U.S. citizen can sometimes derive status from their deceased spouse. But in all of these situations, USCIS must first see documents proving the petitioning person's U.S. citizenship.

The following are accepted as proof:

- a birth certificate showing the place of birth to be any of the 50 U.S. states, Puerto Rico, the U.S. Virgin Islands, or Guam
- a valid U.S. passport. (You can get a U.S. passport even if the petitioner's birth certificate or baptismal certificate cannot be obtained, by including Form DS-10 with the DS-11 passport application. On the DS-10, a U.S. citizen with firsthand information about the petitioner's birth in the U.S. can sign an affidavit providing relevant details.)
- if the birth certificate cannot be obtained, a baptismal certificate with the seal of the church showing the place of birth and date of baptism, which must have occurred within two months after birth
- a certificate of naturalization
- a Department of State-issued form reporting on the birth abroad of a U.S. citizen, or
- a certificate of citizenship issued by the INS or USCIS, which is also adequate proof that someone is a U.S. citizen born abroad.

U.S. Passport

4. Proving U.S. Lawful Permanent Residence

As a green card holder, you have the right to petition for your spouse and unmarried children, by submitting proof that you are a permanent resident. Although USCIS has your file and alien registration number in its records, you must still submit a copy of your green card.

The official name of your green card is Permanent Resident Card (also sometimes called "Form I-551"). The Form I-551 is the best form of proof of lawful permanent residence.

If your green card is lost or not available, your "home country" passport—bearing the USCIS rubber stamp showing lawful admission for permanent residence and your alien registration number—is acceptable proof of your permanent resident status. You should also file Form I-90 with USCIS to request a replacement green card, as described in Chapter 23.

E. Submitting Photographs for Identification

U.S. immigration authorities are quite strict about photo requirements. The style and specifications for USCIS photos are the same ones used for U.S. passport photos.

While it is not essential to hire a professional photographer to take USCIS photos, it can be tough to comply with the picky requirements for size, lighting, clarity, and digital resolution. If you or a friend attempt to take the photos on your own, be sure to take many pictures and to read the requirements (which will be sent to you) first. Vending machine photos won't be accepted, but many pharmacies offer passport- photo services for around $15.

If, as is normally the case, you're asked to submit more than one photo, the photos must be identical—you can't just take a few photos that look quite similar and submit them.

1. The Photographs

The overall size of the picture, including the background, must be at least 5 cm (2 inches) square.

The photographs must be in color—with no shadows, marks, or discolorations on them. The background must be white or off-white; it is not acceptable to be photographed against a patterned or colored background. There must be good lighting; the photo must not appear too light or too dark. And the final image must be original, not retouched in any way, and printed on photo-quality paper.

2. Your Image Within the Photo

The image on the photo—the total size of the head—must be centered and sized between 1 inch and 1⅜ inches (2.5 to 3.5 cm) from the top of the hair to the bottom of the chin.

Make sure the eye height is between 1⅛ inches to 1⅜ inches (2.8 cm to 3.5 cm) from the bottom of the photo. You must be facing forward and a neutral or natural smile is preferred.

Although eyewear was once allowed to be worn in passport photos, new regulations no longer permit wearing glasses unless it's a medical requirement for you to wear them at all times. In such a situation, include a note from your physician with your application.

Do not wear jewelry. You may not wear a hat or head covering unless it's required by your religion or for medical reasons. If so, provide a signed statement detailing that the headwear is customarily worn continuously in public for religious reasons or a medical note discussing why a continual head covering is necessary for medical reasons.

Be sure to face the camera directly, keep your eyes open, and submit a photo taken within the last six months.

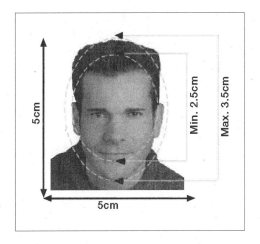

F. Fingerprinting Requirements

USCIS requires fingerprinting (also called "bio-metrics") to accompany a variety of applications, including permanent residence, asylum, and naturalization, among others. Fingerprints are normally reviewed by the FBI and CIA to determine an applicant's actual identity and to determine whether the person has a criminal background that would make him or her inadmissible or ineligible for immigration benefits. USCIS will also check to see whether you've submitted previous applications under a different name.

If the application you are filing requires biometrics, you must include the appropriate fee (currently $85)This is in addition to any fees for the application itself.

USCIS will usually contact you within 45 days by letter, telling you when you should go to a USCIS-authorized site for fingerprinting and the like. You will be given an address and a specific date and time at which you must appear.

If you cannot make it during your appointed time, you can ask to be rescheduled.

If you live abroad and are filing your application outside the United States, in some cases, you may be fingerprinted at a U.S. consulate or military installation. Whether or not you will be fingerprinted abroad depends on the type of application you submit and the particular U.S. consulate.

G. Keep Your Own File

For your own records, make copies of everything that you submit to the U.S. government, including the immigration forms and supporting documents. Also make a copy of the receipt USCIS issues to you after you pay any filing fee.

Keep your own copies and original documents in a safe place. You will need them again when you are called to receive your immigrant visa at the U.S. embassy or when you attend your personal interview for your green card at USCIS.

Also, like any other bureaucracy, USCIS does sometimes misplace files. It will save you headache and heartache if you can show that you have already filed the application with USCIS by presenting a copy of the documents filed and the receipt from USCIS.

H. Tips for Filing Applications

USCIS loses a surprising number of applications, or the documents and checks that came with them. To protect yours, and to make sure they get through the system as smoothly as possible, follow the tips below.

1. Submitting Applications by Mail or Courier

After you've filled out your application forms, assembled the needed documents, and written the checks, you'll be eager to submit everything to USCIS. Most applications must be submitted by mail. But don't just pop yours in the nearest mailbox. First, make complete copies for your files—even copy the checks. Next, choose a mailing method that includes tracking. One option is the U.S. Postal Service's Priority Mail service, or certified mail with return receipt requested. Sending your application via couriers such as FedEx or DHL is another good way to make sure you have proof of its arrival.

However, make sure the USCIS office is equipped to accept this form of delivery. A few never do, because a live person has to be there to sign for the package. Most designate a special address for courier deliveries, which you can find on the USCIS website (www.uscis.gov/forms).

When your application arrives at a USCIS office, the clerical staff will examine your papers to see if everything is in order. Your papers will likely be returned to you if you:

- did not enter your full name, including middle name
- did not sign your application or other papers requiring a signature
- signed a name different from that shown on your attached birth certificate
- used an outdated version of the form(s)
- did not enclose the correct filing fee
- left some questions unanswered, or
- forgot to include some documents.

When your papers are returned, there should be a letter included with them (a Request for Evidence or RFE), telling you what information was incorrect or missing. You will usually have a chance to correct what was wrong and send back your documents and check or money order. When your documents are in order, USCIS will accept your submission and will send you a receipt notice on Form I-797C.

Moving to a New Place? Take Precautions

When files must be transferred between USCIS field offices, they can get lost, at least for a time. No wonder some people postpone moving until after their cases have finished processing! If you don't want to go to such an extreme, at least keep in touch with the new people living at your place, to see whether anything from USCIS arrives.

Also, you must report any change of address to USCIS within ten days. Use Form AR-11, either the paper form or online at www.uscis.gov/ar-11. The online form is easiest for most people. If you have your receipt number, the online system will update your address in the main database as well as with the USCIS office currently processing your application. Select the form that you filed with USCIS and enter the zip code used when filed (if any). Then enter the applicant/petitioner information, citizenship information, old and new addresses, and location and date of your U.S. entry (if any). You can also elect to receive email confirmation of the address change. Keep this email handy in case you have trouble with your address change. You might also want to send a letter to the USCIS office processing your application—just in case. Include your receipt number on the letter.

Applicants in a limited number of visa categories (including self-petitioners under the Violence Against Women Act and serious crime and human trafficking victims) can't use the online address system. They will have to send a letter to the USCIS Vermont Service Center.

If you file a paper AR-11 and have no pending applications, you don't need to do anything else. Otherwise, you also need to call 1-800-375-5283 to update your address.

TIP

Will faster, "premium" processing become available? With USCIS's Premium Processing Service, 15-calendar-day processing is available to people filing certain applications who are willing to pay the premium processing fee (much more than $1,000, with the exact amount dependent on the type of application). Unfortunately, only a few kinds of cases are currently eligible for premium processing, and none of them are covered in this book. (It's mainly available for petitions by companies on behalf of important workers.) However, USCIS might someday make the service more widely available.

2. Some Applications Can Be Filed Online ("e-Filing")

USCIS allows online filing for a growing number of applications. While the technology continues to improve and allows you to upload documents, it can be easier to just mail everything together, as a paper application. The main advantage to e-filing is that you will receive an instant confirmation. The USCIS website will tell you whether online filing is an option for your application when you go to download the form.

3. Always Use Your Alien Registration Number

There are two kinds of numbers by which the Department of Homeland Security identifies every person who comes in contact with it. The first one, an A followed by nine numbers—for example: A093 465 345—is given to those who apply for or receive permanent residence (see Chapter 18) or who have a removal case. It's called an "Alien Registration Number" or "A number."

Until recently, A numbers were issued with only eight numbers. That means that when USCIS needs to enter an "old" A number into its current system, it automatically adds a zero to the beginning. For example, "A93 465 345" becomes "A093 465 345."

Once you have an A number, it never changes. It is even recorded on your Naturalization Certificate if you become a U.S. citizen. However, if you file immigration applications for relatives after becoming a U.S. citizen, you no longer need to use your A number on immigration forms.

The second type of number USCIS assigns is the receipt number, which changes with each application you submit. It starts with the initials of your district or regional service center followed by ten numbers—for example: SRC 2263334455 or EAC 2212345678. Such numbers are given to applications submitted to the various service centers, to track them through processing.

Once your immigration papers are accepted by USCIS, its computer system verifies whether you have ever been assigned an alien number or whether the alien number you wrote on your application is the right one for you.

The clerk then checks the computer files, looking for all the names you might have used, your date and place of birth, and your parents' names. The clerk will confirm the A number you wrote on your application, or if you have other A numbers previously assigned, will note them on your application so that all your files can be consolidated under one number. If you do not have a previous A number, the clerk will give your file a new one.

Keep a record of your immigration case number, because any time you pose a question to USCIS, it will ask you first for your number. And if you send letters—for example, asking why your case is taking so long—you must include your A number or processing number.

4. Use One Check for Each Filing Fee

Occasionally, you might find yourself submitting more than one petition or application at the same time. For example, in a marriage case where your spouse is here in the U.S., you can file Form I-130 and Form I-485 simultaneously. Or, you can file applications for your spouse and your stepchild in the same envelope. In any of these situations, resist the temptation to combine all the filing fees into a single check.

If you submit separate, individual checks for each filing fee, then if you make a mistake on a check (for example, you forget to sign it, or you make it for the wrong amount), USCIS will reject only the filing that is affected by that check. But if you submit a single check covering all fees, and you've made a mistake, you will ruin all of the filings at once.

It's a pain to have to write more than one check for forms and applications being submitted in the same package, but most of the time it's worth it.

5. Looking at Your USCIS File

If you need to see your immigration records or to have a copy of a document you submitted, you can do so by filing Form G-639, Freedom of Information/Privacy Act Request. It's downloadable from the USCIS website (www.uscis.gov/g-639) or you can submit the request online by creating an online account there. If you decide to file Form G-639, mark your envelope "Freedom of Information Request" and send it to: National Records Center, FOIA/PA Office, P.O. Box 648010, Lee's Summit, MO 64064-8010.

Expect a long wait. It's not unheard of for a FOIA request to sit at USCIS for longer than a year.

Tracking Your Application Through the System

A. Understanding U.S. Government Culture..220

B. How to Track Your Application Online..220

C. What to Do When Things Go Wrong...221

D. Inquiring About Delays...222

E. Speeding Up Processing in Emergencies..223

F. Reporting Wrongdoing..225

When you submit an application to U.S. immigration authorities, most likely Citizenship and Immigration Services or an office of the Department of State (such as the National Visa Center), you probably expect to receive an official reply within a few weeks. But a month might pass, then two—and still no reply arrives. You would like to find out why your application is delayed, but each time you contact the government office, you are told to be patient and wait—that your paperwork is "being processed" or "pending."

There are a number of things you can do to be sure that your dealings with U.S. immigration officials move as smoothly and efficiently as possible. Those options are explained in this chapter.

A. Understanding U.S. Government Culture

The officials handling U.S. immigration matters reflect the workforce of any other government bureaucracy. They can generally be divided into two types: those who are earnest and conscientious in doing their jobs, and those who are at their posts in body but not in spirit. You take the luck of the draw as to which kind of bureaucrat will be handling your application or answering your questions.

Although these agencies are governed by law (the Immigration and Nationality Act, Code of Federal Regulations, and Operational Instructions), how these get applied depends upon individual USCIS office workers, who have their own cultural and social biases.

For example, you could be confronted with an immigration officer who is anti-immigrant, and who detests dealing every day with people who do not speak English, who speak with an accent, or who look, dress, or even smell differently from what the officer thinks of as "normal" Americans. This bias might make the worker grumpy, officious, intimidating, unhelpful, unreasonable, discourteous, or downright infuriating.

Furthermore, none of these agencies is very phone accessible, and the people at USCIS's national information line aren't well-informed about local office procedures. Some of them might give you wrong information.

B. How to Track Your Application Online

It's wise to check your case status online before taking further measures, such as picking up the phone or attempting to schedule an in-person appointment. Here are the most helpful case status websites:

- **USCIS:** At https://egov.uscis.gov/casestatus, you can enter your receipt number to receive an update on your application. You can also sign up for automatic email updates by creating a myUSCIS account.
- **Department of State:** Check your visa application status by visiting https://ceac.state.gov and entering your Immigrant Visa Case Number.

Visiting USCIS Offices in Person

The only USCIS offices that you can visit in person are the district or field offices, and even those have restricted entry systems. Each U.S. state usually has one or two such offices (though in a few areas, particularly in New England, you'll have to travel to another state). To find the office that serves you, go to www.uscis.gov and click "Find an Office." Click "Field Offices" and follow the prompts.

Until recently, USCIS allowed people to schedule in-person appointments, but no longer. Now, you need to call the USCIS Contact Center at 800-375-5283 and make your way through a voice-automated system. The most you are likely to achieve during this initial call is to place yourself on a list to be called back. (It's best to start such calls early in the day, and make sure you're phone accessible for the rest of it.) When you're called back, a representative will determine whether you qualify for an appointment and schedule it or direct you to other resources.

C. What to Do When Things Go Wrong

If you're actually at a USCIS office and you feel an immigration officer is being unreasonable, go up the chain of command and appeal to the worker's supervisor. Insist on speaking with the supervisor personally. You can even do this in the middle of an appointment or interview. If that's not possible, try to obtain the supervisor's telephone number and call and explain what happened—or write a detailed letter. Be clear on what action was taken by the worker and what you want the supervising officer to do.

Because the DHS is a bureaucracy with many departments and branches, it is easy to get mixed up in a game of finger-pointing in which each person with whom you speak claims that the problem is not their fault.

When making inquiries, you will need to figure out the exact unit or section where your application is pending. Here are the offices you'll most likely deal with:

- **The USCIS district or field office,** which is open to the public by appointment only, and also schedules and handles green card interviews. Most states have at least one. It is rarely possible for a member of the public to talk to someone at the District or Field Office by telephone, but you might be able to speak to someone face-to-face by making an appointment via the phone Contact Center.
- **The USCIS regional service center,** which is a processing facility that you cannot normally visit, but to which you may be required to send certain applications. There are six service centers nationwide. You can check on the status of applications that you've filed with them by telephone (see the phone number on your receipt notice) or online at the USCIS website (www.uscis.gov), where you'll click "Check Case Status" and enter your receipt number.

- **The National Benefits Center (NBC),** which was created to handle administrative case processing burdens formerly borne by local USCIS district or field offices. Many kinds of petitions and applications that used to be filed directly with local offices are now filed with a lockbox facility located either in Chicago, Illinois; Dallas, Texas; or Phoenix, Arizona. The lockbox handles fee deposits, issues receipts, and enters initial data. After receiving cases from the lockbox, the NBC completes all necessary preinterview processing of Form I-485 applications (including conducting background security checks, performing initial evidence review, and other tasks). Then the NBC forwards the case files to local field offices for a final interview.
- **The National Visa Center (NVC),** which is not actually part of USCIS or the Department of Homeland Security. It is an arm of the Department of State, and is an intermediary that steps in after an initial visa petition has been approved. It collects visa fees and gets cases ready for transfer to a U.S. consulate in one's home country. If you will be processing your case in the U.S. rather than abroad, the NVC will transfer your file to a USCIS office upon your request. As NVC is not part of DHS/USCIS, it will not accept the adjustment of status fees, and if you send it money for consular processing, those fees will not be transferred to your adjustment case or refunded. Depending upon your basis for green card eligibility, your case file might be kept at the NVC for a number of years. The NVC used to be remarkably accessible, but now can basically only be reached via its online form: At https://travel.state.gov, click "Contact Us," then "U.S. Visas Contacts," then one of the links to the NVC's Public Inquiry Form. You will need

your receipt number, the applicant's and the petitioner's full names and dates of birth, and a valid email address. Don't expect a speedy response. With luck you will get at least some information about your case within six to eight weeks.

- **Immigration and Customs Enforcement (ICE),** which is the enforcement arm of the DHS. Its investigators check on whether both employers and employees have complied with the immigration laws. They do surveillance, make arrests, and issue orders to show up for removal hearings—previously called "deportation" or "exclusion" hearings—before the Immigration Court.

- **The detention of Enforcement and Removal Operations (ERO),** which is part of Immigration and Customs Enforcement (ICE), and comes under DHS. Its job is to find removable people, determine whether to hold them in custody, and execute final removal orders. ICE has an online system that allows the public to find out where a particular detainee is being held: Go to www.ice.gov, and click "Online Detainee Locator System," then search either by entering the detainee's A number and country of birth, or the detainee's name, birth date, and country of birth.

- **The Naturalization Section,** which is part of DHS/USCIS, and is responsible for deciding which aliens are eligible for citizenship and who qualifies as a citizen of the United States.

- **The Adjustment of Status Section,** which is part of DHS/USCIS, and is responsible for adjudicating applications for permanent residence.

- **The Litigation Section,** also called the Office of the Chief Counsel. It is under the direction of DHS and Immigration and Customs Enforcement (ICE). It is the legal arm of the DHS and represents the government during hearings involving a foreign national before the Immigration Court and the federal and

state courts. It also counsels the other DHS sections on legal matters.

- **The Immigration Court** (also called the Executive Office of Immigration Review), which is separate from DHS, and under the direction of the Department of Justice. It offers an automated phone system at 800-898-7180, which can tell you about your ext hearing date, time, and location; other case processing information; the Immigration Judge's decision on your case; Board of Immigration Appeals (BIA) case appeal information, including appeal due date, brief due date, decision outcome and date; and filing information. You'll need your A number (and if it's eight rather than nine digits long, enter a zero into the system as the first number).

D. Inquiring About Delays

If you're waiting for an appointment or a decision on an immigration petition or application, you're likely to be frustrated. Action by USCIS and the State Department usually takes longer than anyone thinks it should. The question is, how long is too long? To some extent, this depends on the office you're dealing with.

For U.S. consulates, you'll have to ask other people in your country, or contact the consulate directly, to find out its normal schedule. Some consulates post such information on their websites, which you can locate via www.usembassy.gov.

You can find out how backed up the various USCIS offices are by going to USCIS's online service at www.uscis.gov. Click "Check processing times" to find out the dates of applications filed by other people like you. That lets you at least see whether USCIS is still dealing with people who applied before you, or seems to have skipped over you and is dealing with people who applied after you.

Or, if you have a receipt notice from a service center, click "Check your case status" and follow the prompts.

In general, if waiting for an initial receipt, such as one for an I-129F or I-130 petition filed with a USCIS service center, a month or two is the longest you should wait. After that, there is a good chance something is wrong. If you sent your application by Priority or certified mail, or with some other delivery confirmation, you might be able to trace it. If you sent a check with your application, find out from your bank whether it cleared. If it did, get a copy of the back of the canceled check, which should be stamped with the USCIS receipt number that will help you track your application.

For personal assistance, call the USCIS Contact Center at 800-375-5283 or go through its online chat system, responsive in both English and Spanish (named "Emma"). The online services are available 24 hours a day, but the only times you can potentially be connected with an actual person are Monday through Friday, 8 a.m. to 8 p.m. Eastern.

Have as much information as possible on hand. The USCIS receipt number will make it easier for the agency to find your application, but it might also be able to find it with other information you provide.

Make a note of the referral number or the name of the person with whom you (eventually) speak, as well as the date of the call. It will help to have this information if further inquiries are needed.

Although the USCIS Contact Center will rarely answer your question while you are on the telephone, it can usually make sure that your inquiry gets to someone who can do so. They customarily ask you to wait 45 days for a response, although it will hopefully come more quickly than that.

The other good way to inquire about a delay in your case is to submit an online inquiry at www. uscis.gov. Click "Check your case status" and then scroll down to click "Submit a Case Inquiry." Choose the option that fits your situation. For the "Case outside normal processing times" option, you'll first need to make sure your case receipt date is prior to USCIS's stated "Receipt date for a case inquiry" under the processing times for your type of case. (That date indicates that they're already making decisions on cases filed later than yours, in which case something has gone awry.)

> **CAUTION**
> **Keep your cool.** Be courteous, clear, and to the point. Demonstrate that you're well organized, and that you know exactly when USCIS or the State Department received your materials, and when you should have gotten an answer.

Attorneys can't always get results any faster than you could on your own, but they know how to navigate the bureaucracy and can be a valuable resource.

E. Speeding Up Processing in Emergencies

An emergency could arise in which you need an action expedited or your immigration papers approved very quickly. For example, your wife might still be abroad because your petition for her is not yet approved, when she is stricken with a rare disease for which the only treatment is found in the United States.

In this type of situation, you might need to speak with an information officer face-to-face. Call the USCIS Contact Center to present your situation. You should be connected to a representative who will escalate your call to an information officer. (Note that the Contact Center is staffed by government contractors who merely read from scripts that USCIS prepared for them. In other words, they're just "order takers.")

Once you talk with the information officer however, you will find that USCIS is extremely reluctant to bend its rules and act outside the standard operating procedures. But if your case truly deserves an exception, and you approach the right USCIS worker in the right way, you might get a satisfactory resolution because there is a humanitarian reason to grant your request. It enables USCIS to show its human side.

Unfortunately, it is sometimes difficult to locate USCIS's human side.

For your best chance of success with your expedite request, write a letter explaining your situation and have documents showing why immediate action is necessary. Where appropriate, bring the originals of documents, as well as copies to personally leave with USCIS. The letter you have written gives the information officer something to show supervisors in trying to advocate on your behalf. However, do not expect the officer to read the letter before you have explained your urgent situation. In some cases, you'll simply have to mail or email the documents to USCIS.

Again, be resigned to the fact that there are varying kinds of USCIS workers. Some make decisions strictly according to the letter of the law, while others exercise discretion when appropriate, according to the spirit of the law.

If the USCIS worker fails to respond to your inquiry or denies your request, try to go up the chain of command and speak with a supervisor.

If your request for immediate action is still denied unjustly, you could hire a lawyer to help put the pressure on. As a last resort, the lawyer might file a case of mandamus in the federal district court to force USCIS to act on your request.

Sample Letter to Supervisor

Leona Burgett, Supervisor
USCIS Office
Anytown, Anystate 12345

August 12, 20xx

Dear Ms. Burgett:

My file number is A12345678 and I have an adjustment of status application pending in your office.

I received a letter from my mother, with a certification from the hospital, that my father suffered a heart attack and his prognosis is dim. I filed for Advance Parole two days ago, but my application was denied. The USCIS worker said he believed that the certification from the hospital was fraudulently obtained, and did not accept my mother's letter because it was not translated into English.

Yesterday, I returned with a translation of the letter and my affidavit explaining that in our remote hometown, the most modern equipment available is a manual typewriter, on which some letters might be crooked or spaces might be skipped. The USCIS worker said that my Advance Parole will still be denied regardless of my explanations that my father is truly very ill.

I am married to a U.S. citizen and have been law-abiding—except for overstaying in this country until submitting my adjustment of status application.

Please help me with my Advance Parole request.

Sincerely,

Max Haxsim

Max Haxsim

F. Reporting Wrongdoing

In rare cases, a USCIS worker's actions might be truly reprehensible, perhaps involving gross incompetence, immoral conduct, or unlawful behavior. It's not the normal course of business, but there have even been reports of USCIS workers asking for a bribe. If you encounter anything like this, don't just go along with it. Report the misdeed to the head of the particular USCIS office.

Your letter should specify the name of the USCIS worker, if known. If you did not ask for the name or the USCIS worker refused to answer, describe the person. Also indicate the time, date, and manner of misconduct and the names of any witnesses.

Sometimes, They Surprise You

While it's important to make your dissatisfaction known about a USCIS officer's bad or abusive behavior, the contrary should also be true. If you are served by a USCIS worker who goes the extra mile to be helpful, by all means write to the relevant office and let it know that there is an outstanding worker in their midst.

It might encourage more workers to deliver superlative service to the public.

Although your complaint could lead to an investigation where you might be asked to repeat your facts in front of an investigator or an administrative judge, do not be afraid or unwilling to get involved. The officer's abusive behavior is not likely to stop, and many more people could be injured by it unless you take action. ●

Keeping, Renewing, and Replacing Your Green Card

A. Renewing or Replacing Your Green Card...228

B. When U.S. Immigration Authorities Can Take Away Your Card..229

    1. Failing to Report a Change of Address..229

    2. Failing to Maintain a Residence in the United States...229

    3. Explaining Your Failure to Reenter the United States..231

    4. Becoming Inadmissible to the U.S. 231

    5. Becoming Removable From the U.S. 232

C. Planning to Apply for U.S. Citizenship 232

ow that you have finally obtained that plastic card giving you the right to stay and work in the United States without major hassles, and to leave and return without applying for a visa, make sure you don't you lose the card—or your right to it. If all goes as it should, your green card will give you the right to live in the United States for as long as you want to. However, you need to protect this right by taking such measures as telling USCIS when you move, not remaining too long outside the United States, and not becoming inadmissible or deportable. You should also make sure to renew your green card on time and replace it if it's lost.

> CAUTION
> **Think about applying for U.S. citizenship.**
> After a certain number of years with lawful permanent residence (usually five, but fewer for some people), you can apply for U.S. citizenship. This is a much more secure status—you'll be able to travel for longer periods of time, be safe from deportation, and will gain the right to vote. Start planning now: If you wait until five years go by to start thinking about citizenship, you might discover that there was something you needed to do (or something you did that you shouldn't have done) while you were waiting. For complete guidance, see *Becoming a U.S. Citizen: A Guide to the Law, Exam & Interview,* by Ilona Bray (Nolo).

A. Renewing or Replacing Your Green Card

Whether your green card is lost, mutilated, or expires and needs to be renewed, U.S. Citizenship and Immigration Services (USCIS) requires that you file Form I-90, Application to Replace Permanent Resident Card. (It's available from www.uscis. gov/i-90; and you can download a completed sample at www.nolo.com/back-of-book/GRN.html.)

The filing fee is currently $455, plus $85 for fingerprints (biometrics). (However, you don't need to pay the filing fee if you're getting a replacement green card because of a mistake by USCIS, for example if it misspelled your name on the card.) For where to file, visit USCIS's website at www. uscis.gov/i-90. Consider e-filing this form in order to avoid any confusion about addresses. You can do so at www.uscis.gov/i-90, as long as you are not applying for a fee waiver based on financial hardship or paying by money order. E-filing requires you to enter your bank account or credit card information in order to pay the filing fee.

You can also use Form I-90 to get a new green card when:

- Your name has been changed, due to marriage or divorce, in which case you must include a copy of your marriage or divorce certificate and your old card.
- You turn 14 years of age; USCIS requires that you change your green card for a new one.
- You receive an incorrect card with an erroneous name, birth date, photo, or date of entry.
- You never received your green card.
- Your green card is blue, Form I-151; these old cards were issued during the 1960s and 1970s and expired on August 2, 1996, because of their lack of security features, giving opportunities for fraud.

You must swear that all the answers you give when applying for a green card are correct. If you knowingly falsify or conceal a material fact, or use any false document in submitting the application, you may be fined up to $10,000, imprisoned for up to five years, or both. Try to renew your green card shortly after six months before its expiration date. This way, if an unanticipated processing delay occurs, you'll still have a card for work authorization and travel purposes.

You should receive your new green card (Form I-551) within three to six months after USCIS receives your paperwork and filing fee.

B. When U.S. Immigration Authorities Can Take Away Your Card

As a green card holder, you are expected to be law-abiding. Because you were not born with the right to stay in the United States and have not yet been naturalized, the immigration laws put certain restrictions on you that do not apply to U.S. citizens.

1. Failing to Report a Change of Address

The immigration law says that a foreign national who fails to give written notice to USCIS of a change of address can be deported or removed from the United States. Not only that, the person could be charged with a misdemeanor and if found guilty, fined up to $200, imprisoned up to 30 days, or both.

The person would have to convince the Immigration Judge during removal hearings that failure to notify USCIS of an address change was reasonably excusable or was not willful.

To avoid any possible problem whenever you move to a new address, prepare and submit Form AR-11 (from www.uscis.gov/AR-11). To submit by mail, send it to:

> U.S. Department of Homeland Security
> Citizenship and Immigration Services
> Attn: Change of Address
> 1344 Pleasants Drive
> Harrisonburg, VA 22801

However, you can also submit the form online, by going to www.uscis.gov/AR-11 and clicking "File Online." You'll need:

- your USCIS receipt number (if you have a pending case with USCIS)
- your A number
- your new and old addresses, and

- the names and biographical information for any family members for whom you have filed an immigration petition.

The advantage to submitting online is that you'll receive confirmation that your message got through.

There is no fee for filing Form AR-11.

2. Failing to Maintain a Residence in the United States

You become a U.S. permanent resident presumably because you intend to live in the United States. Sometimes things happen, however, that require you to spend long periods of time outside the United States. To make sure that you do not unintentionally lose your permanent residence, it's important to keep certain things in mind.

First, if you are outside the U.S. for one year or more without getting advance permission, the law will presume that you abandoned your permanent residence. Like any legal presumption, you can show that it is wrong in your particular case, but it is not easy to make this showing, and you might be required to prove your case in Immigration Court. If you are not successful, your right to U.S. residence and green card will be taken away.

To avoid this situation, if you know that you might be out of the U.S. for one year or more, apply for advance permission (a reentry permit) before you leave. Do this by filing Form I-131 (available at www.uscis.gov/i-131; and you can download a completed sample at www.nolo.com/back-of-book/GRN.html). This form is used for several different purposes, so you want to check off the box in Part 2 that shows you are a permanent (or conditional) resident applying for a reentry permit. Be sure to include a copy of your permanent resident card. (Only copy the back of the card if you have the old style card with information written on the back.) The filing fee for this is currently $575, plus an $85 biometrics fee if you are between age 14 and 79.

A few weeks after USCIS receives your Form I-131, it will send you a receipt notice, and then a biometrics appointment notice. You must attend this appointment (where your fingerprints and photo will be taken) before you leave the United States. However, once that's taken care of, USCIS doesn't mind if you leave the U.S. before your reentry permit is actually approved and sent to you.

a. Six-Plus-Month Departures and Inadmissibility

Apart from the one-year rule just discussed, another important thing to know about traveling as a permanent resident is that an absence from the U.S. of more than six months at a time is treated differently than an absence of less than six months. An absence of less than six months at a time is not considered to be a legally significant departure. What this means is that USCIS will not consider whether any of the grounds of inadmissibility apply to you when you return. (See Chapter 4 for a discussion of the grounds of inadmissibility.)

If you are out of the U.S. for more than six months at a time, however, U.S. immigration authorities consider this a legally significant departure and when you (attempt to) return, they will consider whether any of the grounds of inadmissibility now apply to you. If they think you are inadmissible, you will have a chance to show that they are wrong, but you might be required to prove your case in Immigration Court. If you are not successful, your green card (permanent residence) can be taken away.

b. Residence Can Be "Abandoned" After Departures of Any Length

There is one more thing to keep in mind to make sure that you do not unintentionally abandon your U.S. permanent resident status. It is not enough to be sure that you are never outside the U.S. more than one year at a time; it is not even enough to be sure that you are not outside the U.S. more than six months at a time. Even if you take only short trips outside the U.S., if, over the space of several years, you are spending more time outside the U.S. than inside the U.S., at some point border officials will wonder if you are acting more like a tourist in the U.S. than a permanent resident. In a situation like this, you should be ready to demonstrate your strong ties to the United States. The things that the border official will consider are:

- your purpose in leaving the U.S.
- whether your purpose is consistent with a temporary absence
- whether you have been filing U.S. tax returns as a resident
- whether you still have a job, home, or family in the United States, and
- the duration of your trip or trips.

Even if you are not going to be outside the U.S. for one year or more, if you know that you will be away on so many short trips that you will be outside the U.S. much more than inside over the course of several years, getting a reentry permit (using Form I-131, described above) could be a good idea. It creates evidence that you intend to continue living in the United States as a permanent resident. It means that the authorities cannot rely solely on the length of your absences to determine whether you have lost your permanent residence status. However, since they can still look at other facts in your life, you should maintain as many ties to the United States as possible—even if you get a reentry permit.

If you have to go abroad before you receive the permit, you can request that the permit be delivered to your address overseas or, if the mail in your country is not reliable, through the United States embassy or consulate in your country.

A reentry permit is good for two years. However, if you have been outside of the U.S. for four out of the past five years, the permit will be issued for only one year. And if you have been out of the U.S. for that amount of time, you can also expect to receive intense questions at the airport or other port of entry about whether you have maintained your legal residence in the United States.

3. Explaining Your Failure to Reenter the United States

If you stay outside the U.S. longer than the two years allowed by the reentry permit, or if you stay longer than one year without applying for the reentry permit, you will jeopardize your lawful permanent resident status.

Upon arriving at the U.S. port of entry, officials will question you about your right to return as a green card holder. Be ready to present proof of why you did not return to the United States within the time expected, such as one of the reasons named below.

Illness. A permissible delay could be due to your own serious illness or that of a close relative, especially if the illness started after you left.

Convincing evidence of the illness would be copies of a doctor's written diagnosis, medical bills, prescriptions, and letters to you from friends.

Death. A death in the family could be another reason for delay in returning. Bring with you copies of the death certificate, letters from the court or a lawyer on settlement of the estate, life insurance letters concerning distribution of the insurance proceeds, and a court order dividing property of the deceased.

Business reasons. Setting up or closing down a foreign business enterprise could also be a valid reason for delay. Be ready to show bank statements, a contract of sale, invoices, letters from the bank, and letters from your business partners, your lawyer, and your accountant.

In other words, if you are detained at the airport for a more thorough questioning, you must be ready to convince the U.S. immigration officer that you had a very good reason for not returning to the United States when expected. If the officer is still not convinced, you will have another chance to explain your case before the Immigration Judge at your hearing.

Insist on your right to a hearing. Too often, border officers act intimidating, and the scared green card holder signs away all rights to U.S. residence. Once you do this, it is difficult to get a second chance to explain your side before the Immigration Court. Your status will most likely automatically revert to that of a nonimmigrant— and you will have to repeat the process of getting a green card all over again.

However, if you were coerced or forced to sign away your rights, contact an immigration attorney, who might be able to help you fight to keep your green card. Above all else, never, ever sign Form I-407, Record of Abandonment of Lawful Permanent Resident Status, without first consulting an immigration attorney.

4. Becoming Inadmissible to the U.S.

Grounds of inadmissibility are conditions that U.S. immigration authorities can legally use to keep you from entering the United States. You had to prove that you weren't inadmissible (that is, hadn't committed any crimes, didn't have any serious illnesses, and weren't likely to need public assistance) in order to get your green card in the first place. But these same grounds apply to you every time you leave the United States for more than six months at a time and try to return, or if you commit a crime while you're away. Even with your green card, you could be refused reentry. If one of the grounds of inadmissibility applies to you, however, you might be able to get it waived. (See Chapter 4.)

5. Becoming Removable From the U.S.

In addition to the grounds of inadmissibility described above, U.S. immigration laws list numerous grounds of removability. These are actions or circumstances that can cause you to lose your right to the green card and be placed in removal proceedings in the United States. If you lose, you could be deported back to the country you came from.

The grounds of removability are too complex to explain in detail here. We have already discussed one of them, namely your obligation to report your changes of address to USCIS. In general, however, you need to make sure not to violate any immigration or criminal laws and not to get involved with any organizations that the U.S. government believes to be terrorist.

For a complete list of the grounds of removability, see I.N.A. § 237 or 8 U.S.C. § 1227.

C. Planning to Apply for U.S. Citizenship

You can avoid all the hassles and worries about losing your green card by applying for U.S. citizenship as soon as you're eligible. Citizenship is the highest benefit available under U.S. immigration law, and once you're a citizen, your status can't be taken away (unless you committed fraud in your citizenship application). You're not eligible for U.S. citizenship just yet, however—most people must wait between three and five years after getting their green card. But it's not too early to start thinking about citizenship and planning to apply.

The basic requirements for U.S. citizenship include:

- You've had permanent residence (a green card) for the required number of years—usually five, but three years if you've been married to and living with a U.S. citizen all that time. Also, asylees will receive green cards that are backdated one year to give them credit for some of their time spent in the U.S. as an asylee before actually getting approved for permanent residence, so in effect they don't need to wait a full five years after the approval. Similarly, refugees can, after receiving a green card, count all their time in the U.S. since their date of entry toward the required five years of permanent residence.
- You've been "physically present," that is, lived in the U.S., for at least half your required years of permanent residence.
- You've been "continuously present" in the United States since being approved for your green card.
- You've lived in the same U.S. state or USCIS district for three months before applying to the USCIS there.
- You're at least 18 years old at the time of filing the application.
- You've demonstrated good moral character over the years leading up to your application for citizenship—for example, by paying your taxes and child support and not committing any crimes.
- You can speak, read, and write English.
- You pass a brief test covering U.S. history and government.
- You're willing to affirm loyalty to the U.S. and serve in its military if necessary.

For now, the important message is to think twice before taking any long trips outside the U.S., do your best to learn English, and be a responsible member of society. You can start worrying about the details of your eligibility, and start studying for the test, closer to the time when you're allowed to apply.

 RESOURCE

Need complete instructions on the eligibility criteria and how to apply for U.S. citizenship? See *Becoming a U.S. Citizen: A Guide to the Law, Exam & Interview*, by Ilona Bray (Nolo).

How to Find and Work With a Lawyer

A. Where to Look for a Lawyer 234

    1. Immigration Groups 234

    2. Friends and Relatives 234

    3. Embassies or Consulates 234

    4. Ads in Ethnic Newspapers 234

    5. Lawyer Referral Groups 235

    6. State Bar Associations 235

B. Deciding on a Particular Lawyer 235

    1. The Initial Interview 235

    2. Consultation Fees 236

    3. Dealing With Paralegals and Assistants 236

C. Paying the Lawyer 236

    1. Types of Fee Arrangements 236

    2. Get It in Writing 237

D. Managing the Lawyer 237

    1. Carefully Check Every Statement 237

    2. Educate Yourself 237

    3. Keep Your Own Calendar 238

    4. Maintain Your Own File 238

E. Firing a Lawyer 238

Although this book's philosophy is to help you understand the immigration law and procedures, your situation could be too complicated for you to handle on your own—particularly if you've spent time in the U.S. illegally, have a history of drug use or criminal activity, or fit any of the other problem scenarios described in this book. Or you might be unable to get USCIS to respond to a request for action on your application. It could become necessary to hire a lawyer for help. This chapter gives you valuable tips on where to find help—and what to do once you find it.

A. Where to Look for a Lawyer

Look carefully to find a good, competent, honest lawyer who will assist you with your immigration problems without charging you a hefty fee up front and a huge hourly fee as your case proceeds.

There are a number of good places to begin your search.

1. Immigration Groups

Organizations that specialize in helping low-income people with immigration problems might be able to answer your questions, represent you in your case, or refer you to an experienced immigration lawyer if the group does not take on individual cases. Ask your local USCIS office or a church, mosque, or temple whether they know of any such immigration groups.

Many of these organizations are what are called "nonprofits," meaning they exist to help the public, not for anyone's personal gain. They raise money from individuals, businesses, and charitable foundations.

Unfortunately, because the U.S. government gives almost no money to nonprofits that help immigrants, and because other funding is rarely enough to meet the community's need, you'll need to be patient with these groups. They might be understaffed and have difficulties returning your

phone calls within a reasonable time or spending time with you at all. Also realize that they can legally charge you market-rate fees for their services, although most try to offer lower fees for low-income immigrants.

> **CAUTION**
> **Don't rely on advice from someone who is not a lawyer, or at least supervised by a lawyer.** For example, some church groups try to have volunteers help immigrants with their legal problems. Though their efforts might be well meant, immigration law is too complex to be puzzled out by nonlawyers.

2. Friends and Relatives

Ask your friends and relatives about their own experiences with immigration lawyers— whether they were satisfied with the representation, the competency, and the fees charged, and about their personal rapport with their attorney. Never choose a lawyer simply because they're the relative or classmate or friend of your brother or sister or best friend, without having an idea of the lawyer's competency or track record.

3. Embassies or Consulates

Your own country's embassy or consulate might have a list of immigration lawyers to recommend to you. Normally, these consular officers have your interests at heart and would not recommend a lawyer who is incompetent, a rogue, or a cheat.

4. Ads in Ethnic Newspapers

Local ethnic newspapers and journals probably have an array of immigration lawyers offering services directly through advertisements. But beware— anyone can buy ad space. Be sure to investigate the lawyer's reputation on your own.

Beware of the Bad Guys

Nonattorney practitioners, visa consultants, immigration pseudo-experts, travel agents, people posing as attorneys, and nonprofit organizations not authorized by USCIS to represent aliens before USCIS— all of them litter the immigration marketplace.

Some provide decent advice. But for the most part, be wary—especially if they promise you a green card without any hassle for a certain amount of money. Aside from the fact that it is unlawful to practice immigration law without being admitted by a state bar association, there is no way you can check on these individuals' expertise, and nowhere to complain if their services are poor. Many incompetent consultants prey on immigrants and then simply pack up and move when too many people catch on to them.

Report wrongdoers to the attorney general's office in your state so that they will be forced to stop victimizing unsuspecting immigrants.

5. Lawyer Referral Groups

Local bar association and other lawyer groups sometimes offer referral services. Here are some worth checking:

- **The American Immigration Lawyers Association (www.aila.org).** The lawyers who participate in the service are usually competent and knowledgeable, and have access to lots of resources to help them keep up on what's new.
- **Nolo's Lawyer Directory (www.nolo.com/ lawyers).** Nolo has an easy-to-use online directory of lawyers, organized by location and area of expertise.
- **Martindale.com.** This site has an advanced search option allowing you to sort not only by practice area and location, but also by

criteria, like law school. Whether you look for lawyers by name or expertise, you'll find listings with detailed background information, peer and client ratings, and profile visibility.

6. State Bar Associations

You can check with the bar association in your state to see whether it maintains a list of Certified Specialists in Immigration and Nationality Law. This is someone who has passed state requirements demonstrating knowledge of and experience in immigration law, often by taking a written exam, completing extra coursework, and being favorably evaluated by other attorneys and judges. Not all states certify specialists, however.

B. Deciding on a Particular Lawyer

Once you have a referral to a lawyer—or even better, several referrals—contact each to see which one you like best.

A law firm might have a good reputation for its immigration practice, but the individual lawyer assigned to handle your case is the lawyer responsible for its success or failure. Base your decision about whether to hire an individual lawyer on the rapport you feel—not just on the law firm's reputation.

1. The Initial Interview

Start by asking for an appointment. The office might ask you to first discuss your immigration problem over the phone, because the lawyer might not handle cases such as yours.

When you do find a lawyer who agrees to meet with you, go to the meeting with the thought in mind that you are interviewing the lawyer—not the other way around. It will be you who decides whether or not you want to hire that particular lawyer to handle your case.

Rely on your instincts. Does the lawyer seem competent, knowledgeable, fair, efficient, courteous, and personable? It would be unfortunate and unwise for you to feel uneasy every time you are in contact with your lawyer.

Find out in which state (or states) the attorney is licensed to practice law. Because immigration law is based on federal law, an attorney is allowed to practice it in any state, as long as they are licensed to practice in some state. Then you'll need to check the bar association of the attorney's licensing state to see whether any complaints have been filed against the attorney.

2. Consultation Fees

Some lawyers might not charge you any initial consultation fee, but most immigration lawyers charge between $100 and $350, depending on the city where you live, the expertise of the lawyer, and how long the interview lasts. When you call for an appointment, ask whether a consultation fee is charged and how much it is. Also ask how long the lawyer has been in immigration law practice and how many cases like yours the lawyer has handled.

If you take a few minutes to get organized beforehand, 30 minutes to an hour should be enough time to explain your situation and get at least a basic opinion of what the lawyer can do for you and what that help is likely to cost. Bring with you:

- your passport
- Form I-94 (if you entered the U.S. legally; you might have received a small green or white card or you might need to go to the U.S. Customs and Border Protection (CBP) website at www.cbp.gov and click "Get Your I-94 Admission Number")
- records of any arrests
- a copy of any immigration forms you may have filled out and correspondence received from the INS or USCIS, and
- certificates and documents you may need to prove family relationships, such as husband and wife or parent and child.

3. Dealing With Paralegals and Assistants

Because the practice of immigration law usually involves filling out a great number of forms, the lawyer might hire a paralegal or secretary who interviews you to get many of the answers needed to complete your paperwork.

The paralegal or secretary becomes your contact person. At the initial interview, ask to meet the paralegal who will be working on your case, too, so that you have an idea of how comfortable you will be in dealing with that person. Ask whether the paralegal is closely supervised and whether the lawyer normally reviews the forms before submitting them to the U.S. government.

C. Paying the Lawyer

Some law firms or organizations specializing in immigration might take your case *pro bono*, meaning they will provide a lawyer to handle your case without asking for any money; or perhaps asking for only a small amount to cover expenses.

However, due to limited resources and great demand, they might not be able to accept your immigration case and might only be able to tell you what your legal options are and advise you about whether you seem to have a strong case. These groups might refer you to a list of attorneys they feel would be representing you in the same spirit of service as they do and whose fees would be reasonable.

1. Types of Fee Arrangements

Many immigration attorneys charge a "flat fee" for their work. Flat fees are set amounts for specific types of cases. The attorney's hourly rate could be specified in the contract and would become important if you decide to end the attorney's representation before the work is completed. (See "Firing a Lawyer," below.) Most lawyers are guided by the principle that time is money.

Since you are being charged a flat fee for a specific job, be sure you know what that job is. For example, if hiring an attorney for an adjustment of status case, does the flat fee include filling out the forms (including the forms for the work permit and travel document), making sure that USCIS receives the forms, preparing you for the interview, and attending the interview with you? If you are among the few people who get called back for a second or third interview, does the attorney charge for those interviews separately from the quoted flat fee? If USCIS does not decide your case in a timely fashion, are the lawyer's additional inquiries charged for separately? What "incidental" charges will you be expected to pay in addition to the flat fee? For example, you should know whether you will be paying the USCIS filing fees separately from the attorneys' fee, and whether you will be responsible for mail or courier charges and copying costs.

Many lawyers will agree to let you pay a flat fee in installments during the period it takes to process your immigration papers.

Some immigration lawyers do not charge a flat fee. They charge for their work based on quarter-hours, so that if you call and spend seven minutes on the telephone, you will be charged for a minimum of 15 minutes of work. Unless your lawyer is honest, you could end up paying into a bottomless money pit when you agree to pay the lawyer according to an hourly charge.

If you agree to the per-hour billing rate—usually unwise unless you are in a removal proceeding due to grave criminal conduct or some other complicated case—request a schedule of legal work to be done and a maximum you will pay for each task.

2. Get It in Writing

Most disagreements between lawyers and clients involve fees, so be sure to get all the details involving money in writing—the per-hour billing rate or flat maximum fee, how often you will be billed, and how

the attorney will handle any funds you might have deposited in advance to cover expenses.

D. Managing the Lawyer

A great many complaints against lawyers have to do with their failure to communicate with their clients. Your lawyer might be the one with the legal expertise, but the rights that are being pursued are yours—and you are the most important person involved in your case. You have the right to demand that your lawyer be reasonably available to answer your questions and to keep you posted on your case.

You might need to put some energy into managing your lawyer.

1. Carefully Check Every Statement

Each statement or bill should list costs that the lawyer has paid or that you are expected to pay. If any one lacks sufficient detail, call your lawyer and politely demand that a new, more detailed version be sent before you pay it. Don't feel as though you're being too pushy: The laws in many states actually require thorough detail in lawyers' billing statements.

2. Educate Yourself

By learning the most you can about immigration laws and what to expect during the procedure, you'll be able to monitor your lawyer's work and might even be able to do some legwork, make a suggestion, or provide information that will move your case along faster.

Unfortunately, USCIS and the State Department are bureaucracies and oftentimes a case is simply held up until the slow-grinding wheels of procedure get through it. Many people unfairly blame their lawyers for delays that are actually the government's fault—or just a natural result of how the immigration laws are structured.

However, if an immigration application is proceeding much more slowly than your lawyer initially told you it would, ask your lawyer whether it would make sense to contact the appropriate office and find out the reason for the delay.

3. Keep Your Own Calendar

Note when immigration papers and appearances are due, for example in court or as responses to so-called "Requests for Evidence." If you rely on your lawyer to keep your case on schedule, you could be unpleasantly surprised to find that an important deadline has been missed. This could put your immigration status in jeopardy. Call or write to your lawyer at least a week before any important deadline in your case to inquire about plans to meet it.

Of course, you need to do your part, by showing up for appointments with your lawyer on time, with the right documents in hand, so that your case can be adequately prepared.

And you must be especially careful to arrive on time—or better yet, early—for any appointments with immigration officials. If you're not in the room when you're scheduled to be there, your case could be delayed for weeks or months, or, in the case of Immigration Court, you might receive an immediate order of removal (deportation).

Your lawyer will be unable to help you out of this mess, even if the lawyer is in the courtroom at the time.

4. Maintain Your Own File

Try never to give away original documents connected with your case; keep the originals for your own files and give only copies to your lawyer. USCIS will, in most cases, accept copies of the original documents. Also, ask for a copy of every letter and application your lawyer sends to USCIS. By having a well-organized file of your own, you'll be able to discuss your case with your lawyer intelligently and efficiently—even over the telephone.

Being well-informed will help keep your lawyer's effectiveness up and your costs down, especially if your lawyer is working on an hourly basis, in which case telephone consultations are less expensive than office visits.

Also, your lawyer cannot hold your immigration files ransom in case you decide to change legal counsel, because you have copies of everything the office file has on your case.

In any event, you have a right to promptly receive a copy of your file. The attorney might ask you to sign or produce a written authorization and transfer request before turning the file over to you.

E. Firing a Lawyer

Change lawyers if you feel that's necessary. If the relationship between you and the lawyer you chose doesn't seem to be working, or if you feel that your case isn't progressing as it should, think about asking another lawyer to take over.

If you get upset every time you talk to your lawyer because the lawyer does not seem to understand what you are saying about your case, or will not take the time to listen, you will save yourself both money and mental anguish if you look for someone else to represent you.

But be clear with the first lawyer that you are taking your business elsewhere, and immediately put your decision in writing. At that point, your first lawyer should stop working on your case. The lawyer can then give you an accounting of how much time was spent working on your case. If you have paid a lot of money up front, and the lawyer did not yet spend much time on your case, you will probably be due a refund.

If you were paying in installments and the lawyer spent more time working on your case than you have so far paid for, you might still owe money for the work that was performed, even though you are firing the lawyer.

Do not expect your first lawyer to share any of the fee you've paid with your new lawyer. Unless you have a contingency fee arrangement where the lawyer takes a share of the damages won—and very few immigration cases are structured that way—your fee agreement with your new lawyer will be completely separate from your fee agreement with your first lawyer. Between the two lawyers, you might end up paying more than you would have if you had only one lawyer. Both lawyers could claim they handled the lion's share of the work in your case. Do not be embarrassed to negotiate with the lawyers.

Also, be sure that your new lawyer understands whether you have an application or other matter pending with USCIS or a related agency, and quickly advises that agency of the change in attorneys.

What to Do About Bad Legal Advice

Take prompt action against any behavior by a lawyer that appears to be deceptive, unethical, or otherwise illegal. A call to the local bar association, listed in the telephone directory under "Attorneys," should provide you with guidance on what types of lawyer behavior are prohibited and how to file a complaint.

Still, in most states, groups that regulate attorneys are biased toward them. Unless the lawyer's conduct is plainly dishonest or the lawyer has abandoned your case, you will probably not get much satisfaction. However, sometimes the threat of filing a complaint can move your lawyer into action. And if worst comes to worst, filing a formal complaint will create a document that you'll need should you end up later filing a malpractice lawsuit against a lawyer.

How to Access the Sample Filled-In Forms on the Nolo Website

List of Sample Immigration Forms Available on the Nolo Website...242

This book comes with downloadable sample forms that you can access online at: **www.nolo.com/back-of-book/GRN.html**

We provide these samples for illustration only. If you intend to file any application, petition, or other form with the U.S. government, use the forms supplied by U.S. Citizenship and Immigration Services (USCIS) at www.uscis.gov/forms/all-forms; or by the U.S. Department of State (DOS) at

https://travel.state.gov/content/travel/en/us-visas/visa-information-resources/forms.html. Some of these government forms can or must be filled in online. They are always free to download (though in most cases you'll pay a fee upon filing).

To access the sample, illustrative forms that come with this book, your computer must have specific software programs installed. The samples provided by this book are in PDF format. You can view them with Adobe *Reader*, free software from www.adobe.com.

List of Sample Immigration Forms Available on the Nolo Website

To download any of the files listed below, go to **www.nolo.com/back-of-book/GRN.html**

Chapter in Book	Title	File Name
3	I-539, Application to Extend/change Nonimmigrant Status	ch3_i-539_sample.pdf
6	I-129F, Petition for Alien Fiancé	ch6_i129f_sample.pdf
6	G-1145, e-Notification of Application/Petition Acceptance	ch6_g1145_sample.pdf
6	I-134, Affidavit of Support	ch6_i134_sample.pdf
7	I-129F, Petition for Alien Fiancé	ch7_i129f_sample.pdf
7	I-130, Petition for Alien Relative	ch7_i130_sample.pdf
7	I-130A, Supplemental Information for Spouse Beneficiary	ch7_i130A_sample.pdf
7	I-751, Petition to Remove Conditions on Residence	ch7_i751_sample.pdf
8	I-130, Petition for Alien Relative	ch8_i130_sample.pdf
9	I-130, Petition for Alien Relative	ch9_i130_sample.pdf
9	N-600k, Application for Citizenship and Issuance of Certificate Under Section 322	ch9_n600k_sample.pdf
10	I-600A, Application for Advance Processing of an Orphan Petition	ch10_i600A_sample.pdf
12	I-130, Petition for Alien Relative	ch12_i130_sample.pdf
13	I-589, Application for Asylum and for Withholding of Removal	ch13_i589_sample.pdf
13	I-730, Refugee/Asylee Relative Petition	ch13_i730_sample.pdf
14	I-360, Petition for Amerasian, Widow(er), or Special Immigrant	ch14_i360_sample.pdf

List of Sample Immigration Forms Available on the Nolo Website (continued)

Chapter in Book	Title	File Name
16	I-131, Application for Travel Document	ch16_i131_sample.pdf
16	I-485, Application to Register Permanent Residence or Adjust Status	ch16_i485_sample.pdf
16	I-765, Application For Employment Authorization	ch16_i765_sample.pdf
17	I-864, Affidavit of Support Under Section 213A of the INA	ch17_i864_sample.pdf
17	I-864A, Contract Between Sponsor and Household Member	ch17_i864a_sample.pdf
19	I-918, Petition for U Nonimmigrant Status	ch19_i918_sample.pdf
23	I-90, Application to Replace Permanent Resident Card	ch23_i90_sample.pdf
23	I-131, Application for Travel Document	ch23_i131_sample.pdf

Index

A

Abused spouses/children
cancellation of removal, 155
exception to bars of unlawful
presence, 37
exclusion from I-864 requirements,
34
joint petitions, 79
waiver of inadmissibility for, 31
See also U visas (crime victims
aiding law enforcement)
Acquisition of citizenship. *See*
Citizenship, acquisition of
Adam Walsh Child Protection and
Safety Act (2006), 84, 92, 102
Adjustment of status, 158–171
consular processing compared with,
158, 174
for Diversity Visa Lottery winners,
115
documentation of eligibility,
163–164
eligibility, 37–38, 51, 158–162
filing charts, 50–51
filing process, 163–167
I-130, Petition for Alien Relative,
158, 163, 174, 175–176
I-131, Application for Travel
Document, 164–165
I-485, Application to Register
Permanent Residence or Adjust
Status, 49, 53, 74, 75, 115,
164–166, 198, 199, 218, 221
I-693, Medical Examination of
Aliens Seeking Adjustment of
Status, 166–167, 198
I-765, Application for Employment
Authorization, 63, 134, 142, 154,
164, 183–184, 193, 194, 198
I-797C, Interview Appointment
Notice, 164, 167, 170, 216
I-797C, Interview Appointment
Notice sample, 170

I-864, Affidavit of Support,
165–166, 177–178
I-929, Petition for Qualifying
Family Member of a U-1
Nonimmigrant, 197, 198
for immediate relatives who entered
legally, 159–161, 163
for immigrant children, 98–99
interviews and approval process,
168–171
for life changes, 52, 53
after marriage to U.S. citizen, 56,
64, 69–70, 74
for parents of U.S. citizens, 88–89
prohibited applicants, 162–163
proving bona fide marriage, 166,
168, 169, 171
refugee and asylee status, 158, 164,
166, 167
Request for Upgrade to USCIS
(sample), 52
sponsors for, 165–166, 168–169
Sponsor's Job Letter (sample), 166
spouses at interviews, 169
temporary visas, 24
travel outside U.S. while waiting for
interview, 88, 164–165, 168
under 245(i) law, 37–38
two-year time limit for conditional
permanent residence status, 78–79
USCIS notifications, 167, 168, 171,
175
U visas and, 196–199
work permits and, 161, 164, 165
See also Consular processing
Adjustment of Status Section (DHS/
USCIS), 222
Adopted children, as immigrants,
86, 94–97, 100. *See also* Orphan
adoptions in non-Hague
Convention countries
Adoption service providers (ASPs), 95
Adoptive parents, as immediate
relatives, 86

Advance Parole, 141, 165, 168, 183,
184–185
Afghani/Iraqi translators for U.S.
military, 146
African Americans, history of slavery,
6
Aggravated felonies, use of term, 130,
151
Airlines, and VWP passengers, 22
Alcohol-related criminal grounds of
inadmissibility, 38
Alien Registration Number (A#),
209, 210, 217
Alien soldiers, during WWII, 7
Al Otro Lado, 133
American Council for Voluntary
Agencies, 131
American Immigration Lawyers
Association, 235
Amnesties, 15
Amnesty law. *See* Immigration
Reform and Control Act (1986)
Antiterrorism and Effective Death
Penalty Act (AEDPA) (1996), 9
Appeals of denials, 138, 158, 195,
221–222. *See also* Cancellation of
removal; Immigration Court
Application forms
list of sample forms on Nolo
website, 242–243
sources of, 3, 4
See also USCIS forms; U.S. State
Department (DOS)
Application tips. *See* Immigration
application tips
Arrival tickets, 21
Assault convictions, and
inadmissibility, 38
Assisted reproductive technology
(ART), 205
Asylees/asylum. *See* Refugees and
asylees
Asylum Seeker Advocacy Project
(ASAP), 134

Automatic email/text updates, 71, 87, 98, 122, 220

Automatic U.S. citizenship, 99–100, 107

A visas, 14

B

Battered spouses/children. *See* Abused spouses/children

Beneficiary, defined, 51, 70

Blood tests, for paternity, 94

Board of Immigration Appeals (BIA), 138, 142, 165, 222

Boat companies, and VWP passengers, 21

Bona Fide Determination (BFD), 195

Border crossings
  asylum applications and, 132–133
  caution against having this book with you, 25
  fiancé(e) visas and, 63
  Migrant Protection Protocols, 130
  returning after unlawful U.S. presence, 31–32, 37
  status adjustments and, 37–38
  summary exclusion law and, 37
  visa approval documents, 180
  without inspection, 69–70, 74, 75–76, 89, 162–163
  See also U.S. Customs and Border Protection (CBP)

Brothers/sisters. *See* Siblings of U.S. citizens

Business visas
  approved I-130 petitions and, 123
  extension of stay, 24
  See also Entrepreneur immigrants; Temporary visas

B visas. *See* Business visas; Tourist visas

Bystander victims of crime. *See* U visas (crime victims aiding law enforcement)

C

Canada, VWP travel to U.S. from, 21

Cancellation of removal, 150–155
  for abused spouses/children, 155
  court proceedings, 150

eligibility, 150–151
evidence for case, 151–152
filing process, 154–155
judicial approval of application, 155
maximum number of cancellations per year, 151
for permanent residents, 155
prohibited applicants, 151
proof of hardship, 152–154

Casa de Maryland, Inc. v. Wolf (2020), 134

Cash assistance, inadmissibility and, 28

Central Intelligence Agency (CIA), 115, 215

Certificate of citizenship, 206, 213

Certification of helpfulness, and U visas, 188, 192, 193–194, 196–197

Certified Specialists in Immigration and Nationality Law, 235

Change of address, 229

Change of status. *See* Adjustment of status

Child, defined, 92

Child immigrants, 92–100
  adopted children, 94–97
  application process, 97–99
  automatic citizenship, 99–100
  child, defined, 92
  divorced, 92
  eligibility, 81, 92–93
  establishing fatherhood, 93–94
  I-130, Petition for Alien Relative, 77, 93, 97–99
  I-800, Petition to Classify Convention Adoptee as an Immediate Relative, 95, 98
  I-800A, Application for Determination of Suitability to Adopt a Child from a Convention Country, 95, 98
  marriage status of parents, 93–94
  N-600K, Application for Citizen and Issuance of Certificate Under Section 322, 100, 107
  passports for, 100
  petition preparation (Form I-130), 97–98

stepchildren, 77, 94, 97
unmarried parents, 85, 93–94, 202–204
See also Hague Convention on the Protection of Children and Cooperation in Respect of Intercountry Adoption; Orphan adoptions in non-Hague Convention countries

Child Protective Services (CPS), 193

Children
  of asylees, 138–139
  birth certificates of, 76, 79, 93
  born through assisted reproductive technology, 205
  child, defined, 93–97
  child trafficking, 29–30
  of conditional permanent residents, 78
  conviction of specified offenses against, 67, 84
  declared as dependents in U.S. juvenile courts, 14
  in Diversity Visa Lottery, 116–117
  dual citizenship, 206
  of fiancé(e)s of U.S. citizens, 56, 63–64
  in interviews, 168
  legal custody of, 96–97
  listing all, on forms, 208
  marriage-based immigration and, 62, 76–77, 81
  in proof of hardship, 152–153, 154
  unlawful presence of, 37, 96
  See also Adam Walsh Child Protection and Safety Act (2006); Deferred Action for Childhood Arrivals (DACA) (2012); Siblings of U.S. citizens

Children of K-1 visa holders, 56, 63–64

Children of permanent residents
  no category for married children, 51
  over 21 years of age, 48, 51, 92, 98–99
  protection from switching categories, 51, 52

residency requirements of parents, 89

unmarried and under 21 years of age, 49, 51

waiting periods, 12, 48, 92

who qualifies, 92–93

Children of U.S. citizens

automatic citizenship, 99–100

cancellation of removal for abused, 155

married children, 48, 51

over 21 years of age, 47, 52

unmarried and under 21 years of age, 47, 98

waiting periods, 47

who qualifies, 92–93

See also Citizenship, acquisition of

Child Status Protection Act (2002), 47, 52, 77, 93, 99, 139

Child trafficking, 29–30

Chinese Exclusion Act (1882), 7

Chinese immigrants, history of, 7

Citizenship

basic requirements for, 232

renunciation of, 33

Citizenship, acquisition of, 202–206

born to unmarried parents and, 202, 203–205

certificate of citizenship as proof, 206, 213

certificate of consular report of birth, 206

dual citizenship, 206

eligibility based on birth date, 202–205

green cards prior to, 2

passports as proof, 205

retaining citizenship at birth and residency, 205

Civil penalties, for false application information, 208

Civil unions, 57, 67

Complaints

of attorney wrongdoing, 235, 239

of USCIS staff wrongdoing, 221, 225

Concurrent petitions, 42, 121, 163, 197, 218

Conditional permanent resident, 78–79, 81

Consular Electronic Application Center (CEAC), 175, 220

Consular processing, 174–180

adjustment of status compared with, 158, 174

application process, 175–177

approval process, 40, 60–61, 180

arrival in U.S., 180

Consular Electronic Application Center, 175, 220

for Diversity Visa Lottery winners, 115, 176

fiancé(e) visas, 59–62, 68–69, 174

after I-130 approval, 41–42, 174–176

I-864, Affidavit of Support under Section 213A of the Act, 61–62, 177–178

I-864A, Contract Between Sponsor and Household Member, 36, 165–166, 177–178

interviews, 43, 60, 61–63, 68–69, 179–180

NVC transfers, 175–177

original documents at, 211–212, 215, 216

Poverty Guidelines Chart for Immigrants, 34, 35–36

required documents, 58–60, 61–63, 177–179

tracking applications, 221–222

unlawful presence and, 174

unmarried son or daughter, 178–179

See also Adjustment of status

Consulates, lawyer recommendations from, 234

Continuous physical presence, defined, 152, 196, 232

Couriers, use of, 216

Courts. *See* Immigration Court; U.S. Supreme Court

COVID-19 pandemic

bureaucratic delays during, 46

inadmissibility and, 28

interview protocols in, 169

travels delays from, 184

vaccination, 60

Credit card authorization, 87, 105, 122, 146, 167

Crewmen, 151, 159

Crime victims aiding law enforcement. *See* U visas (crime victims aiding law enforcement)

Criminal grounds of inadmissibility

in adjustment of status, 169

in adoption, 104

in cancellation of removal, 151

criminal and related violations, 29–30, 38–39

disclosure of, 57, 208

for refugees and asylees, 8, 130, 139, 141

Criminal penalties, for false application information, 57, 208

Criminal records, of petitioners, 57, 102

Cuban refugees, history of, 8

Customs and Border Protection (CBP), 9, 133, 165, 184

D

DACA. *See* Deferred Action for Childhood Arrivals (DACA) (2012)

Dates for Filing chart, 49–50

Death of petitioner, 54, 75

Declaration of Independence, opening lines, 10

Defense of Marriage Act (DOMA) (1996), 9, 67

Deferred Action for Childhood Arrivals (DACA) (2012), 182–185

Advance Parole for, 183, 184–185

eligibility, 15, 21, 182, 183

renewal process, 182–185

status of law, 182

Deferred Enforced Departure (DED), 142

Delays and waiting periods, 46–54

for adult children of permanent residents, 92

annual limits on categories, 46–48, 92

cancellation of removal, 155

checking processing times, 49, 75, 222

for consular processing, 175

after deportation, 23

family first preference, 47

family fourth preference, 48, 120

family second preference, 48

family third preference, 48

for fiancé(e) visas, 59

inquiring about, 222–223

for military translators, 146

none for immediate relatives of citizens, 12–13, 47

for NVC processing, 175

orphan adoption, 102

Priority Dates, 50–51

processing times on USCIS website, 49, 222

refugees and asylees, 15, 131, 136

Request for Upgrade to USCIS (sample), 52

revocation of petitions/applications, 53–54

for spouses of permanent residents, 75

for spouses of U.S. citizens, 70, 72

switching preference categories, 51–53

U visas (crime victims aiding law enforcement), 195

visa cutoff dates, 49–51

visa process during, 48

for work permits for asylees, 134, 136

See also Tracking applications

Denials

of asylum applications, 137

of provisional waiver applications, 43

of temporary visas, 24

See also Immigration Court; Reversal of inadmissibility findings

Departure tickets, 21

Deportation, 23, 37, 67, 136, 138. *See also* Cancellation of removal; Removal proceedings

Detention section (ICE), 133, 222

Diplomats (A visas), 14

Disease. *See* Health problems, inadmissibility and

Displaced Persons Act (1948), 8

Diversity Immigrant Visa Lottery, 110–117

about, 111

application process, 112–114

confirmation number, 114

eligibility for, 9, 15, 111–112, 117

excluded countries, 110

green card application process, 114–116

inclusion of spouse/children, 116–117

marriage or birth during process, 116

notification of winners, 114, 115

Provisional Waiver Request and, 41, 42

scam detection, 111

Divorce

of children under 21, 92

during conditional status, 79, 81

filing petition during, 80

preference category and, 51, 53, 54

proof of, 71

after receiving permanent green card, 80

DNA testing, 212

Domestic partnerships, 57, 67

Domestic violence, 38, 57, 58, 104, 189. *See also* Abused spouses/children

Draft evasion, 33

DREAMers, 21, 182. *See also* Deferred Action for Childhood Arrivals (DACA) (2012)

Drug-related criminal grounds of inadmissibility, 29–30, 38, 155

D/S (duration of status), 161

Dual citizenship, 206

DUI/DWI convictions, and inadmissibility, 38

E

EB-5 visas. *See* Entrepreneur immigrants

Economic hardship, 153–154

e-Filing, 217

Electronic System for Travel Authorization (ESTA), 21

Email alerts, 53

Embassies, lawyer recommendations from, 234

Employment Authorization Document (EAD). *See* Work permits (EADs)

Employment-based green cards, 2, 13

Employment-based preference categories

fifth preference workers, 14–15

first preference workers, 13

fourth preference workers, 14

second preference workers, 13

third preference workers, 13

Enforcement and Removal Operations (ERO) (ICE), 222

English language requirement, 232

English translation of documents, 60, 135, 213

Enlistees in U.S. military. *See* Military veterans and enlistees

Entrant Status Check (DV), 115

Entrepreneur immigrants, 9, 14–15

Entry fees, 21

e-Passports, 21

Ethnic newspapers, 234

European immigrants, as early settlers, 6

EWI (entered without U.S. inspection), 69–70, 74, 75–76, 89, 162–163

Exceptional and extremely unusual hardship. *See* Extreme hardship

Exchange visitors (J-1 visa), 2, 19, 151

Executive Office for Immigration Review (DOJ)

EOIR-42B, Application for Cancellation of Removal and Adjustment of Status for Certain Nonpermanent Residents, 154

EOIR Administrative Closure orders, 42

EOIR proceedings, 150

Extreme hardship
  cancellation of removal and, 152–154
  derivative U visas for family members, 197
  provisional waiver applications and, 42–43, 85, 89
  waiver of inadmissibility and, 32, 40, 41

F

F-1 visas. *See* Student visas
Failure to prosecute, 53
Family-based green cards
  family-based relationships, 12–13, 89
  name changes, 81, 85, 93, 122
  nonapplicable relative relations, 13
  See also Adopted children, as immigrants; Children of permanent residents; Fiancé(e) of U.S. citizen; Marriage-based green cards; Orphan adoptions in non-Hague Convention countries; Parents as immigrants; Siblings of U.S. citizens
Family-based preference categories
  fourth preference, 48, 120
  immediate relatives as first preference, 47–48, 92
  second preference, 48, 66, 89, 92
  switching preference categories, 51–53
  third preference, 48, 92
Fatherhood, establishing, 93–94
Federal Bureau of Investigation (FBI), 115, 178, 215
Fees
  adjustment of status under 245(i) law, 38
  Affidavit of Support review, 176
  attorneys, 236–237
  biometrics (fingerprint/photo), 105, 167, 215
  cancellation of removal, 154
  certificates of citizenship, 206
  checking for accuracy of, 208
  DACA renewal, 184

Department of State, 42
diversity visa application, 112
diversity visa surcharge, 116, 176
exemption of military veterans, 144
fiancé(e) visas, 59
filing I-130, 64, 97, 122
filing I-131, 229
filing I-192, 192
filing I-485, 167
filing I-539, 23
filing I-600, 106
filing I-601, 40
filing I-751, 78
filing I-765, 141–142, 164, 193, 194
filing I-800A, 95
filing I-821, 141
filing I-824, 42, 105, 213
filing I-929, 197
for green card renewal/replacement, 228
immigrant visas, 175, 176
K-3 visas, 69
for marriage-based green cards, 71
medical examinations and vaccinations, 62
notary publics, 212
NVC processing, 175, 176
one check for multiple applications, 218
payment methods, 71, 208–209
Premium Processing Service, 217
receipts for, 42
for special immigrants, 146
for Visa Waiver Program, 21
Female genital cutting, 128
Fiancé(e) of U.S. citizen, visa for, 56–64
  application process summary, 12, 57–58
  border crossings, 63
  children and, 56, 63–64
  citizenship requirements, 56
  consular interviews, 59–62, 68–69, 174
  criminal record disclosure, 57, 58, 60
  DS-160, Online Nonimmigrant Visa Application, 60–61, 63

  eligibility for, 9, 56–57
  G-1145, e-Notification of Application/Petition Acceptance, 58, 59
  I-129F, Petition for Alien Fiancé(e), 57, 58–60, 60, 63, 73
  I-134, Affidavit of Support, 60, 61–62, 116
  I-864, Affidavit of Support, 61–62
  if already married, 62
  if wedding is canceled, 64
  meeting requirement, 56–57, 58
  online visa application, 60–61
  sending petition for, 59
  USCIS interviews, 59
  wedding within 90-days of entry, 56, 59
  work permits, 63
  See also Marriage-based green cards
Filipino immigrants, history of, 7
Filling out and submitting forms. *See* Appendix A; Immigration application tips
Final Action chart, 49–50
Financial support, proof of, 24, 34–36, 115–116
Fines
  on employers who fail to verify immigration status, 9
  for failure to report a change of address, 229
  for false application information, 208, 228
  for sham marriages, 66
Fingerprints, 23, 46, 67, 88, 105, 137, 151, 215
Firmly resettled, use of term, 130
First preference family members, 47, 92
First preference workers. *See* Priority workers
Forced abortion or sterilization, 30, 128
Forced marriage, 128
Forced migration, 6
Foreign Affairs Manual, 160
Former U.S. government employees, 14

Forms
list of sample forms on Nolo
website, 242–243
sources of, 3, 4
See also Appendix A; USCIS forms;
U.S. State Department (DOS)
Fourth preference family members,
48, 120. *See also* Siblings of U.S.
citizens
Fourth preference workers. *See*
International organization
employees
Fraud. *See* Immigration fraud
Freedom of Information Act (FOIA)
requests, 164, 218

G

Good moral character, proof of,
151–152, 232
Grandfather clause, 37–38, 158
Green card lottery. *See* Diversity
Immigrant Visa Lottery
Green cards
appearance of, 12
changes to, 228
losing rights to, 4, 229–232
planning for citizenship
application, 228, 232
renewing or replacing, 214,
228–229
visas and, 46
G visas. *See* International
organization employees

H

H-1B visas. *See* Specialty workers
Hague Convention on the Protection
of Children and Cooperation in
Respect of Intercountry Adoption,
33, 94–95, 98, 102. *See also*
Orphan adoptions in non-Hague
Convention countries
Half-brothers/sisters, as immigrants,
120–121
Hardship. *See* Extreme hardship
Health care workers, admissibility
of, 31
Health problems, inadmissibility
and, 29, 31, 38, 39, 178, 184

Home study, adoption requirement,
95, 104, 105
Hong Kong, employees of U.S.
consulate in, 14
Humanitarian parole, in orphan
adoption, 106
Human rights violations,
inadmissibility and, 30
Human trafficking, 29–30, 188, 189

I

Illegal aliens. *See* Undocumented
aliens
Illegal Immigration Reform and
Immigrant Responsibility Act
(IIRIRA) (1996), 9
Illness. *See* Health problems,
inadmissibility and; Tuberculosis
(TB)
Immediate relatives of U.S. citizens
adjustment of status for, 159–161,
163
adopted parents as, 86
defined, 47
no designated waiting period for,
12–13, 47
stepparents as, 86
unlimited green cards awarded to
spouses, 46
unmarried children, 178–179
widows/widowers, 47
Immigrant visas, 18, 46, 175, 176
Immigration Act (1917), 7
Immigration Act (1924), 7
Immigration Act (1990), 9, 15
Immigration and Nationality Act
(1952), 8–10, 145
Immigration application tips,
208–218
addendum page, 210
additional required documents, 216
Alien Registration Number (A#),
209, 210, 217
copies and original documents,
211–212, 215, 216
documents not in English, 213
e-filing, 217
filing by mail or courier, 216

fingerprints, 215
FOIA requests for copy of file/
documents, 164, 218
if answers are unknown, 209
keeping records, 87, 215, 216, 217
moving during the application
process, 216
one check for multiple applications,
218
online form completion, 209, 210
payment methods, 71, 208–209
penalties for false answers, 208
photographs, 113, 214–215
phrasing of identifying
information, 209–210
proof of family relationship,
210–212
proof of INS or USCIS approval,
212–213
proof of lawful residence, 214
proof of U.S. citizenship, 71, 72,
213–214
Sworn Statement (sample), 212
use of current forms and fee
amounts, 208–209
See also Tracking applications
Immigration attorneys, 234–239
bad advice from, 235, 239
fee arrangements, 236–237
finding, 234–235
firing, 238–239
managing, 237–238
selecting, 235–236
See also Immigration attorneys,
consultation topics
Immigration attorneys, consultation
topics
adjustment of status, 23
adoption of child from Hague
Convention countries, 95, 115
adoption of child from non-Hague
Convention countries, 95
adoption of child living in U.S., 96
Advance Parole, 165
automatic citizenship for overseas
children, 100
cancellation of removal, 150, 154,
155

completion of affidavits, 37

criminal grounds of inadmissibility, 3, 40, 58, 67

criminal record of petitioner, 84, 92

after death of petitioner, 54

denial of adjustment of status, 171

diversity visa applicants, 115, 116

divorce during conditional status, 81

employment-based green cards, 13–15

after entering U.S. without inspection, 70, 74

evidence of residency, 89

extension of temporary visa, 24

filing case of mandamus, 224

finding, 234–325

humanitarian parole, 106

if spouse does not sign joint petition, 79

K-3 visas for spouses of U.S. citizens, 68

name changes, 81

permanent bar status, 37

private bills, 16

provisional waivers, 38, 84, 85, 89, 174

qualifying for a green card on investment, 15

refugee and asylee status, 127, 128, 132, 133, 134, 136, 137

removal of conditions, 79

removal proceedings, 3

revocation of green card, 231

special immigrants, 14

unmarried child who marries, 178–179

U visas, 194, 195

waiver of inadmissibility, 39, 40

waiver of meeting requirement for fiancé(e)s, 57

Immigration Court
in asylum denials, 137–138

cancellation of removal cases, 150, 151–155

under DOJ direction, 222

failure to maintain residence, 229–230

in removal proceedings, 150, 171, 192, 222

signing away rights at border crossings, 231

in tracking applications, 222

in work permit applications, 134

Immigration fraud
by asylees, 139

fraud interviews, 169

fraudulent marriages, 12, 56, 66, 67, 80–81, 179

overstaying, 96

providing false information, 208, 211

proving bona fide marriage, 166, 168, 169, 171, 179

simultaneous petitions, 123

visa fraud, 24, 88, 160–161, 162

Immigration groups, help from, 234

Immigration Marriage Fraud Amendments (1986), 66

Immigration Reform and Control Act (1986), 9

Immigration to U.S., history of
current immigration laws, 8–10

earliest settlers, 6

early immigration restrictions, 7–8

Trump executive orders, contestation of, 21, 130, 134, 182

Imprisonment, for false application information, 208

Inadmissibility, 28–43
30/60 rule, 160

COVID-19 pandemic and, 28

defined, 28

grounds for, 28, 29–33

immigration violations, 31–33

life changes and, 51

Poverty Guidelines Chart for Immigrants, 34, 35–36

remaining outside for required amount of time, 43

reversal of finding, 39–43

summary exclusion law, 37

unlawful U.S. presence, 31–32, 37, 40, 41, 43, 132

waiver of, 28–34, 43, 192, 197

See also Criminal grounds of inadmissibility; Reversal of inadmissibility findings; specific grounds

Income tax records, 153

Indentured servants, history of, 6

Indochinese immigrants, history of, 7, 8

Institutionalization, inadmissibility and, 28

Intercountry Adoption Accreditation and Maintenance Entity, Inc. (IAAME), 102

International broadcasting employees, 14

International Marriage Brokers Regulation Act (2005), 57

International organization employees, 14

Interpreters, 136, 169, 179. See also Translators, for U.S. military

Intra-company transferees, 14

IR-3 and IR-4 visas, 102, 107. See also Orphan adoptions in non-Hague Convention countries

Iraqi/Afghani translators for U.S. military, 146

Iraqi translators for U.S. military, 146

J

Japanese immigrants, history of, 7

Job offers, DOL certification of, 13

Joint sponsors, 36

K

K-1 visas. See Fiancé(e) of U.S. citizen

K-2 visas. See Children of K-1 visa holders

K-3 visas, 19, 69. See also Marriage-based green cards; Spouses of U.S. citizens

Kentucky Consular Center (KCC), 115

Kidnapping, 103, 189

L

L-1/L-2 visas. *See* Intra-company transferees
Labor certification, 13, 31
Lawyer referral groups, 235
Lawyers. *See* Immigration attorneys; Immigration attorneys, consultation topics
Legal assistants, 236
Legal status, importance of, 23, 25
Legitimated child, defined, 202
Legitimation laws, 203
Liberian Refugee Immigration Fairness (LRIF), 141
Liberians, and DED program, 141, 142
LIFE Act (Legal Immigration Family Equity Act) (2000), 75–76
Lottery. *See* Diversity Immigrant Visa Lottery
Lottery scams, 111

M

M-1 visas. *See* Student visas
Mail/couriers, use of, 216
Marriage-based green cards, 66–81
  application process, 67–72
  children and, 62, 76–77, 81
  common questions/answers, 80–81
  consular processing and, 61–63, 68–70
  divorce and, 80
  documents for interviews, 60, 61–63, 177–179
  eligibility for, 9–10, 66–67
  fraudulent marriages, 12, 56, 66, 67, 80–81, 179
  G-1145, e-Notification of Application/Petition Acceptance, 71
  I-129F, Petition for Alien Fiancé(e), 68, 70, 72
  I-130, Petition for Alien Relative, 12, 64, 67–75, 85, 87–88
  I-130A, Supplemental Information for Spouse Beneficiary, 71
  I-751, Petition To Remove Conditions on Residence, 78–79

  if marriage is less than two years old, 64, 78–79
  if spouse does not sign joint petition, 79
  living apart, 80–81
  living outside the U.S. after marriage, 66
  marriage documentation, 76, 78–79
  marriage to a U.S. citizen, 68–69
  marriage to a U.S. permanent resident, 66, 68–70
  proving bona fide marriage, 166, 168, 169, 171, 179
  for same-sex couples, 67
  special rules in court proceedings, 67
  spouse in U.S. illegally, 70, 74
  summary chart of process, 73–74
  using fiancée visa method, 68–69, 72, 77
  See also Fiancé(e) of U.S. citizen; Spouses of permanent residents; Spouses of U.S. citizens; Widow/ widowers of U.S. citizens
Marriage brokers, 57
Marriage by proxy, 71
Marriage certificates, 64, 71, 85, 93
Married children of U.S. citizens, 48, 51
Martindale.com, 235
Matchmaking services, 57
Matter of Arrabally Yerrabelly (2012), 165
Medical doctors, 14, 31
Medical examinations
  adjustment of status and, 166–167, 177, 178
  consular processing, 60, 177
  fiancé(e) visas, 60, 62, 69
  incorrect findings, 40
  spouses of U.S. citizens, 69
Mental illness, and reversal of inadmissibility, 29, 39
Mexico–U.S. border
  asylum applications and, 133
  CBP misinformation at, 133
  immigration detention, 133

  Migrant Protection Protocols, 130
  VWP travel to U.S., 21
Migrant Protection Protocols, 130
Military veterans and enlistees, 144–147
  additional resources for, 147
  application for citizenship after green card, 147
  application for citizenship without green card, 144
  continuous physical presence requirement, 152
  eligibility for permanent residence, 145–146
  fee exemption, 144
  filing for permanent residence, 146–147
  I-360, Petition for Amerasian, Widow(er), or Special Immigrant, 146–147
  Iraqi/Afghani translators, 146
  spouse or children of, 35, 146–147
  USCIS contact information, 145
  Visa Waiver Program and, 22
Millionaire entrepreneurs. *See* Entrepreneur immigrants
Moral turpitude, 29, 39–40, 41

N

National Benefits Center (NBC), 221
National Defense Authorization Act (2011), 146
National Origins Act (1924), 7
National-origins quota system, 7, 49, 128
National Records Center, 218
National Visa Center (NVC)
  in consular processing, 176
  contact information, 59, 176, 221
  fiancé(e) visas, 58, 60
  file transfers from USCIS, 42
  mailing address, 52
  one-year contact rule, 54
  tracking applications, 221–222
  visa cutoff dates, 49–51
  See also Consular processing; U.S. embassy/consulate

Native Americans, U.S. possession of ancestral lands of, 6

Nativity qualifications, 111

Natural disasters. *See* Temporary Protected Status (TPS)

Naturalization Section (DHS/ USCIS), 222

Nicaraguan Adjustment and Central American Relief Act (1997), 150

90-day rule (DOS), 160

Nolo's Lawyer Directory, 235

Nolo Website, downloadable forms on, 242–243

Nonavailability certificate, 211

Nonimmigrant visas
classifications of, 19–20
as short-term option, 18–19
See also Fiancé(e) of U.S. citizen

Nonorphan adoptions, 95–96. *See also* Orphan adoptions in non-Hague Convention countries

Notary publics, 212

Notice to Appear (NTA), 150

O

Obergefell v. Hodges (2015), 10, 57, 67

Office of the Chief Counsel (DHS/ ICE), 222

O*NET database, 112

One-year contact rule, 54

Online dating websites, 57

Orphan adoptions in non-Hague Convention countries, 102–107
advance processing applications, 105
application process, 104–106
automatic citizenship, 107
bringing child to U.S. on temporary visa, 106
eligibility to petition, 103–104
home country approval, 106
home study preadoption requirements, 104, 105
I-600, Petition to Classify Orphan as an Immediate Relative, 106
I-600A, Application for Advance Processing of Orphan Petition, 105, 106

by lesbians and gays, 104
list of parties to Hague Convention, 95, 102
meeting face-to-face, 107
orphan child, defined, 103
state requirements, 105
visa filing, 107
visa types, 102, 103

Orphan child, defined, 103

P

Panama Canal Zone, former employees, 14

Paralegals, 236

Parents as immigrants, 84–89
adjustment of status, 88–89
application process, 86–89
cultural changes for, 88
I-130, Petition for Alien Relative, 85–86, 87–88
residency requirement, 89
subsequent family immigration strategies, 89
travel during application period, 88
who qualifies as parent, 85–86
who qualifies as petitioner, 84–85

Particularly serious crime, use of term, 130

Particular social group (PSG), 128

Passports, U.S., 21, 22, 58, 60, 213–214

Passports from home country, 214

Paternity, establishing, 93–94, 212

Permanent bar, 37, 158–159, 184

Permanent Resident Card (Form I-551), 12, 214, 229

Persecution, defined, 127–128

Petitioner, defined, 70. *See also* Sponsors

Photographs, 60–61, 71, 72, 113, 214–215

Physical illness, and reversal of inadmissibility, 29, 39. *See also* Tuberculosis (TB)

Plane tickets, and temporary visas, 24

Police clearance, 60, 177

Political asylum and refugee status. *See* Refugees and asylees

Political opinion, persecution and, 128

Polygamists, 33

Poverty Guidelines Chart for Immigrants, 34, 35–36

Preconceived intent, 24, **69**

Preference immigrants, 47. *See also* Employment-based preference categories; Family-based preference categories

Premium Processing Service (USCIS), 217

Priority Dates, 50–51, 52, 69, 99

Priority workers, 13

Private bills, 16

Pro bono representation, 236

Professional workers. *See* Specialty workers

Provisional waiver applications
denial options, 43
eligibility for, 41, 84–85
entry without inspection and, 38, 163
extreme hardship, 42–43, 85, 89
repeat applications, 43
Requests for Evidence for incomplete applications, 43
required documents, 42–43
timing of filing, 41–42
for undocumented parents of U.S. citizens, 84–85

Psychological hardship, 154

Public charge rules, 28, 31, 34

Q

Qualifying criminal activity, for U visas, 189, 191

Quotas on green cards
DOS oversight of, 128
family preference categories and, 47
historical, 7–8
for spouses of U.S. permanent residents, 48
waiting times from, 49, **53**

R

REAL ID Act (2005), 129
Receipt Number (USCIS), 59, 122, 175, 216, 217, 220, 223
Records, keeping, 237–238
Refugee Act (1980), 8, 127
Refugee Relief Act (1953), 8
Refugee Resettlement Agency (RRA), 131
Refugees and asylees, 127–142
    adjustment of status, 139, 158, 164, 166, 167
    alternatives to asylum, 130–131
    application process for asylum, 132–137
    application process for refugee status, 131–132
    asylum requests for spouses/children, 138–139
    criminal grounds of inadmissibility, 8, 130, 141
    Deferred Enforced Departure, 142
    denial of application, 137
    distinction between, 15, 128
    eligibility for, 8, 127–129
    green card application process, 132, 139
    I-131, Application for Travel Document, 137
    I-589, Application for Asylum and for Withholding of Removal, 132, 134, 135, 136, 139
    I-590, Registration for Classification as Refugee, 131
    I-730, Refugee/Asylee Relative Petition, 138–139
    I-864, Affidavit of Support, 139
    Immigration Court hearings of denials, 137–138
    interview process, 131, 136–137
    limits on number of applicants, 8, 127
    medical examinations and vaccinations, 131
    one-year deadline, 130
    persons prohibited from eligibility, 129–130
    revocation of status, 139
    right of appeal by, 22
    status during pending applications, 37
    Temporary Protected Status, 127, 140–142
    traveling after grant of asylum, 137
    waiting periods, 14, 131
    withdrawing request for entry, 133
    work permits, 134, 136, 138
Refugee Support Center (RSC), 131
Religious workers, 14
Remain in Mexico policy, 130, 133
Removal proceedings
    admissibility after, 32
    for asylum claims at Mexican border, 132
    cancellation of removal only after, 150
    children, 96
    for failure to report address change, 229
    getting married during, 67
    inadmissibility after, 31–33
    lawyer assistance with, 3
    pending U visas and, 192
    removability of green card holders, 232
    TPS benefits and, 140
    See also Cancellation of removal
Renewal/replacement of green cards
    I-90, Application to Replace Permanent Resident Card, 214, 228
    preparation for citizenship application and, 232
    process of, 228–229
    revocation of cards by USCIS, 229–232
Requests for Evidence (RFEs), 43, 168, 216, 238
Reversal of inadmissibility findings, 39–43
    application for waiver, 40
    correction of grounds of, 39
    proof of inapplicability of, 39–40
    proof of incorrect finding, 40
    provisional waivers, 38
Revocation of green cards
    applicable conditions, 4
    failure to maintain U.S. residence, 229–231
    failure to report change of address, 229
    grounds for inadmissibility, 230, 231
    grounds for removability, 232
    proof of rationale for failures at reentry, 231
Revocation of petitions/applications, 53–54

S

Safe third countries, 130
Same-sex marriage, 9–10, 57, 67, 104
Secondary evidence, 212
Second preference family members, 48, 66, 89, 92
Second preference workers, 13
Security checks, 46, 62, 115, 144, 221
Self-petitioning abused/battered spouses/children. See Abused spouses/children
Self-petitioning widows/widowers, 12, 34, 54, 75
Servicemembers. See Military veterans and enlistees
Sessions v. Morales-Santana (2017), 203
Sexual orientation
    asylum based on persecution, 128, 133
    as bar to adoption, 104
    same-sex marriage, 9–10, 57, 67, 104
Sham marriages, 12, 56, 66, 67, 80–81, 179
Siblings of U.S. citizens, 120–123
    adopted brothers/sisters, 96, 121
    application process, 121–123
    eligibility for, 120–121
    I-130, Petition for Alien Relative, 89, 121–123
    as second preference family members, 48, 66, 89, 92
    simultaneous petitions for, 123
    tourist visas during application process, 123
    in the U.S. illegally, 123
    waiting periods, 48, 123

Skilled worker preference, 8, 9

Slave trade, history of, 6

Special immigrants

    filing for permanent residence, 14, 146–147

    former U.S. government employees, 14

    I-360, Petition for Amerasian, Widow(er), or Special Immigrant, 146–147

Specialty workers, 14, 19, 48

Sponsors

    in adjustment of status, 165–166, 168–169

    death of, 54

    for diversity visa applicants, 116

    I-864A, Contract Between Sponsor and Household Member, 36

    joint, 36

    personal assets of, 34, 36

    for refugees, 131

    residency requirements, 89

    responsibilities of, 34–36

    Sponsor's Job Letter (sample), 166

Spouses of permanent residents

    abused, 31, 34, 37, 79, 155

    adjustment of status interviews, 68–70, 169

    annual limit to green cards awarded to, 46

    application process, 12, 74

    children of, 77

    if married less than two years, 78–79

    marriage documentation, 76, 78–79

    waiting periods, 12, 48

    See also Marriage-based green cards

Spouses of U.S. citizens

    abused, 31, 34, 37, 79, 155

    adjustment of status interviews, 69, 169

    advice for, 75

    application process, 73–74

    cancellation of removal for abused, 155

    children of, 76–77

    if married less than two years, 78–79

    K-3 visa option for, 68–69, 73–74

    living apart, 80–81

    marriage documentation, 76, 78–79

    nonimmigrant visas during waiting period, 48

    unlimited green cards awarded to, 46

    vaccinations, 60, 62

    visa fees, 72

    who entered U.S. without inspection, 74, 75–76

    work permits for, 68

    See also Fiancé(e) of U.S. citizen; Marriage-based green cards

State bar associations, 235

Stateside waivers. *See* Provisional waiver applications

Stepchildren, as immigrants, 77, 94, 97

Stepparents, as immediate relatives, 86

Student visas, 19, 24, 32, 97, 159, 161–162

Substantial mental anguish. *See* U visas (crime victims aiding law enforcement)

Substantial physical injury. *See* U visas (crime victims aiding law enforcement)

Summary exclusion law, 37

Supplemental Security Income (SSI), 28

Suspension of deportation. *See* Cancellation of removal

T

Temporary Protected Status (TPS)

    application process, 141–142

    benefits of, 140

    departure from U.S. requires advance parole, 141

    designated countries, 140, 141

    eligibility for, 9, 127, 140, 141

    period of protection, 140

    termination of status, 142

Temporary visas

    adjustment of status, 24

    application process, 25

    contesting denial of extension, 24

    Deferred Action for Childhood Arrivals, 15, 21

    denial of, 24

    extension of visitor visas, 23–24

    I-539, Application to Extend/Change Nonimmigrant Status, 23–24, 25, 199

    immigrant visas, 18

    importance of legal status, 23

    nonimmigrant U visas, 21

    nonimmigrant visas, 18–20, 21

    undocumented aliens, 9, 18

    Visa Waiver Program, 21–22

    work limitations of, 18–19

    See also specific visas and programs

Temporary worker visas, 23–24

Ten-year bar, 23, 43

Ten-year green card scams, 150

Terrorism, countries with ties to

    grounds for inadmissibility, 9, 30, 38–39, 130, 141

    nationals exclusion from VWP, 22

    U.S. Homeland Security Department list, 38

Terrorist, defined, 39

Text alerts, 53

Third preference family members, 48, 92

Third preference workers, 13

30/60 rule (DOS), 160

Three-year bar, 32, 43

Title 8, U.S. Code, 8

Torture. *See* United Nations Convention Against Torture (CAT)

Tourist visas

    during application for immigration, 123

    approved I-130 petitions and, 123

    extension of stay, 23–24, 25

    Form I-539, Application to Extend/Change Nonimmigrant Status, 23–24, 25, 199

    preconceived intent and, 24

"prospective student" notations, 24
terrorism country exclusions and, 22
tourists who can visit without, 21–22
work restrictions of, 18–19
See also Adjustment of status; Temporary visas; Visa Waiver Program (VWP)
Tracking applications, 220–225
complaints of staff wrongdoing, 221, 225
expedited processing in emergencies, 223–224
inquiring about delays, 222–223
Letter to Supervisor (sample), 224
offices involved in processing, 221–222
online tracking, 220
reporting outstanding service, 225
understanding government culture, 220, 224
at USCIS field offices, 220, 221
Translating services, 136, 213. *See also* Interpreters
Translators, for U.S. military, 146
Tuberculosis (TB), 29, 39, 178
T visas. *See* Human trafficking
245(i) law, 37–38

U
Undocumented aliens
adjustment of status, 158
amnesty for workers in the 1980s, 9
asylum applications, 132
defined, 18
deportation of, 33, 66
parents of U.S. citizens as, 84–85
See also Unlawful U.S. presence, and inadmissibility
United Nations Convention Against Torture (CAT), 130–131, 136, 137
United Nations High Commissioner for Refugees (UNHCR), 128, 131
Unlawful U.S. presence, and inadmissibility
asylum applications, 132
green card seekers not eligible to adjust status, 41

ten-year bar, 23, 43
unlawfully present for 180 days before leaving, 37
waivers for, 31–32, 40
Unmarried parents, children of, 85, 93–94, 202, 203–205
USA Patriot Act (2002), 9
U.S. Armed Forces. *See* Military veterans and enlistees
USCIS forms
AR-11, Change of Address, 216, 229
G-325A, Biographical Information, 154
G-639, Freedom of Information/ Privacy Act Request, 164, 218
G-1145, e-Notification of Application/Petition Acceptance, 58, 59, 71, 87, 97, 122
G-1450, Authorization for Credit Card Transactions, 59, 71, 122, 146, 167, 209
I-90, Application to Replace Permanent Resident Card, 214, 228
I-102, Application for Replacement/ Initial Nonimmigrant Arrival-Departure Document, 164
I-129F, Petition for Alien Fiancé(e), 57, 58–60, 63, 68, 70, 72
I-130, Petition for Alien Relative, 12, 41–42, 47, 49, 52–53, 64, 67–75, 77, 85–86, 87–88, 89, 93, 97–99, 121–123, 130, 152, 158, 163, 174–176
I-130A, Supplemental Information for Spouse Beneficiary, 71
I-131, Application for Travel Document, 137, 141, 164–165, 185, 198, 229–231
I-134, Affidavit of Support, 24, 60, 61–62, 116, 178
I-140, Immigrant Petition for Alien Worker, 41, 42
I-192, Application for Advance Permission to Enter as a Non-Immigrant, 188, 191, 192

I-360, Petition for Amerasian, Widow(er), or Special Immigrant, 146
I-485, Application to Register Permanent Residence or Adjust Status, 53, 74, 75, 115, 164–166, 198, 199, 218, 221
I-485A, Supplement for Form I-485, 164, 167
I-512L, Authorization for Parole of an Alien into the United States, 185
I-539, Application to Extend/ Change Nonimmigrant Status, 23–24, 25, 199
I-551, Permanent Resident Card, 12, 214, 229
I-589, Application for Asylum and for Withholding of Removal, 132, 134, 135, 136, 139
I-590, Classification as Refugee, 131
I-600, Petition to Classify Orphan as an Immediate Relative, 106
I-600A, Application for Advance Processing of Orphan Petition, 105, 106
I-601, Application for Waiver of Grounds of Inadmissibility, 40–41, 43
I-601A, Provisional Waiver Application, 41, 42–43
I-693, Report of Medical Examination and Vaccination Record, 166–167, 198
I-730, Refugee/Asylee Relative Petition, 138–139
I-751, Petition To Remove Conditions on Residence, 78–79
I-765, Application for Employment Authorization, 63, 134, 142, 154, 164, 183–184, 193, 194, 198
I-765WS, Application for Employment Authorization Worksheet, 183
I-797, Notice of Action, 52, 59, 72, 165, 185, 198

I-797C, Interview Appointment Notice, 164, 167, 170, 216

I-800, Petition to Classify Convention Adoptee as an Immediate Relative, 95, 98

I-800A, Application for Determination of Suitability to Adopt a Child from a Convention Country, 95, 98

I-821, Application for Temporary Protected Status, 141–142

I-821D, Consideration of Deferred Action for Childhood Arrivals, 183–184

I-824, Application for Action on an Approved Application or Petition, 42, 105–106, 147, 213

I-864, Affidavit of Support under Section 213A of the Act, 31, 34, 36, 61–62, 116, 139, 165–166, 177–178

I-864A, Contract Between Sponsor and Household Member, 36, 165

I-864 EZ, Affidavit of Support, 34, 166, 177–178

I-864W, Request for Exemption for Intending Immigrant's Affidavit of Support, 34, 165, 178

I-918, Petition for U Nonimmigrant Status, 192, 193, 194, 195

I-918A, Petition for Qualifying Family Member of U-1 Recipient, 192, 193

I-918B, U Nonimmigrant Status Certification, 190, 192, 193, 196–197, 198

I-929, Petition for Qualifying Family Member of a U-1 Nonimmigrant, 197, 198

N-400, Application for Naturalization, 144, 147

N-426, Request for Certification for Military or Naval Service, 144, 146–147

N-600, Application for Certificate of Citizenship, 206

N-600K, Application for Citizen and Issuance of Certificate Under Section 322, 100, 107

Requests for Evidence (RFEs), 43
See also Appendix A; U.S. Citizenship and Immigration Services (USCIS)

USCIS website
Adjustment of Status Filing charts, 50–51
automatic email updates, 71, 87, 98, 122, 220
Check Processing Times, 49, 75, 222
Check Your Case Status, 223
phone numbers, 79, 145, 166, 220, 223
tracking applications, 220–221
Visa Availability and Priority Dates, 49–51, 52, 69, 99
See also USCIS forms; U.S. Citizenship and Immigration Services (USCIS)

U.S. citizen, defined, 84

U.S. citizenship, proof of, 71, 72, 213–214

U.S. Citizenship and Immigration Services (USCIS)
automatic email/text alert signup, 71, 87, 98, 122, 220
culture of, 220, 224
Customer Contact Center, 79, 166, 220, 223
formation of, 9
offices in which applications may be pending, 221–222
phone numbers, 79, 145, 166, 220, 223
public charge rules, 28, 31, 34
regional asylum service centers, 135
See also Tracking applications; USCIS forms; USCIS website

U.S. Code, Title 8, 8

U.S. Congress
automatic citizenship for some children, 99
DACA policies, 15, 21, 182

Deferred Enforced Departure (DED), 142

Diversity Immigrant Visa Lottery, 110–111

passage of private bills, 16

Temporary Protected Status, 140–142

terrorism watch list, 22

U.S. Customs and Border Protection (CBP)
enforcement role, 9
I-94, Arrival-Departure Record Card, 23–24, 96–97, 142, 161, 163–164, 198, 236
misinformation by at Mexican border, 133
See also Border crossings

U.S. embassy/consulate
certificates of report of birth, 206
documents for interviews, 60, 61–63, 215
fiancé(e) visas, 59–62, 68–69
interview questions, 62
in Kabul, 146
referrals to United Nations High Commissioner for Refugees, 131
U visas (crime victims aiding law enforcement), 195
See also Consular processing

U.S. Health and Human Services Department (HHS)
Poverty Guidelines Chart for Immigrants, 34, 35–36

U.S. Homeland Security Department (DHS)
Immigration and Customs Enforcement (ICE), 9, 150, 195, 222
list of countries with ties to terrorism, 38
in removal proceedings, 150

U.S. Immigration and Customs Enforcement (ICE), 9, 150, 195, 222

U.S. Justice Department (DOJ), 128, 222
Executive Office for Immigration Review (EOIR), 154
See also Immigration Court

U.S. Labor Department (DOL)
certification of workers, 13, 31, 76,
162
U.S. Refugee Admissions Program
(USRAP), 131
U.S. State Department (DOS)
30/60 rule, 160
90-day rule, 160
Bureau of Human Rights and
Humanitarian Affairs, 137
Consular Electronic Application
Center (CEAC), 175, 220
Dates for Filing charts, 49–50
DS-10, Birth Affidavit, 213
DS-160, Online Nonimmigrant
Visa Application, 60–61, 63
DS-260, Online Immigrant
Visa and Alien Registration
Application, 115, 175–176, 177
DS-261, Online Choice of Address
and Agent, 175
DS-1350, Certification of Report of
Birth, 206
DV Entrant Status Check, 115
Final Action charts, 49–50
Foreign Affairs Manual, 160
former employees with 15 years
minimum of service as special
immigrants, 14
FS-240, Consular Report of Birth
Abroad, 71, 72, 206
FS-545, Certificate of Birth
Abroad, 206
intercountry child adoption, 102
list of countries eligible for VWP,
22
list of parties to Hague
Convention, 95, 102
obtain documents from other
countries, 211
oversight of quotas, 128
public charge rules, 28, 31, 34
tracking applications online, 220
Visa Bulletin, 49–51, 75, 115
website, 176

See also Diversity Immigrant Visa
Lottery; National Visa Center
(NVC)
U.S. Supreme Court
on DACA, 182
on Defense of Marriage Act, 9–10,
67
on gender-based legitimation laws,
203
on nationwide right to same-sex
marriage, 10, 57
U.S. v. Windsor (2013), 9–10, 67
U visas (crime victims aiding law
enforcement), 188–189
aiding of law enforcement, 190–191
application process, 192–195
burden of proof of crimes, 190
certification of helpfulness, 188,
192, 193–194, 196–197
derivative visas for family members,
189, 191–192, 194, 199
eligibility for, 21, 188–192
expiration of, 199
filing for green cards, 198–199
green card options after approval of
visa, 196–197
green cards for immediate relatives,
197
I-918, Petition for U Nonimmigrant Status, 190, 192, 193,
194, 195, 196–197, 198
I-929, Petition for Qualifying
Family Member of a U-1
Nonimmigrant, 197, 198
indirect/bystander victims, 189–190
legal status while pending, 195
qualifying crimes, 189, 191
required documents, 190, 194
visa interviews, 195
waiver of inadmissibility, 188, 191
work permits (EADs), 193, 194

V

Vaccinations, 29, 60, 62, 166
Veterans. *See* Military veterans and
enlistees

Victims of Trafficking and Violence
Protection Act (2000), 188
Violence Against Women Act (1994),
155
Visa, use of term, 18, 46, 188
Visa Bulletin (DOS), 49–51, 75, 115
Visa fraud, 24, 88, 159–161, 162
Visa lottery. *See* Diversity Immigrant
Visa Lottery
Visa numbers, 46
Visa Waiver Program (VWP)
adjustment of status on, 160, 161
disadvantages of, 22
list of eligible countries, 22
requirements for, 21–22
terrorism country exclusions, 22

W

Waiting periods. *See* Delays and
waiting periods
Waiver of Grounds of
Inadmissibility, 192
Waiver of Inadmissibility, 28–34, 43,
197
War Brides Act (1945), 7
Widow/widowers of U.S. citizens
application process, 12
I-360, Petition for Amerasian,
Widow(er), or Special Immigrant,
146–147
no designated waiting period for, 47
self-petitioning, 12, 34, 54, 75
Withholding of Removal. *See* United
Nations Convention Against
Torture (CAT)
Women applicants, protection for, 137
Work in U.S., previous history of, 34
Work permits (EADs)
adjustment of status and, 161, 164,
165
asylees and, 134, 136
cancellation of removal and, 154
certification of workers, 13, 31, 76,
162
DACA renewal and, 184
fiancé(e) visas and, 63
U visas and, 193, 194

DISCARD